ADVANCE PRAISE

"*House Poor No More* is the perfect handbook to prepare yourself as a homeowner. After reading *House Poor No More*, I know what renovations are worth the investment and how to prioritize maintenance, plus so many other homeownership secrets you could never find with a Google search or internet-deep-dive. Romana King's 20 years of real estate experience and homeownership knowledge are pared down into digestible takeaways extremely valuable for the average homeowner."

—Alyssa Davies, creator of the award-winning personal finance website MixedUpMoney and author of The 100-Day Financial Goal Journal

"Romana King offers readers important tools for making strategic real estate decisions. She shows how to fulfil our emotional desire for homeownership while also building long-term wealth—without having to pinch our lifestyle or compromise other financial goals."

—Rita Silvan, Chartered Investment Manager (CIM) and personal finance expert, and former Editor-in-Chief at *ELLE CANADA* and *Golden Girl Finance*

"Romana dismisses the notion that homeownership is either a good decision or a bad decision. Instead, she helps us acknowledge the emotional need for owning a home and then sets out a plan to help all homeowners make smarter, more strategic decisions when it comes to their home."

—Karin Mizgala, CEO Money Coaches Canada and author of
Unstuck: How to Get Out of Your Money Rut and Start Living the Life You Want

"In her new book, Romana King helps readers understand if homeownership is the right decision for them (right now). In *House Poor No More*, she discusses how to set a goal of homeownership and to use it to build your wealth long term. Most importantly she provides much-needed tools to help you navigate today's overheated housing market."

—Rubina Ahmed-Haq, personal finance expert, 20-year business and finance
reporter and creator of Always Save Money

"*House Poor No More* does an excellent job of explaining how and why homeownership is a smart, strategic tool for our emotional and financial well-being. Following the tips and tactics outlined in this book, anyone can become a smarter homeowner and grow their personal net worth."

—Robert R. Brown, author of *Wealthing Like Rabbits*

HOUSE POOR
NO MORE

HAPPY
HOMEOWNERSHIP

BEST
Romana

HOUSE POOR NO MORE

9 Steps that Grow the Value of Your Home and Net Worth

Romana King

HOUNDSTOOTH PRESS

HOUSE POOR NO MORE

9 Steps That Grow the Value of Your Home and Net Worth

ISBN   978-1-5445-2628-7   *Paperback*

       978-1-5445-2629-4   *Ebook*

*This book is dedicated to five men in my life
who have profoundly changed who I am
and my reason for being:*

My father

My brother

My husband

My two sons

*As a feminist, I fought the idea of being defined by my roles
as daughter, sister, wife and mother. Yet, it is these very relationships that helped to shape me into the strong, capable,
resilient and vulnerable woman that I am today. Thank you,
Mark, Connor, Jaxon, John and Conrad. My home and heart
are with you, always.*

...And then there's you, the reader...

*This book is dedicated to you. All of you. For almost 20 years,
you have written me letters (on paper!), called my phone,
emailed and messaged me, even as brands, technology and
platforms changed. Your desire for answers fuelled my fire.
Thank you for always pointing me in the right direction so
that together we can all become smarter homeowners.*

TABLE OF CONTENTS

Table of Contents

Table of Contents

ACKNOWLEDGEMENTS

This book, my career and my passion did not emerge and blossom in isolation. Many people played a part and I'd like to publicly and personally thank these individuals.

A big, heartfelt thank you to my immediate Zolo team: Alyssa Davies, Kristan Bauer and Jason Billingsley (and their incredible spouses: Nick, Brian and Amy). I've learned so much and consider myself blessed to work alongside such hard-working, dedicated professionals. You make each week a bit brighter. Truly.

A shout-out to Nikki Manthey, who helped remove the extra everything in her edits!

To my original MoneySense crew: Duncan Hood and Sarah Efron. Thanks for taking a chance and letting my passion for real estate blossom. Our time together changed me—for the better.

To Don Bisch: You taught me that leaders can be kind and considerate and still move mountains and overcome odds. You are the best and the brightest. Thank you.

For the better part of two decades, I've worked with and learned from some of Canada's brightest financial journalists and experts. At MoneySense: Bruce Sellery, Dan Bortolotti, David Aston, David Fielding, David Hodges, David Thomas, Jason Heath, Jonathan Chevreau, Julie Cazzin, Mark Brown, Norm Rothery, Prajakta Dhopade, Robert Brown, Sandra E. Martin, Stefania Di Verdi, and my insightful source D. G. Southen. At Advisor: Phil Porado, Mark Noble, Bryan Borzykowsi, Deanne Gage, Scott Blythe, Donna Power and Steve Lamb. During my time with you, I learned the importance of financial reporting and the power of money management. We laughed. We debated. We watched markets implode and sometimes explode. It was awesome.

I'd also like to extend my gratitude to people who helped me grow personally:

To Mildred Frank, Linda Udovicic, Marlene McLafferty, Hanna and Catherine Pervan: You are strong, intelligent, creative and hard-working women. Thank you for the gift of your time, love and friendship. To dear friends (some here, some gone): Tom Miller, Dragan and Tanya Stojanovic, Rebecca Johnston and Neal Armstrong. Thank you for the many, many, many chats. I couldn't be more blessed. To my N.Van family: Curtis, Cindy, Dan, Kristi, Margaret and Michelle—to love and feel loved by a group of once-were-strangers is one of the most healing salves a soul can find. I love you all.

Finally, to Bill and Bob and their wives, Lois and Anne. It starts with recognizing what we don't know and can't control—from there we learn a life based on principles. None of this was possible without you...both then and now.

FOREWORD

By Bruce Sellery,
CEO, Credit Canada and Money Columnist
for CBC Radio and Cityline

I bought my first piece of real estate at the age of 30. Not Doogie-Howser, child-prodigy early. But not late either. It was a tiny, unwinterized A-frame cottage, and when my new co-owner and I signed the deal we had been dating for just six months. I was young, the property was impractical, and the decision was slightly irresponsible—but for $104,000, we decided it was a risk worth taking.

Well, that is just not the mental math that buyers have to do these days. House prices are at all-time highs, interest rates are at all-time lows, and no one really knows where the holy moly things will go from here. That is why the book you're holding in your hands is so essential. Romana King's *House Poor No More* brings together her decades of experience as a personal finance and real estate journalist to help readers see the entire picture.

Real estate can be complicated—which house, where and for how much. Then add in the financial tradeoffs you will inevitably have to make in your life, and the societal pressures you'll need to endure. There are plenty of books on how to buy, sell or invest in real estate. There isn't one that brings together homeownership with money management, investing and retirement planning.

This *is* that book.

House Poor No More will help you think through your goals, create a holistic financial plan and provide you with the non-judgemental emotional support required for the task ahead of you.

I have read most of the major personal finance books written in the last two decades. And as a business journalist, I have interviewed a good percentage of the authors. So I can say with some credibility that Romana King's book is different and that it provides the reader with something different. I have also known Romana professionally for many years. Her writing is clear, compelling, thoughtful, balanced and friendly. And oh, she actually cares. She really does care about helping people find their way—*THEIR* way based on THEIR financial circumstances, emotional needs, goals and dreams.

Pour yourself the beverage of your choice, turn off your phone, grab a pen, and get to work on this book. You'll be so glad you did.

INTRODUCTION

YOUR HOME IS YOUR KEY TO WELL-BEING

I can't remember a time when real estate—or, more specifically, a home—hasn't factored prominently in my life. My parents and I immigrated to Canada in the 1970s and, like many immigrants, began our journey in this country renting apartments in large urban centres close to transit hubs. As our life became more established and more secure, my parents aspired to that North American dream of homeownership. After spending a few years in London, United Kingdom, where I was born, my parents were keen to become masters of their domain, kings of their castle.

Their first attempt was to purchase a bungalow perched on the bluffs of Scarborough in the east end of Toronto, Ontario. As part of the negotiation, they put down $1,000 as a deposit and then got a home inspection. The report prompted my father to cancel the deal and walk away from his deposit money (worth about $6,000 in today's dollars). Turns out, the inspector and my father were not comfortable with the crumbling sandstone that surrounded the foundation and footings that held up the home.

The second attempt was a single-family home with a large mortgage helper that took up the second floor and attic. It was a semi-duplex in a fantastic neighbourhood in the heart of midtown Toronto. The Summerhill neighbourhood was quiet and known for its excellent schools; it felt residential but was also completely accessible to both public transit and the downtown core. My parents stretched their budget to get the home—assured that the mortgage helper would help pay the bills. A few short months later they received a notice from the fire department: upgrade to meet today's fire code standards or remove the tenants and convert the home back to a single-family residence. The upgrades would've cost tens of thousands—money my single-income family did not have—and within the year, my parents were back to renting an apartment.

My parents would become property owners again but not before learning a few vital lessons—lessons my father passed on to me and lessons I have used to make better decisions not just about buying property but about debt management and regarding the achievement of all financial goals.

Believe it or not, the first lesson I learned wasn't about finding the best property (you know, location, location, location) or following the obvious advice of buying low and selling high.

The first lesson I learned is that the fear of losing out (or losing, in general) is the worst reason to make a decision or stick with a plan. My father may have lost deposit money on that first house, but he saved himself tens of thousands in repair costs trying to shore up piers built on an eroding landmass.

The second lesson I learned: don't trust anyone else with your own best interests. My father trusted a banker and an agent when it came to the duplex. He believed that these professionals gave him all the pertinent information about the house he was buying for his family; he trusted that no important details were kept from him since they were theoretically working for him. Sadly, that wasn't the case.

I'm not saying every real estate professional would've acted the same way. Some would; many others wouldn't. I'm also not saying that real estate professionals aren't integral. Real estate agents, mortgage brokers, accountants, bookkeepers and lawyers are all important professionals who get involved in the home buying and selling process, but like with all professionals, some are better than others. For every story of a real estate pro going above and beyond to help, there's another tale of someone skirting the line of ethics.

What does that mean for us Joes and Janes of the world? It means we can't rely on others to give us answers. Although we might have questions—Is now a good time to buy? Should I renovate my home? Should I pay down my mortgage or invest?—don't expect someone to give you the answer. Nor will you find it reading general opinions, applying generic formulas or using shortcuts or rules of thumb. These are useful but only as guides. In the end, the answers will only be found in the application of knowledge—when you take generic information and apply it to your specific situation. Then you will have answers—the right answers.

This is the ultimate aim of this book—to help you find, assess and decide what is best for you and your family using your single largest and most expensive asset in the best possible way.

YOUR HOME: THE KEYSTONE TO YOUR WELL-BEING

To start, we must first appreciate the role our home plays in our lives.

In every ecosystem or community, there is a keystone. A keystone is a critical or vital part that helps hold the entire system together. In an ecosystem, keystone species can be either huge predators, such as grey wolves, or unassuming microorganisms such as zooplankton. Regardless of their size, the elimination of a keystone means the entire system would look and be quite different.

In North American communities, our homes are the keystone to our well-being.

On the most fundamental level, housing helps to satisfy our physiological needs: it gives us a place to sleep and protects us from the elements. But housing satisfies more than our base needs. Examine housing through the lens of Abraham Maslow's pyramid of needs and we can begin to appreciate how comprehensive housing is at satisfying all of our needs—how it lays the foundation and sets the path for our personal and familial well-being.

HOW HOUSING HELPS OVERALL WELL-BEING

Housing can help each of us to progress through each level of motivation, as identified through Maslow's hierarchy of needs.

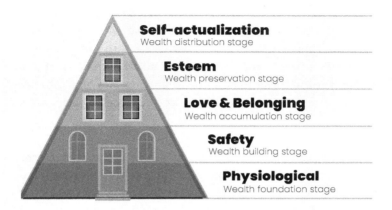

Starting at the base:

Physiological: At the most basic level, the home provides our most basic needs. It's a place we can sleep, eat and rest while being sheltered from the environmental conditions. The home satisfies our physiological needs if we can store, prepare and eat food as well as keep our belongings and ourselves safe.

Safety: The home offers security and protection for ourselves, our loved ones and our accumulated belongings. Knowing that we can explore and define our lives—through the hobbies, sports and activities we enjoy—and that we have a safe, happy place to return is an integral part of a home.

Love & Belonging: A home gives a person a chance to feel a part of—a connection to a place, a community and a city. This attachment enables homeowners the ability to focus on allowing other relationships with friends, family, neighbours and community to blossom.

Esteem: Does the home offer a sense of meaning and accomplishment? Does the owner feel a sense of pride and value about their home? Whether it's a first home or part of a retirement plan, the home offers the owner the ability to set and achieve goals and gain respect from being successful at this.

Self-actualization: How will this home bring someone closer to their dreams and aspirations? How will this home help the owner to be creative and spontaneous, responsible and free, live within their ethics and abide by their principles? How will this home help the owner move towards becoming the most capable, best self?

It's easy to dismiss the idea that housing meets our needs—unless you start to read the science that examines the link between emotions and the space we occupy.

For the last 40 years, academics and social scientists have been studying a concept known as "place attachment"—this is the emotional bond a person feels towards a specific space.

The theory suggests that by finding meaning and connection to a place, our self-esteem increases while our sense of meaning and belonging grows stronger. Some of these social experts will even suggest that place attachment is one of the most influential factors in humans' psychological health, powerful enough to be a significant factor in constructing a person's identity.

Remember Maslow's hierarchy? The path of fulfilment goes from the satisfaction of our physical needs to the realization of our full potential as human beings. Our home enables us to find shelter in a safe space where we can develop our relationships and sense of connection, which promotes a sense of self, which leads us to develop our talents and strengths (and hopefully give back).

Through this lens, the success of HGTV and our aspirations for a Martha Stewart– or Marie Kondo–approved home starts to make sense. Our desire to own property is so strong because of our desire to define and belong to our community and to reach our full potential.

YOUR HOME: THE KEYSTONE TO YOUR WEALTH

What does all this have to do with buying a home and growing our net worth?

Everything.

Of course, if you've been involved in any conversation over the last 10 years regarding real estate, you'd be left with one of two impressions: either buying a home is smart or buying a home is foolish. Either you bought low and sold high or you simply opted not to take that foolish step and take on that financial burden of mortgage debt.

This oversimplification of a very important decision is not only useless but harmful. By reducing this important decision, we end up eliminating the possibility that someone *can purchase a home* as a *smart financial decision* even in a *very expensive real estate market*.

THE WEALTHY RENTER

Truth be told, you don't have to buy in a down market and sell in an up market to have your home be the cornerstone of your nest egg—a keystone to your net worth.

But is owning a home a requirement to finding well-being or to attain financial freedom? Not necessarily. In the book The Wealthy Renter, author and top-ranked institutional equity research analyst Alex Avery explains how renters can grow their net worth without real estate. Avery shows how a renter can surpass the net worth of a homeowner through smart investment decisions.

History proves Avery's argument. If we consider a balanced portfolio, consisting of 50% bonds and 50% stocks split evenly between Canada, the US and international holdings, we can see that the average annual growth rate between 1982 and 2019 was 10.12%. Examine Canadian housing data for the same 37-year time period and the average annual growth rate is 1.7% per year (a number that trailed the average annual inflation rate of 2.46% for the same time period).

Homeownership is not the fastest or most direct route to wealth accumulation. So why bother owning a home? Why not rent and cash in on those juicy stock market returns? Why do so many North Americans and others from all over the world strive to own their own home?

Your Home Is Your Key to Well-Being

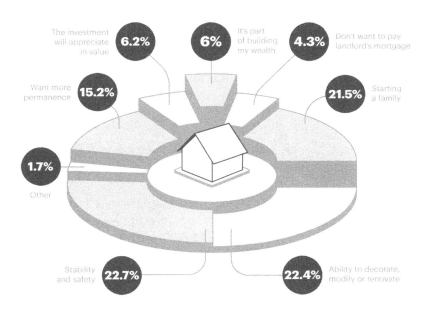

Reasons We Buy Homes

6.2% The investment will appreciate in value

6% It's part of building my wealth

4.3% Don't want to pay landlord's mortgage

15.2% Want more permanence

21.5% Starting a family

1.7% Other

22.7% Stability and safety

22.4% Ability to decorate, modify or renovate

The desire for homeownership continues to be very high in most North American markets. The assumption is that the desire to get into the housing market is primarily led by financial reasons. This is not the case. More than 6,500 potential buyers were asked to list their primary reason for buying a home in a study released in November 2020. Turns out 1 in 5 motives were financial, and the rest had to do with psychological and emotional stability and control.

Source: Financial Literacy vs. Financial Sufficiency study, Zolo

Even though I had my suspicions as to why the drive for home-ownership is so strong, I wanted to validate those suspicions. To do this, I worked with Alyssa Davies, the award-winning personal finance blogger behind *Mixed Up Money* and my colleague for the last three years at Zolo.

Through an online survey, we asked more than 6,500 Canadians a lot of questions regarding their finances, including the motivation and the impact of property purchases and the rationale for homeownership.

By and large, the biggest, most significant reason for owning a home wasn't financial security; it was emotional stability.

This makes sense to me. It also helps explain why buyers kept rushing into the market over the last decade despite frothy price escalations, predictions of bubbles and market crashes and persistent arguments that homeownership is an unwise financial decision.

Let's be clear: I'm not saying buying a house is a bad investment. It can be an incredibly powerful tool that allows you to use leverage, not just to buy the home but to jump-start your investment savings. But buying property isn't the only way to accumulate wealth; however, done smartly and homeownership can be a keystone—a solid tool that can fortify your financial and psychological foundation, allowing you to build.

WHAT THIS BOOK WILL GIVE YOU

This does not mean that the act of buying a home is, in and of itself, a smart decision. That's the problem. Just because you buy a home—or buy stock or save money—doesn't make it smart. It's what you do with the asset—whether it's a home or stock purchase or savings in some account—that is smart. It's whether the asset ends up being an investment that works to grow your net worth or just an expensive product you own.

To make sure your home satisfies all your emotional needs and your financial goals, you'll need a plan and a course of action. This is what this book will help you do. Consider it the blueprint for smart homeownership.

What you'll find in this book are strategies for maintaining, protecting and increasing the value of your home, while finding small and big ways to save money. Broken down into eight steps, with a final step that wraps up what we've learned:

1. **Why homeownership?:** Stop justifying, identify goals and take action.

2. **Your home is an asset:** Learn how to assess its value.

3. **Spend money to make money:** Learn how to maintain and even increase your property's value through home maintenance and strategic budgeting.

4. **The real value is in problem-solving:** Learn how and when to make strategic home renovations and upgrades.

5. **Save more by using less:** 35 tips to help you save more than $6,000 per year through efficient upgrades, new habits and rebates.

6. **Home equity is a tool:** Use smart strategies to help you tackle the debt side of homeownership to help lower your borrowing costs and increase your net worth.

7. **Pay for the unexpected:** Insurance tips and strategies to protect your single-largest asset, while saving you money.

8. **Make tax savings a priority:** Learn to use tax rates and deductions to minimize your overall tax burden, plus learn strategies to reduce or avoid capital gains tax.

9. **The Big Takeaway:** Your home, your castle, your cash. A few reminders to keep you focused on the positive.

By using these nine steps you will develop a smart strategy to take your money and buy a home, then grow the value of your home, the single largest asset you own and make better wealth accumulation decisions. This book can help you make smart financial decisions even if you live in an expensive property market. Consider it your financial blueprint to help you manage, repair, upgrade and protect your single largest and most expensive asset, all while growing your net worth.

A Note About Pricing, Rates of Return and Timelines

Where and when possible, I've tried to provide costs, percentages and timelines—quantitative information that is extremely useful when making strategic financial decisions.

Even though it may be obvious, I still need to point out that actual costs are going to vary widely based on location, circumstances and how much time has passed. The ratio of budget and proportions of spending is still going to be relatively accurate. That means that costs, rates of return and timelines listed in this book should give you a good basis for understanding the costs associated with being a smart homeowner.

If you want to account for differences over time, here are some guidelines:

- **Prices tend to go up, not down, over time.** Even if labour costs drop, material costs go up. For each year beyond 2021, consider adding 1.86% to the quoted price, which reflects the average annual inflation rate in Canada over the last 20 years.

- **Rates of return will change but usually very slowly.** There are a variety of factors that impact the return on investment (ROI), but the ratios are typically pretty stable over a long time. When in doubt, stop and research.

- **Timelines don't tend to change all that much.** Timelines related to homeownership rarely change, making this data a good, stable constant you can rely on.

Armed with this information, you can now use the data and costs included in this book at any time during your homeownership life cycle.

Although the situations and events in this book are all true, names and personal details have been changed to protect privacy, except where noted.

1

WHY HOMEOWNERSHIP?

FIND YOUR NORTH STAR BY IDENTIFYING YOUR GOALS

We all need goals.

To illustrate the importance and power of goals, let's turn to a well-known Canadian-born actor and comedian, Jim Carrey. Before Carrey became famous, he would drive out to the eastern Santa Monica mountains near Los Angeles in Southern California and park on Mulholland Drive. He would sit there and visualize living on this famous street. A few years later, Carrey would hit it big in Hollywood. Now, not only can he afford to live on this famous street, but he can easily afford more than one home in this historic neighbourhood. For Carrey, visualizing his success as a house on Mulholland Drive helped him solidify the work and determination needed to achieve his aim of becoming a Hollywood A-lister.

Carrey isn't the only one to tap the power of visualization and goal-setting.

Oprah Winfrey created a vision board in 2008 to conceptualize Barack Obama's election. On January 20, 2009, Obama was sworn in as the 44th President of the United States of America. (He was also the first black man to be elected President.)

Then there's Katy Perry. By all accounts, the once-unknown singer-songwriter created a dream board at the early age of nine. The board helped her visualize her dreams of fame. Now, if you're unfamiliar with Perry, just Google her name and quite quickly you'll learn how her childhood musical aspirations helped her turn into a globally famous pop star.

Even Jack Canfield, the famous American author who wrote *Success Principles*, promotes the use of vision boards and goal-setting; he has an entire web page dedicated to the practice.[1] According to Canfield, "The best way to achieve your goals is to keep them top of mind, so you're always looking for ways to move closer to them—and a vision board is a perfect tool to help you do that."

To sum up: Setting goals—visually or otherwise—has long been a strategy for many entertainers, Olympians, sports heroes and business CEOs. The practice continues to be the go-to practice when establishing a plan to win or succeed, partly because it's accessible to just about everyone, partly because there is so much anecdotal evidence that it helps, and partly because science proves that goal-setting works.

THE SCIENCE BEHIND GOAL-SETTING

In a 1967 study published in the *Journal of Applied Psychology*, researchers found that setting goals will increase moti-

---

1   Jack Canfield, "How to Create an Empowering Vision Board," Maximizing Your Potential, accessed June 22, 2021, https://www.jackcanfield.com/blog/how-to-create-an-empowering-vision-book.

vation. The study found that having a specific goal—rather than a vague notion of success—increases motivation, which increases the achievement of those goals, by as much as 30%.[2]

In another, more recent study, published by the American Psychological Association, a team of researchers decided to test whether the process of writing down goals had an impact. Researchers asked struggling university students to complete an online goal-setting program. After four months, students in the goal-setting program enjoyed a 30% average increase in academic performance over the control group.[3]

There are plenty of other studies that support the idea that goal-setting is a powerful motivator and a precursor of increased success—add in a public declaration and those results increase. In a study released in 1985 (by Earley and Kanfer)[4] and another released in 1989 (by Hollenbeck, Williams & Klein[5]), researchers found that peer influence and public admission of desired goals help us commit to the goal and enhance our efforts to achieve that goal. In other words, what our family, friends and neighbours see and know about our desires and objectives helps us stay the course and achieve our aim.

---

2 J. F. Bryan and E. A. Locke, "Goal Setting as a Means of Increasing Motivation," Journal of Applied Psychology 51, no. 3 (1967): 274–77.

3 Dominique Morisano, Jacob B. Hirsh and Jordan B. Peterson, "Setting, Elaborating, and Reflecting on Personal Goals Improves Academic Performance," *Journal of Applied Psychology* 95, no. 2 (2010): 255–64.

4 Earley and Kanfer study cited in https://ie.technion.ac.il/~merez/papers/locke.pdf.

5 J. R. Hollenbeck, C. R. Williams and H. J. Klein, "An Empirical Examination of the Antecedents of Commitment to Difficult Goals," *Journal of Applied Psychology* 74, no. 1 (1989): 18–23.

The idea behind visualizing goals is that if you "see" your goal, you are more likely to achieve it.

Visualizing goals teaches our brain to recognize the resources needed to achieve those goals while filtering out the noise—distractions that can't or won't help us achieve our aspirations.

Goal-setting also creates inner motivation and promotes positive thinking, which also helps us stay on track and be successful in the long run.

So it should come as no surprise that many financial planners and money coaches insist on a financial plan. By identifying your financial goals, you can determine and start to establish the steps required to meet those goals.

For instance, if your goal is to retire early, your actions may be very different from someone with a goal to reach a certain professional standard, or buy a car, or start a family.

So how does homeownership fall into goal-setting and the financial plan?

In part, owning a home is a goal all by itself. Saving up a down payment, shopping for the right (at least for now) home and maintaining a property, once you've bought it, are all monumental undertakings all on their own. But owning a home shouldn't be the final destination or the ultimate goal.

Although some argue that homeownership is a poor substitute for saving and a substandard way to achieve financial independence, studies consistently show that homeownership affects investment, consumption and savings decisions of households, and plays a major role in post-retirement well-being.

Wait. There's more.

Homeownership has been linked to better educational outcomes and superior future income prospects for kids who grow up in owner-occupied homes. At the larger, community level, homeownership appears to provide a stability that allows residents to act as informed and engaged citizens, according to a 1999 study by DiPasquale and Glaeser.[6] No wonder boosting the rate of homeownership has been a public policy goal in many OECD countries over the last few decades! (The OECD is the Organisation for Economic Co-operation and Development, an international organisation that works to build better policies for better lives.)

WHAT DOES THIS MEAN FOR MY FINANCIAL WELL-BEING?

Here's the thing: **money is a tool, not a goal.**

And financial independence is also a tool, not a goal.

Now, before you polish your pitchfork or light that torch, hear me out.

Financial independence is the status of having enough income that you can pay your living expenses now and into the future without having to be employed or dependent on others. The end goal is to live well without having to rely on others; a critical tool to achieve this is financial independence.

---

6 Denise DiPasquale and Edward L. Glaeser, "Incentives and Social Capital: Are Homeowners Better Citizens?" *Journal of Urban Economics* 45, no. 2 (March 1999): 354–84.

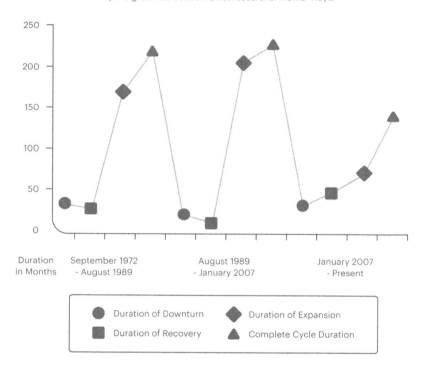

Long-Term Real Estate Market Cycle Pattern

The complete real estate market cycle has an average duration of about 18 years. This pattern was first observed in 1933 by the great real estate market researcher Homer Hoyt.

Ultimately, the end goal for all of us is to achieve all five levels of Maslow's hierarchy. The critical tool to help achieve this goal is money.

But to use money effectively—and to achieve your end goal—you need to develop milestones along the way. To do this, you establish a set of short-, mid- and long-term goals; then you need to identify how your home—your tool—can help meet these goals.

Ask yourself what you want to accomplish. Get specific and write down your goals and aspirations. Which goals are most important to you? Which goals are aspirations? And which goals are necessary for risk mitigation? (Both are important.) Remember, identifying and prioritizing your goals acts as a motivator and seriously increases your chances of successfully achieving those goals.

When dealing specifically with real estate, keep the short-term within 1 to 5 years, mid-term between 6 and 14 years and long-term anything over 14 years. The theory behind this is that one complete real estate market cycle lasts about 18 years, with the expansion stage lasting about 12 to 14 years.[7] To maximize the expansion—or profit—stage, you need to be active in the market for that time period.

If you need a bit of structure when creating your goals, consider following the S.M.A.R.T. philosophy:

Simple (or specific)

Motivational (or measurable)

Action-oriented

Reachable

Time-based

---

7 Brad Case, "Looking Carefully at the Current Real Estate Market Cycle," *Market Commentary* (blog), Nareit, September 19, 2017, https://www.reit.com/news/blog/market-commentary/looking-carefully-at-the-current-real-estate-market-cycle.

Examples of S.M.A.R.T. goals include:

- Increase my savings by 20% in the next 6 months.

- Save up $60,000 to use as a down payment on a home with a maximum price of $600,000.

Another powerful goal-setting method comes from John Doerr, venture capitalist and author of the *New York Times* bestseller *Measure What Matters*. Doerr believes in the Objectives & Key Results (OKR) goal-setting method—a tool used by senior decision-makers at IBM, Google, LinkedIn, Twitter, Dropbox, Spotify, Disney and BMW.

Objectives describe where you're going. Key results are the steps you take to get there.

Here's an example:

Objective: Run a marathon in under four hours.

Key results:

- Join a marathon training group.

- Train five days per week with one long run each week.

- Increase mileage by five miles per week.

- Drink at least three litres of water every day.

- Sleep at least eight hours every night.

Why Homeownership?

The idea is to determine your wishes—these are your objectives—and then identify the specific actions to take to meet those objectives. As Doerr explains, objectives are just wishes if there are no results, while those results are merely check marks on a to-do list without ambitions to ground them.

It's the difference between saving money for a down payment on a home versus saving money to have a large bank balance. It's why high-level goals motivate us and short-term actions drive us—but you need both to level up and be successful.

The great thing about OKRs is that the goals *need to be measurable*—data and numbers rule this method of goal-setting.

Regardless of the method used, the idea is to develop a list of:

Short-term goals (up to one year);

Mid-term goals (one to seven years); and

Long-term goals (seven years or longer).

These lists are your objectives; now you need to prioritize. An easy way to do this is to use a decision matrix, where you weigh each goal against the next until all the important ones are high on your list. Another option is to use the Eisenhower Matrix.

THE EISENHOWER MATRIX METHOD
OF FINANCIAL PLANNING GOAL-SETTING

The Eisenhower Matrix is a method of prioritizing your tasks on the basis of their urgency. The matrix categorizes your tasks into four quadrants according to the urgency and priority of each task or goal.

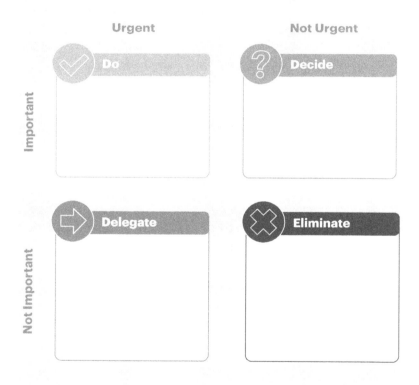

The four quadrants are:

1. DO

The first quadrant includes important goals and urgent tasks.

Goal examples: Cut debt, reduce expenses, increase income

Task examples: Make a budget, monetise a side hustle

2. DECIDE

The second quadrant includes the important but not so urgent tasks and goals.

Goal examples: Long-term planning, saving for retirement, reducing risk

Task examples: Call insurance agent, set up an RRSP or TFSA account

3. DELEGATE

The third quadrant are not important but (apparently) urgent tasks and goals.

Goal examples: Strategize your explore portion of your investment portfolio

Task examples: Buy a new car, comparison shop credit cards

4. ELIMINATE

The last category includes all goals and tasks that are not urgent and not important or don't get you closer to your goals.

Goal examples: Get a Tesla, buy a bigger house

Task examples: Increase your spending because you got a raise

Why is all this goal-setting so important? Because without goals and clear, actionable steps, we tend to get distracted, so much so that we can misjudge what's required to get where we want to go. In a recent survey, 46% of more than 6,500 survey respondents failed a basic literacy test and 78% said they'd run out of money in 90 days or less if they lost their job today—and yet, 70% of these respondents reported feeling confident about their overall financial knowledge and 82% reported that they were good at "keeping track of money."[8]

And **once the pandemic hit**, almost three-quarters (74%) of these 6,651 survey respondents expressed **more interest in buying a home**.[9]

---

8 Romana King and Alyssa Davies, "Study: Financial Literacy vs Financial Sufficiency: How Canadians Overestimate Their Financial Knowledge—and Pay the Price," *Zolo Homebase* (blog), Nov 2, 2020, https://www.zolo.ca/blog/financial-literacy-canada.

9 Romana King and Alyssa Davies, "Study: Financial Literacy vs Financial Sufficiency: How Canadians Overestimate Their Financial Knowledge—and Pay the Price," *Zolo Homebase* (blog), Nov 2, 2020, https://www.zolo.ca/blog/financial-literacy-canada.

If your goal is to buy a home, or if you're already a homeowner but your goal is to grow your net worth, then start putting pen to paper and writing down your specific, measurable objectives and the actions required to achieve those objectives.

MAKE HOME BUYING AND GOAL-SETTING A PRIORITY

Don't skip this step. Identifying your goals will set the agenda for where money should go. Remember, money is a tool. How you use that tool will determine how well your money works to achieve your goals.

There's another reason why writing down our goals is important: it helps us identify our objectives and the actions to take to obtain those objectives. This helps us act on principle, not emotion.

Having a plan is key when it comes to building wealth because it can prevent us from taking fear-based action.

To illustrate the danger of panic selling—when someone sells during a declining market to mitigate losses—the Wells Fargo investment team ran four hypothetical investment scenarios, showing the results of four different investor strategies.

The investor who capitalized on the stock market dip outperformed all other investors—and when compared to the investor who sold it all in a panic and decreased their portfolio by 6%, the equity investor has more than a 20–percentage point margin.

This idea of not panicking is also important when moving from property acquisition to smart homeownership. The principle behind smart homeownership is to keep our money working for us, not to rely on just working for our money. Part of that is learning to use our home; we need to see beyond the utilitarian use of a home as a roof over our heads and to see this asset as a way to fundamentally help us grow our net worth.

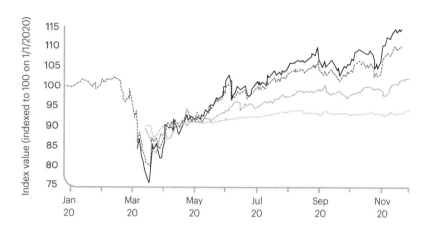

To establish how costly panic selling is to investor portfolios, Wells Fargo Investment Institute analysed four hypothetical investment scenarios:

— Investor 1 didn't panic and followed their investment plan, which included selling 30% of fixed-income and buying into the falling equity market.

···· Investor 2 also followed their more conservative investment plan and rebalanced in order to keep their strategic allocations.

— Investor 3 started to panic, sold half their equities and bought fixed-income.

— Investor 4 panicked and sold their entire equity portfolio.

HOW MUCH CAN YOU REALISTICALLY AFFORD?

When the goal is to buy your first home, the actions you need to take to get to that goal can seem almost insurmountable. Saving up a large down payment is hard; paying down debt is hard; shopping for a property is hard (but also fun, at times). And one of the hardest questions to answer is how much home can you afford?

There are loads of guidelines or rules about the best way to calculate how much you should spend on a house.

One rule of thumb is to multiply your gross annual income by 3.5 to give you the maximum mortgage loan you should borrow. (Before the 2020–2021 market surge, the rule of thum was to multiply your gross annual income by 2.5.)

Based on this calculation, the average American household could max out their mortgage loan at $157,500 USD for a one-income household with average annual earnings of just under $63,000 USD (for 2019). For double-income households, the maximum mortgage is closer to $315,000 USD.

In Canada, the maximum mortgage for one-income households with an average household income of $61,600 CDN (in 2019) is closer to $154,000 CDN, or $308,000 CDN for two-income households.

Given these limits, here's what buyers would need to earn in some of North America's most expensive cities to afford each city's median home price.

CITY	MEDIAN HOME SALE PRICE	REQUIRED ANNUAL EARNINGS
Vancouver, BC, CA	$1,440,849 (CDN)	$576,339 (CDN)
San Francisco, CA, US	$1,275,000 (USD)	$510,000 (USD)
Manhattan, NY, US	$1,207,500 (USD)	$483,000 (USD)
Brooklyn, NY, US	$725,000 (USD)	$290,000 (USD)
Seattle, WA, US	$699,000 (USD)	$279,600 (USD)
New York, NY, US	$675,000 (USD)	$270,000 (USD)
Mississauga, ON, CA	$650,000 (CDN)	$260,000 (CDN)
Los Angeles, CA, US	$628,750 (USD)	$251,500 (USD)
Toronto, ON, CA	$613,080 (CDN)	$245,232 (CDN)
Boston, MA, US	$610,000 (USD)	$244,000 (USD)
Washington, DC, US	$570,000 (USD)	$228,000 (USD)
San Diego, CA, US	$560,000 (USD)	$224,000 (USD)

Annual average income USD: $ 63,000 (USD)

Max house price: $393,750 (USD)

Annual average income CDN: $ 61,600 (CDN)

Max house price: $385,000 (CDN)

Source: The International Housing Affordability Survey, December 2018. Currency conversion based on USD $1 = CDN $1.30. The median sales price for average annual income assumes 20% down.

For those looking for property to purchase, this guide to home affordability may seem ridiculously out of touch.

Another option is to follow Senator Elizabeth Warren's 50-30-20 budget rule. As a former law school professor who specialized in bankruptcy law, Warren laid out her popular budget method in her book *All Your Worth: The Ultimate Lifetime Money Plan*.

In the simplest terms, Warren suggests dividing up your after-tax income and allocating 50% to your needs, 30% to your wants and 20% to savings.

According to this budget, a home shopper should spend no more than 50% of their after-tax income on the necessities in life, including housing, food, transportation costs and utility bills. The great thing about this allocation is that it allows you to adjust. So if you live in a higher-priced city but live close enough to work that you can walk, then more of this portion of your budget can go to rent or mortgage, and less to transit costs. The second category enables you to spend 30% on those lifestyle choices that bring you joy. (In financial terms, this category is often called "discretionary income.") This could include cell phone costs, cable or streaming subscriptions, takeout meals, travel and even clothes. Regardless of what you choose to spend on, this category should take up only 30% of your after-tax income. Keep in mind, the more you trim your spending in this category, the faster you can pay down outstanding debt and the more you can save for large purchases, like a house, or future plans.

The final is your "get-ahead" category, which requires you to dedicate 20% of your take-home pay towards savings. This includes retirement accounts, debt payments, emergency funds and large purchase savings. In terms of priority, you should pay into this category once you've paid for your necessities and before you consider any discretionary costs.

Sometimes also referred to as the 50/20/30 rule, this budget method can help you keep your housing purchase price within reasonable and realistic spending limits—and still provides a buffer for living expenses such as Netflix, Spotify and specialty coffee drinks.

This 50/20/30 budgeting strategy not only allows you to continue living and saving but also helps foster overall financial health— good financial habits that can last a lifetime. (Better still, you don't need a high income to follow this budget guide. Since it's a percentage-based system, you simply have to follow the framework to watch your habits harden and your savings grow.)

Now let's look at the above list again to see how the 50/20/30 rule enables homebuyers to stretch their house-buying budget. Using the same cities mentioned above, the maximum mortgage a household could afford is as follows:

CITY	MEDIAN HOME SALE PRICE (IN CITY IN 2019)	APPROX. ANNUAL EARNINGS REQUIRED
Vancouver, BC, CA	$1,440,849 (CDN)	$152,520 (CDN)
San Francisco, CA, US	$1,275,000 (USD)	$271,008 (USD)
Manhattan, NY, US	$1,207,500 (USD)	$257,088 (USD)
Brooklyn, NY, US	$725,000 (USD)	$156,888 (USD)
Seattle, WA, US	$699,000 (USD)	$151,488 (USD)
New York, NY, US	$675,000 (USD)	$146,520 (USD)
Mississauga, ON, CA	$650,000 (CDN)	$ 76,709 (CDN)
Los Angeles, CA, US	$628,750 (USD)	$137,016 (USD)
Toronto, ON, CA	$613,080 (CDN)	$ 73,170 (CDN)
Boston, MA, US	$610,000 (USD)	$133,368 (USD)
Washington, DC, US	$570,000 (USD)	$125,160(USD)
San Diego, CA, US	$560,000 (USD)	$123,072 (USD)

Note: Assumes 20% down. In the United States, assumes a 10-year fixed-rate mortgage with a rate of 3.7%. In Canada, assumes a 5-year fixed-rate mortgage based on a 25-year amortization with a rate of 3.5%.

To calculate the Approximate Annual Earnings Required in the United States we used the Bankrate mortgage calculator, which included property taxes and homeowner insurance. We added $200 for utility costs, then doubled this monthly payment (as housing costs make up 50% of the budget) and multiplied the result by 12 to arrive at Approximate Annual Earnings Required.

To calculate CDN we used Karl's Mortgage Calculator, added $600 (to include property taxes, home insurance and $200 for utilities), then doubled this and multiplied by 12 to arrive at Approximate Annual Earnings Required.

Based on Warren's 50/20/30 budget, homeownership suddenly appears more accessible, even in some of North America's most expensive cities.

Better still, this budget is simple and helps you become a homeowner, while also saving for the future and continuing to enjoy today.

TAKEAWAY: Calculating how much the bank or mortgage provider will lend you and how much you can realistically pay each month is the smart way to buy a home and achieve your financial and emotional goals.

SUM IT UP

Trying to figure out what the real estate market is doing is a pastime for some and an obsession for others. It's easy to get wrapped up in trying to time the market when deciding whether or not to buy or sell—and to be fair, it's important.

Understanding what the real estate market is doing in your current neck of the woods helps determine if it's a buyer's market or a seller's market. This knowledge helps you select the right strategy when putting in an offer on a home or when listing a home for sale. The right strategy can help you save (or earn) thousands, tens of thousands or even hundreds of thousands. This makes knowledge of the market cycle important but not vital.

But whether you buy or sell should not be based on where the current housing market is in the real estate cycle. Making a decision based on market timing is akin to choosing an investment based on tax savings. Even though tax savings may be an important factor in determining what type of investment to hold, the main reason to invest is to earn a return, not save on taxes. This same rationale applies to buying and selling a home. The primary reason to buy or sell should be based on your needs and your personal finance plan—not on the speculative assessment of where the market currently sits in the long-term real estate market cycle (or the short-term microcycles).

That's not to say we should ignore the markets or the data. All data is good when used appropriately. Trying to time bubbles and bursts is not an appropriate way of using this data—and even very smart people have lost out on housing gains and returns by trying to time the market. Instead, consider using current market data and knowledge as a way to guide your actions—a tool to help determine the ***best possible action today, on a decision you've already made***. In hindsight, there's always a chance of seeing that another, perhaps better decision was possible. But there's also a really good chance that whatever decision you make will work for you, regardless of the market conditions (now and in the future). Things work out as long as you focus on your needs, your goals and your plans. In the end, knowledge of the real estate market and its cycles is a tool. Use the tool to meet your goals—don't let the tool dictate your actions.

TAKEAWAYS

Stop Justifying Your Decision. It's easy to justify the purchase of a home as a wise—or unwise—financial decision. Stop it. We buy homes to meet our emotional needs. Good enough.

You Have to Start to Get Ahead. To reach any goal, you must set specific, relevant goals that are personal to you. Financial independence, retire early (FIRE) by 40? Great. Write it down. Mortgage-free by 50? Write it down. No matter the goal, write it down. Use specific numbers, specific dates and specific outcomes. Don't worry if things work out differently. The point isn't to get it right. There are no grades or gold stars. The point is to be focused and accountable—to yourself. By setting goals, you have a better chance of making smart decisions about every dollar you earn, save and spend.

Your Home Is Your Keystone. Buying a home isn't the fastest or only path to financial freedom. But it can be a smart, strategic tool to help you achieve this goal. Use it wisely—such as a keystone or foundation—to grow your wealth.

All You've Got Is Today. It's important to consider what you learned in the past and to plan for the future. But when you think too far ahead or expect a resolution or change overnight, you're wasting your efforts. By focusing on yesterday—the coulda, shoulda, woulda regrets—or worrying about the future, you end up pissing on today. It's a crass cliché, but it's a good reminder to tackle each day and each decision as it comes.

There Are No Shortcuts. There is no right way to build wealth or gain financial independence, so stop looking for that mental shortcut or the perfect formula to follow. Instead, find your North Star—the goal that keeps you motivated—and build your plan accordingly.

2

TAKING STOCK
OF YOUR HOME

FINDING YOUR HOME'S VALUE
BY IDENTIFYING ITS ASSETS
AND LIABILITIES

I'm about to make a shocking statement:

Property doesn't appreciate in value. Land does.

Before you scoff, let me explain.

Like all physical property, buildings depreciate over time; it's why businesses deduct depreciation on any building (or other physical assets) used to earn an income.

However, homeowners aren't trying to earn an income from their home and, unless they want to lose their exemption and end up paying capital gains tax (more on that in Chapter 8), homeowners don't use the capital cost allowance (CCA) to capture the depreciation on their property. But just because you can't capture the tax deduction doesn't mean your property isn't depreciating.

UNDERSTANDING HOME DEPRECIATION AND PROPERTY VALUE

If my home depreciates, then why is it worth more over time?

Great question! Like your regular mortgage payment, which is broken into two segments—the principal and the interest—your property's value can be broken up into two segments: the land and the structures on the land.

Highest Use for Real Property

To get maximum value out of raw land—known as the highest and best use of real property—land use and real estate structures must meet four critical criteria:

1. Legal Permissibility
2. Physical Possibility
3. Financial Feasability
4. Maximum Productivity

Highest & Best Use

The land portion makes up the bulk of your property's value, but your home can add or detract from this value, based on the structural attributes of the home and whether this structure is in line with the highest and best use for the location.

Although this distinction may seem trivial, it isn't—and understanding the difference can help you make much better decisions when it comes to home buying, renovating and selling.

DIFFERENCE BETWEEN MARKET VALUE AND MARKET PRICE

Value is not always equal to cost. Value refers to the economic worth of an item. Cost refers to the price someone is willing to pay for the item. That means the value of your property could be $850,000 (with the majority of that value tied up in the land's value), but a buyer may be willing to buy the property for $900,000.

On the flip side, if your home has a cracked and faulty foundation, the value of the home can drop since the structure doesn't make the best possible use of the land. The cost, or the price someone is willing to pay, may also drop. This is one example of how the market price does not always reflect market value when it comes to residential real estate.

Still, if a physical structure depreciates over time, why does the land underneath it appreciate in value? Because land is finite (buildings are replaceable), and the value of finite resources will feel more pressure from the market forces of supply and demand—forces that are impacted by demographics, regulations and economic realities.

7 FACTORS THAT INFLUENCE YOUR PROPERTY'S VALUE

A variety of factors impact what your home is worth, both on paper and in the market. Although the most significant factors are the internal factors—where the home is located, how many bedrooms it has and if it's updated—external factors also play a big role. The difference is, you can't influence external factors. Still, it pays to have a good idea of how these external factors influence property values. It helps you make the big decisions, like whether you should add an expensive addition to your home, or if it's worth investing in a rental property.

Here's a brief overview of the top seven factors that influence your property's value.

#1: Demographics

As a city's population increases, builders look for ways to develop and build housing. Depending on the location of the city, access to land can range from plentiful to extremely limited. The larger the population and the more limited the access is to land (for development), the more valuable land will be—and this will increase the price of housing.

To illustrate, let's consider the impact of fear and panic in March 2020, when the novel coronavirus SARS-CoV-2, the virus that causes COVID-19, was officially reported by the World Health Organization (WHO).

As people got wind of the dangers of COVID-19 and began to realize how it would impact our lives, they began to buy toilet paper. Lots of toilet paper. Some bought it and then resold it at a massive markup. Others bought it and held on to it out of fear. Eventually, grocery stores restocked shelves and imposed limits. The entities that were price gouging were stopped, partly due to new rules and regulations and partly because demand decreased. It was a basic life lesson on supply and demand: as supply became limited, the price of that item started to go up. This same situation plays out in just about any other commodity, asset or service in the marketplace, including housing. It's also why Lord Harold Samuel, a British real estate tycoon, was credited with uttering that famous phrase "location, location, location" sometime back in the mid-1900s. Although the attributes or use of a building can change, its location cannot, which makes land a valuable commodity, not necessarily the structures built on the land.

Coming back to demographics, if a population in a city or neighbourhood begins to increase, demand for housing will also increase. This will increase the demand for current housing stock, as well as land for future housing stock. The demand-supply relationship also explains why housing in urban centres appreciates faster than in rural locations or vacation property areas. More jobs in larger urban centres attract more workers who need accommodation—both in the rental sector and to purchase.

Of course, population size isn't the only factor. Attributes of a population can also impact residential real estate values.

For instance, the demographic group with the most impact on housing markets is first-time home buyers—typically people between the ages of 25 and 40. This generation of home buyers is considered the "engine of the housing market" because it drives all other activities within the overall real estate sector. As first-time buyers enter the market, it pushes each cohort through the various stages of the property ladder, from move-on-uppers to downsizers to those cashing out. According to a survey by the Mortgage Professionals of Canada, 94% of renters in this age cohort intend to buy a home. That's a lot of power under the hood of the primary engine that drives the housing market supply and demand.

Age is not the only factor. Life events also play a big role. The life events with the biggest impact on the decision to move from renter to homeowner include:

- getting married (29%);

- starting a family (33%);

- getting a permanent job or getting a promotion (30%); and

- receiving an inheritance (8%).

These demographic factors, and the relationship they have with property values, can get complicated. Add in additional considerations such as immigration numbers, birth and death statistics, and access to healthcare, and the complexity of this relationship increases tenfold. Still, at a very basic level, all we need to remember is that any major shifts in the demographics of an area can have a large impact on real estate trends and prices for several decades.

#2: Regulation—Zoning

Another key factor in determining land values is the zoning bylaws that identify what can be built and where. Officially known as "land-use controls," these legislative-based restrictions dictate how the property is built and used. Although local municipality zoning is often considered to determine what a property may be used for, other land-use restrictions can also be found in Official Community Plans (OCPs), Local Area Plans (LAP), flood-plain restrictions, view plan restrictions, and agricultural reserve and heritage designations, among others.

The primary aim of these land-use restrictions is to determine the "highest and best use" of the land. The concept was adopted from the teachings of American economist Irving Fisher. As a statistician and economist, Fisher believed that land was a finite resource and that its value was intrinsically tied to the maximum productivity of that land.

Fisher's concept is still used. For instance, the US-based Appraisal Institute defines the highest and best use as the reasonably probable and legal use of vacant land or an improved property that is physically possible, appropriately supported, financially feasible, and that results in the highest value.

In plain speak: the value of a property is based on the most profitable use of that piece of land.

In practical terms:

- If a house is built on land designated for single-family residential use, then the highest and best use of the property is a single-family home.

- If a house is built on land that may also be used for multi-residential complexes or commercial structures, then the value of the land may increase, even if the property is in relatively poor shape.

This valuation helps explain headlines like these:

- An "uninhabitable" shack in San Francisco that's missing a wall just sold for $2 million, and it showcases the real value of land in the Bay Area[10]

- Vancouver teardown in Point Grey sells for almost $2.5M[11]

- This tiny Toronto house just sold for $800K over asking[12]

- East Vancouver shack selling for $1.1 million[13]

Why is the highest and best use so important? Because it helps determine the most profitable use of a property site, and this helps determine both the intrinsic and perceived value of a residential home. A good example of how this knowledge can help is when a property owner with a home on a busier street finds out that local zoning permits both residential and commercial use. Before this knowledge, the home may have a lower perceived value from potential buyers because it's on a busier street, but once the homeowner learns that potential business owners may find the property a good buy, the value of this property can shift.

---

10 Libertina Brandt and Katie Canales, "An 'Uninhabitable' Shack in San Francisco That's Missing a Wall Just Sold for $2 Million, and It Showcases the Real Value of Land in the Bay Area," *Business Insider*, March 5, 2020, https://www.businessinsider.com/shack-in-san-francisco-asking-nearly-two-million-dollars-2019-12.

11 Karin Larson, "Vancouver Teardown in Point Grey Sells for Almost $2.5M," *CBC News*, February 16, 2016, https://www.cbc.ca/news/canada/british-columbia/vancouver-teardown-real-estate-1.3449869.

12 Sean Davidson, "This Tiny Toronto House Just Sold for $800K Over Asking," *CTV News*, August 20, 2020, https://toronto.ctvnews.ca/this-tiny-toronto-house-just-sold-for-800k-over-asking-1.5072243.

13 Paula Baker, "East Vancouver Shack Selling for $1.1 Million," *Global News*, May 12, 2016, https://globalnews.ca/news/2698519/east-vancouver-shack-selling-for-1-1-million.

#3: Regulation—Government Policies and Subsidies

Legislation is another factor that makes a sizable impact on property values. Tax credits, deductions and subsidies are a few of the ways different levels of government can temporarily boost demand or curtail sales activity.

For example, in 2009, the US government introduced a first-time home buyer's tax credit to jump-start a stalled housing market and a sluggish economy. This tax incentive prompted the purchase of 900,000 homes that year, according to the National Association of Realtors (NAR). It was a sizable increase in sales activity at a time when foreclosures and price cuts were the norm.

In Canada, the federal government helped to slow resale housing activity, particularly in the nation's two hottest markets—Greater Toronto and Greater Vancouver—when it introduced the "Canadian mortgage stress test." Implemented on January 1, 2018, this test required banks to check that any borrower applying for a new or refinance loan is capable of making the loan repayment at a rate that's higher than they pay. Initially, the stress test required buyers to qualify at the posted rate, which hovered around 4% to 4.5%. Later, the rules for the stress test were amended so that:

- If a homebuyer needs mortgage loan insurance, the bank must use the higher interest rate of either:

    * the Bank of Canada's conventional five-year mortgage rate; or

    * the interest rate you negotiate with your lender.

- If the buyer does not need mortgage loan insurance, the bank must use the higher interest rate of either:

    * the Bank of Canada's conventional five-year mortgage rate; or

    * the interest rate you negotiate with your lender plus 2%.

Will Dunning, Chief Economist for the Mortgage Professionals of Canada, analyzed the Greater Toronto housing market. According to the data, sales dropped off almost as soon as the stress test was implemented, as seen in the GTA Resale Activity chart.

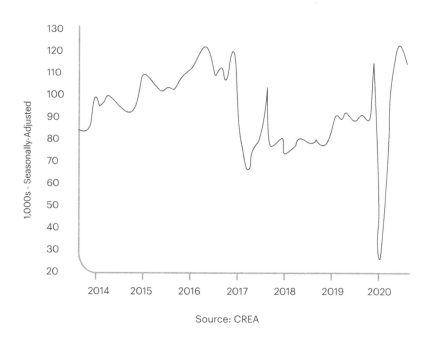

Source: CREA

By and large, government policies and subsidies will only impact the housing market as long as they are in effect.

#4: Economy

An area's or city's or nation's overall economic health is also a significant factor that affects the value of real estate and the price of your property. In general, economic health is measured through economic indicators such as the GDP, employment data, manufacturing activity, the price of goods and so on. Broadly speaking, when the economy is sluggish, so is real estate.

However, not all real estate property types are impacted the same way at the same time when it comes to economic factors.

For instance, in an economic downturn, hotels and other vacation accommodations can drop in value, while office space can maintain its value. Why? Because a vacation rental is a form of a short-term lease, whereas office space is typically leased out using longer-term contracts. During an economic downturn, people and companies will curb their spending through cost-cutting measures, such as avoiding short-term lease agreements. However, these same decisions won't impact office leases, as they are legal contracts with a much longer timeline.

For homeowners, the single largest economic factor that influences the value of your home is employment rates. In general, if unemployment is low and people feel safe and secure in their employment prospects, buyers will demand housing, which will push up residential housing value. On the flip side, if unemployment figures are high and people feel insecure about their job prospects, demand for housing will drop, and this can decrease the value of residential housing in the area (and reduce what you could sell your home for at that time).

It's also why analysts, developers, brokers and agents watch economic factors like job growth, unemployment rates and housing affordability.

#5: Interest Rates

Interest rates also have a major impact on property values.

Changes in interest rates can greatly influence what a person can afford. As rates rise, it costs more to borrow and a buyer can afford less.

Keep in mind, this is a simplified explanation. There is no causal relationship between mortgage rates and property prices. Just because rates go down doesn't mean that property prices go up. However, low rates do incentivize buyers to consider bigger budgets, and for most markets in Canada, this typically means shopping for the most in-demand property type, the single-family house.

#6: Location

C'mon, you didn't think we could skip over the most obvious factor to impact property values!

The community your home is located in, along with the size of your particular plot of land, is one of the biggest influences on property value. If you live in a desirable location, the value of your property increases.

An easy example is my current home. I live on a minor arterial road in a cloistered community in North Vancouver. Vehicles are allowed to travel 50 km/hr on this street, compared to 30 or 40 km/hr on adjacent residential roads. If you were to examine comparable homes on my street versus a neighbouring residential street, you would notice a 15% to 35% increase in the prices. In other words, buyers who desire a quieter street are willing to pay $200,000 to almost $500,000 more to get off the less desirable, busier road.

This is just an example, but the premise plays out in cities, neighbourhoods and streets all over North America.

How Does This Impact You as a Homeowner?

Understanding these six factors (and all the other facets that impact property values) is important but not integral to the ultimate goal: to use your home to grow your net worth.

Remember, your home is a tool, just like money. We can passively own these tools, or we can actively use these tools.

To illustrate, let's assume I earn $6,000 from a side hustle project I complete before year-end. To increase my net worth, I could:

- deposit this money into a savings account;

- deposit it into my Tax-Free Savings Account (TFSA), where I then use it to invest in a low-fee exchange-traded fund (ETF) that aligns with my financial plan; or

- use it to upgrade my outdated upstairs bathroom.

The first choice is a passive way to grow my net worth. I've earned the money, now I save the money, but it isn't working for me over the long term. If I'm not careful, inflation could erode the value of these savings.

The second choice is a more active way to grow my net worth. I've earned the money and now I'm using that money to actively increase my savings by investing according to my personal goals and financial plan. I'm getting the money to work for me (not just me working for it).

The third choice is the trickiest to decipher. Does it provide a return? Would I get more money if I sold the house by upgrading this bathroom? Or is it a sunk cost? This is a cost I pay as a homeowner so that I can enjoy an upgraded bathroom, even if the money spent doesn't grow the home's value (and, subsequently, my net worth).

The first two options are easy to decide between. Even the most risk-averse investor needs to consider how to get their savings to work for them over the long haul. Neglect to do this and the $1 you earn today will be worth $0.82 in 10 years due to erosion from inflation.[14]

It's the third option that trips us up. It's possible to earn money in real estate. We all know this, but to be a smart homeowner you need a method or formula for determining whether the money you spend on your home is a smart investment or a sunk cost (or a bit of both).

Thankfully, there is a seventh factor that influences your property's value and gives you the most control: your property's attributes.

---

14 Based on an average annual inflation of 1.9%.

#7: Property Attributes

The size of your home, its curb appeal and whether it offers what buyers in the area want all influence property values. Also, the age and condition of your home will impact the sale price (and the overall value of the property). Although newer homes tend to command higher square foot prices, a well-maintained home can sell for just as much as a newer home or more—so your home's condition does matter!

HOW MUCH IS YOUR HOME WORTH?

When trying to find out how much your home is worth, the best place to start is online, using free tools and calculators. The next step is to go offline and get the expertise of professionals—using both free and paid services.

Determining your home's value is the first solid step to becoming a smart homeowner. It allows you to make smarter, more strategic decisions that impact not only your current cash flow but also your future savings. The great news is, you can start this process whether you're a first-time buyer who hasn't quite sealed the deal on a property yet or a seasoned homeowner with more than a few purchases and sales under your belt.

Free Tools and Calculators

There are loads of free tools and calculators in the market. There are so many that it's impossible to list the best one right now; wait a minute and a new one will be added to the list. Instead, here is a summary of the type of tools you can use, along with the pros and cons of each.

#1: Online House Value Calculators

Do an online search of "how much is my house worth?" and you'll find dozens of home value estimators. In fact, 22% of US homeowners who determined their home's value used an online estimator. The technical term for these tools is automated valuation model (AVM), and they're typically offered by lenders or real estate sites.

The tools rely on a variety of data points to develop a formula for predicting and calculating the value of your home. The data used can include public records like property transfers, deeds of ownership and tax assessments along with some mathematical modelling. Although each tool may be built slightly differently, the overall aim is to predict your home's value based on recent sales and current listing prices in the area.

There's a catch: Generally speaking, most AVMs are for marketing and lead generation purposes. They are built to provide a value for just about every property even when data is limited. And this waters down the accuracy of their results.

That doesn't mean all AVMs are useless. Quite often, AVMs built by lenders and real estate professionals use slightly different standards. These online calculators use a "confidence score" to indicate how close the AVM provider thinks an estimate is to market value. For example, a confidence score of 90% means the estimate is within 10% of market value, though each AVM has its own way of calculating confidence.

Professional-grade AVMs with confidence scores are a step up from the real estate sites but still lack complete accuracy.

AMERICAN LOCAL OR NATIONAL HOUSE PRICE INDEX

If you live in America and you're wary of AVMs but still want a quick estimate of what your home is worth, the Federal Housing Financing Agency (FHFA) offers their house price index (HPI) calculator that applies a more scientific approach.

The tool uses the repeat sales method. Armed with millions of mortgage transactions gathered since the 1970s, the FHFA tracks a house's change in value from one sale to the next. Then it uses this information to estimate how values fluctuate in a given market.

Although this method can be more accurate, its accuracy depends on whether the home (and mortgage associated with the home) conforms with the "typical" home. For more American markets, that means the FHFA AVM works best for properties with loans less than $510,400 (up to $765,600 in high-cost areas). Plus, the value estimates offered are not seasonally adjusted or adjusted for inflation.

These are certain limits. Still, if you have a conventional, conforming loan, the HPI calculator is an easy way to see how much your house may have appreciated over time and where its current value lies today.

#2: Comparative Market Analysis

Another option is to ask a local real estate agent for a comparative market analysis (CMA).

Although not as detailed as a professional appraisal, a CMA provides an evaluation of the home and current market trends based on parameters chosen by a real estate agent. A CMA is good at providing an estimate of your home's value.

Local real estate agents may provide a CMA for little or no cost, typically because they are vying to get your business as a potential property seller.

You don't have to rely on a real estate agent to get a CMA. These days, a variety of sites offer "sold" information that can help you find sale prices and other information about comparable properties, often called "comps."

Pulling comps is one way to determine market value without paying an appraiser, but use good judgement. Just because the property next door sold doesn't mean it's a comp.

To choose accurate comps, you must employ an "apples to apples" approach. Think about which properties would interest a buyer if yours weren't available. Look for similar size, location, condition and upgrades.

To get started:

Browse a site where MLS listings are displayed to find the recent sale prices of comparable houses in your neighbourhood.

If there aren't enough recent sales, look at listing prices, but remember they might not be realistic.

You'll need at least three valid comps to come up with a market value range for your home.

#3: Tax Assessments

Finally, if you are already a homeowner, consider using your property tax assessment record number—referred to as a roll number—to access password-protected property tax information. Although each municipality will have its restrictions, most allow homeowners to register a property tax account, which you can then use to peek into the city's official documentation on neighbouring properties.

In the past, I've suggested using this information to launch a tax assessment appeal, but the information could also be used to find comparable properties—similar square footage, lot size and housing attributes—and to determine the official value of these properties using tax assessment data.

If you do opt to use this information, keep in mind that tax assessment data is limited. Although it's illegal, many homeowners still don't report upgrades and renovations, which can artificially deflate the city's value assessment of the property. Also, in prior years, tax assessments weren't always in line with market values. This is because the assessments were set at a particular point in time, while market value adapted to current, real-time trends.

What to Do with These Tools

Once you've chosen the appropriate comparable properties, things get a little tricky. You'll need to adjust for differences between your home and the comps, such as adding value to the comp price if your home has more bedrooms, or subtracting value if your home's interior is outdated.

How much you add or subtract depends on conditions in your market; as you can imagine, these can vary widely. After adjusting values, look at your highest and lowest comps. A rough estimate of your home's value is somewhere in the middle.

Unfortunately, there are no free, online tools in Canada to help you make these adjustments easily and quickly. Don't get me wrong, there are tools, but each one has significant enough limitations that it makes them pretty useless for most home-owners in most circumstances. For instance, one online tool offers cost guides for fewer than 10 Canadian cities (as well as a national average, but that's not nearly accurate enough for this type of valuation exercise) but you can only select from a handful of remodelling and update projects. Plus, this tool only gives you a cost to add or upgrade; it doesn't provide a potential return on the expense—the answer to that all-important "how much value will this add to my home?" question.

If you want an accurate answer as to how much a potential reno-vation would add to the value of your home or a precise value as to how much your home is worth in the current market, you'll need to pay a professional.

Paid Professional: Hire an Appraiser

Lenders hire appraisers before they approve a mortgage primarily because they do not want to overvalue a property and extend a loan that is out of sync with the property's actual value.

As a property owner, you can hire an appraiser to estimate the home value at any time. More than a quarter (28%) of US homeowners determined their home's value through an appraisal (while just over half, 56%, used comp valuations).

Among other things, appraisers evaluate:

- **Market:** The region, city and neighbourhood in which a home is located.

- **Property:** Characteristics of the house, including improvements and the land it sits on.

- **Comparable properties:** Sales, listings, vacancies, cost, depreciation and other factors for similar houses in the same market.

- **Impact of current trends:** Are the demographics changing in your neighbourhood? Are more homes being renovated? And other changes to the area.

This information is combined to create a final opinion of the market value for your home and delivered as an official, date-stamped report.

WHY KNOWING YOUR HOME'S VALUE IS IMPORTANT

Knowing your home's value allows you to evaluate what you can afford, determine whether a listing is priced appropriately, decide how to price your own home (if you are selling) and make smart decisions when it comes to your home.

And the benefits of finding a property's value doesn't end with a purchase or sale: refinances, home equity lines of credit,[15] insurance premiums and annual property taxes are all based on your home's value.

Determining your home's value means greater control over all of these processes. Knowing how to calculate your home's value better prepares you to buy, sell, refinance, tap into your home's equity, decide what and when to remodel, make renovation decisions or even negotiate lower property taxes.

It can also provide a better, clearer picture of your overall financial health. This is key, given that your home is an important tool in establishing and growing your net worth.

SUM IT UP

Most homeowners know what they paid for their property and how much their monthly mortgage is, but not everyone knows the current value of their property.

Why does it matter? If you are living in your home, intending

---

15 Holden Lewis and Kate Wood, "HELOC: Home Equity Line of Credit FAQs," *Nerd-Wallet*, June 5, 2020, https://www.nerdwallet.com/article/mortgages/heloc-home-equity-line-of-credit.

to continue living there for the foreseeable future and making the mortgage payments, why would you care about its current market value?

Knowledge of current market value is important for a whole host of reasons. Your home's current market value plays a role in how your insurance premiums are calculated; how your property tax rate is determined; methods you can use to strategically plan for your financial future; and whether you can sell, downsize or trade up.

Knowing your home's value can also help you make smart, strategic decisions that can help you save money as well as time. What your home is worth and the price of homes recently sold in the neighbourhood are important factors used when comparing and contrasting your home, which helps determine the potential market demand, and value, of your home. This information can then be used to make more strategic decisions when it comes to repairs and renovations— homeowner costs that can hurt or help your bottom line.

TAKEAWAYS

Your Home Is an Asset—Know It's Value. This isn't a debate about what side of the ledger your home should sit. This is about making smart decisions using all information and tools at your disposal. Learn how property is valued, understand how depreciation works and research the value of your home in relation to current neighbourhood conditions and market trends. Do this, and you'll end up making wiser wealth-building decisions, including the money you spend and save on your home.

Become a Pragmatic Optimist. There are many reasons to follow or get embroiled in housing market debates, but making decisions about homeownership isn't one of them. Instead of focusing on what was, what could have been or how it should be, focus on what is and what you have. Your budget, your goals, your risk tolerance and your knowledge are all powerful mechanisms that can help you achieve your milestones and goals. Remember, you can't fix a bike with tools you wish you had.

3

MANAGING HOUSEHOLD EXPENSES

LEARN HOW TO MAINTAIN (AND EVEN INCREASE!) YOUR PROPERTY'S VALUE THROUGH HOME MAINTENANCE AND STRATEGIC BUDGETING

When my husband and I bought our first home, we knew it was a fixer-upper. We'd bought the home at a modest discount because of the blanket of mould that had covered the basement. (To get the mortgage, we had to show complete mould remediation including air quality samples before and after the work—the level of mould growth was *that* bad.) Even though we knew the repair and remediation would be pricey, we never appreciated the amount of time and money it would take to diagnose and fix *every* problem.

We had bought the downtown Toronto rowhouse in the winter months. By the spring thaw, we knew we had to tackle the large leak in our basement—the leak that was the primary cause of the massive mould growth. At that time, we didn't know about the plumbing and electrical issues or the need to repair and replace the foundation to shore up the home's structural integrity. Although unaware, we also were not caught off guard. We had already taken stock and accounted for these major expenses, and factored these into the purchase price and overall plan for the home. Still, had my husband not completed most of the work himself, all of these repairs would have easily cost us $200,000 or more. Even with his labour, we had to take out a line of credit to pay for ongoing material and labour costs.

Back then, it was a labour of love. We were a young couple, early in our careers, childless and full of energy and grit. But even with all this time and energy, on one of the many work weekends, when pulling nails or removing rotted wood from the walls was par for the course, I started to wonder, how much does it cost to repair and maintain the average home?

HOW MUCH SHOULD YOU BUDGET FOR HOME MAINTENANCE?

Truth be told, it's impossible to predict *exactly* what maintenance your home will need, how much it will cost and when it will become necessary, but you can use data and a bit of knowledge to increase your odds.

Once you know the average home maintenance budget, you can use it as a starting point—adjusting it to your unique circumstances, such as the location and age of the property, the seasonal impact on the home, how the home was treated by the previous owners and your home's general condition.

In general, six factors impact your home's general condition:

#1: Age of the property

A newer home, say one built or extensively remodelled in the last ten years, will probably need far less maintenance than a home built a few decades or a century ago. That's because each of your home's major components, as well as all the interior and exterior facets, have a lifespan. The older the home, the more likely one or more of these components are coming to the end of that lifespan and will need to be repaired or replaced.

For example, gas or electric water heaters only last about 10 years, according to the Life Expectancy of Home Components study that's collected and compiled by the National Association of Home Builders. Aluminium windows only last 15 or 20 years, while wood windows can last 30 years or more if cared for properly (and old-growth window frames can last much, much longer).

#2: Seasonal variations

If you live in an area with distinct seasons or extreme temperatures, this will put a much greater strain on your home.

For instance, in just about every city in Canada, homeowners need a home that can provide a cool retreat in summer when temperatures can hit 30°C or more. This same home must also provide an impenetrable barrier from –20°C or colder.

#3: Extreme weather conditions

Although temperature fluctuations can put stress on the home, so do extreme weather conditions. Homes in areas that experience ice storms or heavy snowfall are subject to more strain than homes that are not exposed to cold weather. Similarly, homeowners living in climates that experience high winds, heavy rains and other extreme weather conditions can expect a faster degradation of their home's structure than homeowners in areas not prone to these extremes.

#4: Geographical factors

There are geographical features that can either hurt or help property values. For example, if your home was built on a floodplain or in an area prone to landslides, you may need to disclose this to potential buyers, who may consider these problems as less than attractive. Other issues can include erosion around cliffs and overhangs; the potential for earthquakes, tornados or hurricanes; or a higher risk of pest infestations, such as rats or termites. Not only do geographic circumstances impact the perceived value of your home, but the damage done can also impact your home's integrity and, consequently, its value on the market.

#5: How well the property was treated

The more a property ages, the more important it is to maintain it well. If the prior owner (or owners) didn't maintain the home, this would mean spending more time and money on repairs as well as regular maintenance.

#6: The size of the property

Yes, size does matter. Larger homes and larger plots of land will typically cost more to maintain.

Using the 1% to 5% Rule to Budget Home Maintenance Costs

Calculating average costs gives you a starting point for building your home maintenance savings, and real estate rules of thumb can help you do this. One popular rule of thumb is to put aside between 1% and 5% of the purchase price of your home each year for ongoing maintenance.

Is the 1% to 5% Rule Realistic?

Follow the rule-of-thumb approach and you'll be setting aside between $7,165 and $35,840 each year. This is based on 1% to 5% of the Canadian Real Estate Association's national benchmark price of $716,828, as of March 2021.

Over five years this unrealistic shortcut to home maintenance budgeting means setting aside as much as $180,000 in "just in case" repair money! Ask any homeowner who didn't buy a money pit or dilapidated fixer-upper and they'll tell you, this budget line item is not realistic.

What About Larger Upgrades and Repairs?

But what about the larger upgrades and repairs? The costs that can blow a hole through your budget? Chances are, most homeowners will end up paying for at least one larger repair or upgrade—if not more than one, quips my husband.

Does the 1% to 5% Rule factor in these costs? If not, then how do you factor in these larger, more expensive repairs and upgrades, such as replacing a roof, repairing or replacing plumbing or upgrading electrical?

Challenging the 1% to 5% Rule to Budget for Home Maintenance Costs

Since my first house (and subsequent homes) have all been fixer-uppers, I decided to challenge the 1% to 5% Rule.

I suspected this rule-of-thumb calculation wasn't too accurate and wanted a more realistic method for homeowners to create a home maintenance budget. Not only that, but I also wanted to nail down *exactly* what tasks and jobs were required to properly maintain a property. By developing a must-do list, along with a more accurate budgeting tool, smart homeowners could then allocate the right amount to household costs and use the remaining money to strategically grow their net worth. Win-win, right?

To keep me on track, I broke down a home's vital components into seven basic categories. I considered each of these components integral because:

- they add to the overall structural integrity of the home, helping prevent minor and major damage caused by time, use and environmental impact;

- almost all of these components can lead to very expensive repair and replacement costs if not properly maintained;

- typically, each component has a long shelf life, meaning that replacement costs can be minimized with proper upkeep; and

- each component costs a great deal to replace.

The idea was to create a systematized process and budget to ensure that each of these seven components is up to date and thoroughly maintained. Doing this helps mitigate potentially expensive problems and helps maintain the value of your property.

Using the Per Square Foot Contractor Method

To develop a more realistic maintenance task list and budget, I first had to divide household maintenance expenses into two broad categories:

- Regular or ongoing tasks

- One-off or major upgrade tasks

Why bother making this distinction? The first reason is that it's really hard for most homeowners to budget for repeated maintenance tasks, let alone unexpected repairs or necessary upgrades. Sure, the smart homeowner has an emergency fund of at least three months' worth of living expenses stashed in a high-interest savings account, but will those funds cover the cost of a blown furnace? A leaking roof? Or fixing a sinking foundation? Since it's these costs that can often throw off even the most finely tuned budget, it was important to figure out a way to budget for both known and not-yet-known home maintenance projects.

Annual Maintenance Tasks and Amortized Strategic Updates

To differentiate, I consider the known, regular tasks to be "Annual Maintenance Tasks," while the less structured and more expensive upgrades are "Amortized Strategic Updates."

To be clear, the Annual Maintenance Tasks are typically the easy items to plan and budget for. Still, I am sure many homeowners will find one or two tasks (and costs) not yet on their home maintenance task list.

The Amortized Strategic Update list was harder to ascertain. Many of the more expensive upgrades and repairs involve components with a multiyear lifespan. Given the length of time it takes before facing this type of cost, how can a smart homeowner budget for these line items but still not trap good money in bad situations (picture the value of your dollar eroding as it sits for months and years waiting for the roof repair bill)? To calculate the costs in the Amortized Strategic Update list, I found the average or cost range of the most common upgrades or repairs and then divided this cost over the lifespan of the component.

For example, if you need to replace your roof and it will cost you $18,000 but should last 25 years, then the annual cost of that roof replacement is $720.

Are there holes in this method? Absolutely! We know that labour and material costs tend to increase over time and this inflation can erode your purchasing power. Plus, most home renos and upgrades aren't precise. Price ranges and how long an upgrade lasts can vary, sometimes quite dramatically. Still, this method of finding the amortized cost of a major repair does help develop a more realistic budget for average home maintenance costs.

For more on the lifespan of components, please go online to www. zolo.ca/house-poor-no-more.

Putting Annual and Amortized Together to Create a Budget

Once the research and calculations were complete, I had a cost range—from the complete handy homeowner to the pay-the-pros homeowner—for each task and component in the complete home maintenance task list.

Great. And if you lived in my sample house, you could copy these costs directly into your household budget. But what if you didn't live in my sample house? (See the Appendix for the defining features of my sample house.) Then what?

To overcome our differences in property types and sizes, I chose to calculate the per square foot costs for both the Annual tasks and Amortized tasks. This means that all you have to do is use the per square foot cost to calculate the cost range for those tasks. For ease of use, I refer to this method of creating a home maintenance budget as the Per Square Foot Contractor (PSFC) method.

The reference to "contractor" is an homage to my husband, who has taught me about home maintenance and renovation, and a reference to real estate investment terminology.

In the real estate investment world, there are five main methods for evaluating a property investment: the Comparison method, the Profits method, the Residual method, the Investment method and the Contractor method. The Contractor method is often used as a last resort by real estate investors since costs and projected earnings can easily be swayed by economic forces. Still, the method relies on providing a property evaluation based on the cost of providing a modern equivalent to what exists. For more on these methods of property evaluation, please go online to www.zolo.ca/house-poor-no-more.

For ease of use, I've broken out the seven home expenses into separate sections. Each section includes the associated Annual Maintenance Tasks and costs and Amortized Strategic Updates and costs for that housing component, as well as the breakdown of per square foot costs.

Please keep in mind, every homeowner has their level of comfort and desire for getting their hands dirty. To help cover this vast spectrum, I provide cost ranges. The lowest end reflects the handy do-it-yourself homeowner. The upper end reflects the hands-off homeowner who would prefer to pay the pros for virtually all tasks.

To sum up, I provide an overall annual budget range at the end of this chapter. Use this range to plan and pay for home maintenance in a smart, strategic way.

7 COMPONENTS TO INCLUDE IN YOUR HOME MAINTENANCE PLAN

Your home shelters you and your belongings from the elements—elements that can be harsh and unforgiving. That means your number one priority is to preserve the exterior envelope of your home while keeping the interior components working optimally. The key to doing this is preventative maintenance. Here are the seven components in your home that require preventative maintenance—the seven areas where you need to spend time and money to maintain the integrity and value of your property:

Expense 1: External structure (including external plumbing, windows, doors, walls and seams)

Expense 2: Roof

Expense 3: Landscaping and grading

Expense 4: Foundation

Expense 5: Heating, ventilation and air conditioning (HVAC)

Expense 6: Electrical

Expense 7: Plumbing

Expense 1: External Structure

You need to make sure your home's exterior envelope is watertight and weatherproof. The exterior envelope is the outer structure of your home that defends it against fluctuating temperatures, changing seasons and the weaknesses introduced by various protrusions, sharp angles and different materials used in the construction of your home.

Your job is to keep the exterior as seamless as possible, a task even the most novice do-it-yourselfer can accomplish. The key is consistent, persistent observation followed by quick remedial action.

To illustrate, let's assume an outside tap starts a slow drip. The homeowner notices this drip, but rather than spend $0.19 on a new washer and 15 minutes to repair the faucet seal, the homeowner places a bucket under the leaky tap. For the first few months, the water in the bucket is diligently dumped onto the lawn. Over time, the homeowner forgets about the bucket and the leak. Fast forward 10 years and this small drip manages to destabilize the home's foundation and cause structural damage. Now the repair cost is closer to $15,000 and includes excavation, shoring up the foundation and waterproofing. Although the homeowner avoided having to deal with the leaking outside tap for a decade, the cost of doing so was an almost eight-million-percent increase when compared to the initial repair cost. Ouch.

This scenario is not uncommon and highlights how that old cliché "An ounce of prevention is worth a pound of cure" is really applicable when it comes to maintaining your home.

There's another reason for maintaining the external structure of your home: to significantly reduce the chance of expensive or harmful damage to your home's interior and your own health.

When a property suffers damage to its exterior envelope (or to its foundation), other problems may occur. For instance, elevated humidity levels, moisture problems and flooding can lead to rot in wood used for framing or other organic materials used to build the home. Elevated levels of moisture in a house can also lead to mould and mildew problems, which can become so significant that a home can be considered unlivable.

Ideally, we want to keep the home's external structure impenetrable but still able to breathe.

6 PROBLEM SIGNS CAUSED BY YOUR HOME'S BROKEN WEEPING TILE SYSTEM

#1: UNUSUAL ODOUR

If you notice a musty or damp smell in your basement or crawl-space, there could be mould or mildew caused by a build-up of moisture. Pay close attention to joists, walls and flooring. Signs of mould and mildew include stained or peeling drywall or paint, as well as separation of flooring or wall materials.

#2: POOLING WATER AROUND YOUR EXTERIOR

Pooling water around the exterior can be a sign that your yard is not properly sloped away from your home and not able to do its job (which is to move water away from your foundation). Another culprit is that downspouts are not directing water from the roof out into the garden but dumping water too close to your foundation. Another culprit for pooling water is that your home's weeping tile—the drainage system designed to create an easy underground path for water to move away from your home—is clogged or broken.

#3: CRACKS IN YOUR FOUNDATION

Look for horizontal, vertical or diagonal cracks. The force of water pooling against the foundation can cause small cracks in your foundation. Even small hairline cracks can be an indication of a problem. Watch and monitor all cracks to see if they get bigger or show signs of water seepage.

#4: WATER STAINS ON YOUR BASEMENT WALLS

This is an indication that something is wrong. If ignored, this could lead to serious flooding.

#5: LEAKS IN YOUR BASEMENT

Although there are few sources for leaks in the basement, the primary culprit is a home with an ineffective or non-existent perimeter drain. This becomes a more urgent problem if the leak is persistent, but that doesn't mean you should ignore a leak if it happens only once or twice a year.

#6: EMPTY SUMP PUMP PIT

There should always be some water at the bottom of your sump pump pit. If your pit is not filling with water, this is a sign that the weeping tile is clogged and needs immediate attention.

Annual Maintenance Tasks: External Structure

Most home improvement professionals recommend that homeowners take inventory of their home's exterior at least once a year, given that serious weather and even average wear and tear can lead to bigger issues if left unchecked.

Walk the perimeter of your home. Check for damage or potential issues. Keep an eye out for any large cracks or dents, major mildew build-up, and stains caused by leaks.

Ideally, this first step is best done in the spring, when the weather starts to warm up and snow and rain have melted. In climates that don't experience cold spells, consider taking this step in the winter, when temperatures are cooler and it's easier to stay outside during daylight.

Regardless of when you schedule this walk around, make sure you systematically complete this step at least once per year.

Take a power washer and clean off the dirt and debris that's accumulated over the year. Not only does this protect your home's curb appeal, but it can also help prolong the life of your home's external cladding and, by washing away debris, expose any potential problems you may have missed during the initial visual inspection.

For vinyl or metal siding and stone, the highest power washer setting should suffice. For stucco, older wood-clad homes and older brick homes, it's recommended that you use the lowest possible setting on a power washer so you don't risk damaging your home's exterior cladding. If your stucco or brick is really dirty or risks crumbling and decaying at the slightest pressure, you may have to call in professionals to do this external cleaning for you.

Once clean, it's time to do another visual inspection. Again, check for cracks, holes, mould or mildew spots that didn't come off during the power wash.

Then check all external protrusions from the home. Check vents (for dryers, ovens and fireplaces) and external taps (called bibs), as well as window wells and door trims. Check weather stripping (inside and outside of doors and windows) and the effectiveness of door sweeps (the rubberized attachment at the bottom of the door that creates an airtight seal).

Lubricate door hinges and garage door springs. Clean out all window and patio door tracks.

What Is Mould and Why Is It Bad?

Mention mould, and many people either visualize a past-its-due-date slice of bread or rush straight to catastrophic visions of hazmat suits and months living in a hotel. Just because you may notice a mould spot on or in your home doesn't mean you'll need a remediation crew.

Turns out, roughly 50% of North American homes have some type of mould despite a lack of smell or any visible infestation, according to a Harvard study.

That means if you notice mould or discolouration, it's time to do an assessment. The first step is to learn what mould is and what causes it to grow.

What is mould?

Moulds are part of a group of microorganisms called fungi, like mushrooms and yeasts. Mould is one of nature's decomposers, destroying anything organic from food products to wood, carpet and other materials. If allowed to grow, it can cause significant damage to your home's structure by disintegrating less-stable products, such as drywall, and rotting wooden beams and posts. Mould will also stain and discolour fabrics.

Then there's your health: according to Health Canada, mould can seriously impact your overall health and wellness, causing headaches and allergic reactions, as well as asthma and allergic rhinitis.

How mould grows

However, mould needs a few precise conditions to grow:

- Presence of mould spores (which are always present both indoors and outdoors)

- A temperature range between 2° and 40°C (or 35.6° to 104°F)

- A food supply (anything organic such as books, carpets, clothing, wood, drywall)

- A source of moisture

There is only one factor that a homeowner can control when it comes to mould: the level of moisture in your home, and that moisture can come from the unlikeliest places.

Moisture can come from excessive condensation on uninsulated pipes, a lack of insulation in the walls, or a lack of vents in the roof (which allow for air circulation throughout the home). Moisture can also result from water penetrating your home's exterior structure, seeping up from the earth into a basement floor, coming from a leaking interior wall pipe, or coming through holes in walls or the roof.

Remember, the link between moisture and mould is that too much moisture combined with too little ventilation becomes a breeding ground for mould.

Turns out, most mould growth is simply a flag—a sign that you need to address a moisture problem in your home before it becomes a major issue or expense. In these circumstances:

- Your main concern should be finding out how and where the moisture is coming from.

- Your secondary concern is how to get rid of the mould.

Right way to get rid of mould

Let's say you find a patch of mould and you've identified and fixed the source of the moisture problems. Now, how do you get rid of this spore breeding ground?

For most homeowners, the go-to solution for mould and mildew removal is bleach. There's science to back this up. A 2012 study, published in the *Journal of Occupational and Environmental Hygiene,* found that the use of sodium hypochlorite (bleach-based) disinfectants was "effective and recommended."[16]

Another study, published in the same journal, compared gamma irradiation (the process of sterilizing growth and currently used to treat potatoes and onions to prevent sprouting)[17] to

16   Kelly A. Reynolds, Stephanie Boone, Kelly R. Bright, and Charles P. Gerba, "Occurrence of Household Mold and Efficacy of Sodium Hypochlorite Disinfectant," *Journal of Occupational and Environmental Hygiene* 9, no. 11 (2012): 663–69.

17   "FAQs: The Foods Irradiated in Canada and the Safety Issues," *CBC News*, May 30, 2016, https://www.cbc.ca/news/health/food-irradiation-faq-1.3608013.

steam-cleaning to cleaning with a detergent/bleach wash. The most effective method for cleaning mould was to use a detergent/bleach solution; the least effective was steam-cleaning.[18]

The problem is, these studies were testing bleach with chlorine. According to many studies, the most effective method of eradicating mould spores is to use chlorine dioxide, a yellow-green to orange gas or liquid. Although this compound is very effective as a biocide, it can be deadly and should only be used by professionals under precise conditions. As a result, bleach found in consumer stores may smell like chlorine, but these products don't actually contain chlorine dioxide (which doesn't actually smell like chlorine). Instead, bleach detergents contain either calcium hypochlorite or sodium hypochlorite—both of which are good but not 100% effective in eradicating mould spores (even in undiluted form).

Only a bleach-chlorine solution of 10% or more will kill 100% of mould spores. However, this strength of bleach is not available to consumers and must be purchased through an industrial supplier and used only by properly trained and equipped people.

For the regular homeowner, this means the safest method of getting rid of mildew and mould is still good ol'-fashioned soap and water. The good news is that this cleaning solution is gentle enough to be used on porous surfaces but effective enough to kill the spores anywhere.

18 S. C. Wilson et al., "An Investigation into Techniques for Cleaning Mold-Contaminated Home Contents," *Journal of Occupational and Environmental Hygiene* 1, no. 7 (2004): 442–47.

Mould-Killing Formula: Mix two parts water to one part detergent. Wear protective safety glasses (or goggles), rubber gloves and a disposable dust mask. Remember, when spores are disturbed, they float into the air. To stop them, a liquid cleaning solution is applied, but to prevent inhaling, it's best to wear a mask.

Whether you use soap and water or bleach, remember to dry the area quickly and completely. The idea is to remove the visible mould and remove the wet conditions to prevent additional spores from germinating.

HOW TO CLEAN MOULD ON DIFFERENT SURFACES

Floor: Clean the area using a high-efficiency particulate air (HEPA) filter vacuum. Then scrub or brush the mouldy area with the detergent solution (one part detergent, two parts water). Rinse with a clean, wet rag. Repeat. Dry the area quickly. Vacuum the affected surface and the surrounding area again to get rid of mould spores and inhibit regrowth.

Wood: Clean the area using a HEPA filter vacuum. (You can also use an externally exhausted vacuum such as a shop vac with hose attachment). Clean the wood with the detergent and water mixture, rinse with a clean, damp rag, and dry quickly using towels and fans. If the mould does not come off, sand the wood's surface and vacuum with a vacuum-sander combination. It is important to vacuum at the same time to prevent mould spores from being dispersed into the air. If the mould has turned into wood rot, you won't be able to clean it. You'll need to replace the affected areas.

Concrete: Vacuum and then clean with the detergent and water mixture. If the surface is still visibly mouldy, use TSP (trisodium phosphate)—a cheap but strong cleanser sold in any hardware store. Dissolve one cup of TSP in two gallons of warm water, and stir for two minutes (wear gloves and do not let TSP come in contact with skin or eyes). Saturate the concrete surface with the TSP solution using a sponge or rag, and keep the surface wet for at least 15 minutes. Rinse the concrete surface twice with clean water, and dry as quickly as possible using rags and fans.

Drywall: The paper facings of gypsum wallboard (drywall) grow mould when they get wet repeatedly and don't dry quickly. Cleaning with water and detergent not only adds moisture to the paper but can also damage the drywall. Still, if it's the first time you've noticed mould on your drywall, start by cleaning the surface with a damp rag using baking soda or a bit of detergent, but do not allow the drywall to get too wet. If the mould comes back after the cleaning, it means that the source of the moisture has not been removed. At this point, you may need professional help.

Since the work you do to prevent and remove mould can be combined with other house maintenance tasks or with regular cleaning tasks, there are relatively few extra costs when it comes to mould remediation. For that reason, I did not add annual maintenance or replacement costs due to mould remediation into the home maintenance final tally.

36 TIPS FOR PREVENTING MOULD IN YOUR HOME

- Keep your home dry.

- Find and fix water leaks as soon as possible.

- Clean and maintain your home regularly.

- Remove moisture using exhaust fans or by opening windows for a short time.

- Reduce clutter. Moulds grow on fabrics, paper, wood and practically anything that collects dust and holds moisture.

- Dehumidify the basement during warmer months.

- Avoid slab-on-grade installation of carpets.

- Periodically clean the drain in your basement floor. Use half a cup of bleach, let it stand for a few minutes and then flush with plenty of water. Keep the drain trap filled with water.

- Avoid standing water. Keep sump pits covered. (You can buy or get custom covers or use plywood wrapped in plastic.)

- Regularly clean and replace furnace filters. Use a pleated one-inch filter, not a coarse filter.

- If you have a heat recovery ventilator (HRV), clean the filter often.

- If you notice moulds or signs of dampness, such as water on your windows or wet spots, do not humidify. Disconnect furnace humidifiers that are no longer used.

- If you have electric baseboards, vacuum the units or have a professional clean them.

- Check that your clothes dryer exhausts outside of the house.

- Remove lint every time you use the dryer.

- Don't hang-dry laundry indoors.

- Check the bathroom fan to make sure it exhausts outside of the home.

- Turn the bathroom fan on when you shower. Keep it running after you finish your shower (to remove excess moisture from the home).

- Towel-dry shower stalls and bathtubs after use.

- If there is a carpet in your bathroom, remove it.

- Remove debris from external and internal drains.

- Clean drains regularly (aim for once per season, at least). Pour a handful of baking soda and then add a cup of vinegar before putting a plug into the drain.

- If the fan over your stove exhausts outside, use it when you cook.

- Minimize open boiling of water.

- Clean the drip pan at the back of the refrigerator. Pull the fridge out to do this; at the same time, vacuum the dust from the coils or back casing behind the fridge.

- Check under the kitchen sink to make sure there are no water leaks.

- Get rid of clothes and items you don't use. Keeping your closets and bedrooms tidy makes it easier for air to circulate and harder for mould to grow.

- Close the windows when the dehumidifier is running.

- When family and friends come to the home, ask them to take off their shoes.

- Vacuum often. If you are buying a vacuum cleaner, get one with a HEPA filter.

- Clean hard floors with a damp mop.

- Do not bring items that have been stored in a mouldy place into your home.

- Reduce the number of potted plants in the house; soil is a good place for mould to grow.

- Regularly check the roof and exterior finish for places where water might enter.

- Make sure that eavestroughs and downspouts are connected and working properly and that they are free of debris.

- Install downspout extensions to lead water away from your home.

Now that we've got a handle on mould and how to prevent these spores from germinating, let's review the required maintenance tasks for your home's external structure.

Annual Maintenance Costs: External Structure

- Replace weather-stripping around windows and doors, replace door sweeps: $150 to $500

- Fill holes with spray foam and recaulk foundation seams as well as window and doorframes: $10 to $35

- Power wash siding and exterior structures: $0 to $200

- Lubricate garage door: $15 to $150

Total Annual Costs: $175 to $885

Per Square Foot Cost: $0.09 to $0.44

Amortized Strategic Updates: External Structure

For example, installing new vinyl windows can cost between $3,000 and $12,000 but will eliminate the annual sanding, priming and painting old wooden frames require, while also increasing energy efficiency.

Just ***don't*** replace century-old wood window frames; even though you will need to perform annual maintenance on them, they are more resistant to rot and vermin than newer window frames (and are a sought-after feature in character homes).

The idea with these updates is that most homeowners will need to spend money on at least one if not many more home upgrades or replacements to keep their property in optimal shape. Ideally, the less you need to replace, the better for your pocketbook, but that doesn't mean you should put off all these tasks. If you do, expect a larger hit to your pocketbook at some point in time or watch the market value of your home decrease as potential buyers factor in all the replacements and updates that are still required to get your home up to current standards.

Although a comprehensive list of all upgrade costs and life expectancy for components and material can be found online at www.zolo.ca/house-poor-no-more, here are the most common costs most homeowners experience.

Amortized Strategic Update Costs: External Structure

- Replace 10 new, double-pane vinyl windows every 8 to 20 years ($3,000 to $12,000): $215 to $857

Managing Household Expenses

- Replace 3 external vinyl doors, every 15 to 20 years ($2,400 to $4,500): $137 to $257

- Replace or install new vinyl siding, every 20 to 40 years ($4,300 to $15,800): $143 to $527

- Replace sliding glass/patio exterior door, every 20 years ($1,200 to $5,000): $60 to $250

- Replace garage door, every 20 to 25 years ($650 to $2,000): $29 to $89

- Replace garage door opener, every 10 to 15 years ($120 to $500): $9.60 to $40

- Replace extension springs in garage door, every 7 years ($30 to $300): $4 to $43

- Replace hose bib (tap) with antifreeze bib, every 20 to 30 years ($30 to $200): $1.20 to $8

- Add or rebuild single-car garage, one-time cost ($8,000 to $24,000): $320 to $960

- Repaint the exterior, every 7 to 10 years ($3,000 to $10,000): $353 to $1,177

Total Amortization Cost per Year: $1,272 to $4,208

Per Square Foot Cost: $0.64 to $2.14

EXPENSE 2: THE ROOF

The roof is integral to the external envelope. It's the cap that, combined with the walls and foundation, helps create an impervious barrier to the elements. It's also one of the most expensive components to replace. The cost to replace a standard 1,500-square-foot roof can range from $4,200 to $13,500, depending on the roof grade, time of the year, type and quality of materials, and company. Then there are all the systems and components designed to keep your roof watertight and secure: the eavestroughs, gutters, fascia, soffits and even bargeboard.

Annual Maintenance Tasks: The Roof

The good news is, you can prolong the life of your roof and its accompanying components by implementing a few ongoing maintenance routines.

1. Visually inspect your roof. Look for curled and separating shingles. Another way is to examine the amount of grit and gravel that collects in your eaves and gutters. That grit is bits of asphalt rolling off the roof during wind and rainstorms. If you find more than a quarter inch of sediment, it's time to look at a new roof.

2. Also, look for waves or dips, which are indicators of rot. If you catch it early enough, you can eliminate rot with the simple addition of more roof vents (rather than tearing off the roof shingles and replacing the trusses and beams).

3. Secure or replace loose shingles. If getting on the roof is a terrifying thought, it's time to hire a roofer.

4. Inspect the chimney and its mortar to verify that the chimney cap is securely fastened. If not, critters will use this as an entrance to your home or as a place to set up a home.

5. Inspect your flashing seals. Flashing is the thin, continuous piece of metal (or other impervious material) that's installed at every angle or roof joint to prevent water from seeping under the roof material, such as asphalt tiles. A sealant is used to strengthen this barrier and must be retouched regularly. Remember, for a roof to be effective, it has to be seamlessly watertight and weather resistant.

6. Inspect the components that are designed to keep water from entering the roof and your home. This includes eavestroughs (the cap that protects your roof's structure, known as trusses), gutters (the component that attaches to the eaves to collect and move water away from your home), fascia (also known as the roofline), soffits (underside of fascia) and bargeboard (the side where the roofline meets the wall). Look for holes or damage. If you find any, make a note to repair or replace the damaged components ASAP.

7. Inspect downspouts and drains (along with the gutters). Look for holes and other damage that would minimize the effectiveness of these components.

8. Twice a year—in the spring and fall—clear the debris from all of the components mentioned above: clean out the leaves, twigs and animal waste.

9. Twice a year—in the spring and fall—check for blockages. Do this when it's raining or turn on a hose and run it up to the gutter. The water should flow freely through the

gutter to the downspout and away from your home. If this doesn't happen, pay attention to where water gets stuck, backs up or doesn't drain. This is where you need to focus your maintenance and repair efforts.

10. In the winter, visually inspect your gutters and down-spouts. Look for areas where water is pooling or ice is building up as this is where water can freeze and form ice dams. An ice dam is a ridge of ice that forms at the edge of a roof and prevents melting snow (water) from draining off the roof. The water that backs up behind the dam can leak into your home and damage walls, ceilings, insulation and other areas.

KEY COMPONENTS OF THE ROOF

There are many different parts of the roof as well as different types of roofs (from gable, to flat to mansard). Typically, though, all roof structures will consist of similar components, all of which are integral to keeping your roof impervious to weather conditions and your home watertight.

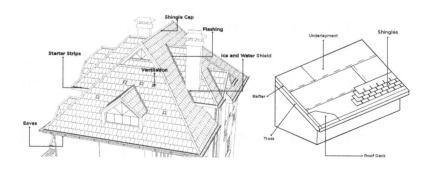

The key components of the roof, as illustrated, are:

Truss: The "skeleton" of the roof, made of a series of parallel beams.

Rafters: The supporting beams that run from the apex (top) of the roof to the bottom. Rafters hold up the truss.

Sheathing: These are the flat panels attached to the roof truss, which forms the base layer of your roof. Usually made of construction-grade plywood or particle board. The sheathing adds structural integrity to the roof frame.

Underlayment: Felt paper or rubber membrane installed on exposed roof decking for better strength, longevity and breathability.

Ice and Water Shield: Installed on your roof system's more vulnerable areas to keep the roof leak-free. Usually found around vents, skylights, chimneys and soil stacks.

Starter Strips: Installed on all edges of the roofline to prevent water and wind intrusion under the shingles.

Shingles: The outer covering that is the most visible part of a roof. Shingles come in a variety of materials including asphalt, fibreglass, tile, wood, metal or slate. Flat roofs do not use shingles but require waterproof membranes, usually made with tar.

Flashing: Refers to the metal seals placed around vent pipes, chimneys and other leak-prone areas of the roof.

Ventilation: Prevents excessive heat build-up in the attic space, helping reduce wear and tear on the roofing materials, while allowing for a more consistent temperature.

Shingle Cap: Special shingle used to cover the peaks in your roof, giving it an enhanced, more finished appearance.

Eaves: The edges of the roof, typically overhanging the vertical exterior walls of a home (or building). The eaves are one structure made up of three components: fascia, soffits and drip edges.

Here's a trick for estimating your roof size: Multiply the square footage of your home by 1.5. For example, a basic box-style one-storey house with a 1,000-square-foot base (although, you could have 2,000 square feet of living space stacked on two floors) will have a roof that is approximately 1,500 square feet (based on a 26.5-degree pitch roof). To determine the minimum linear feet of gutters you'll need to replace on your home, divide the home's square footage by 10.

Annual Maintenance Costs: The Roof

- Replace loose or worn shingles and recaulk flashing: $150 to $1,000

- Chimney maintenance, cleaning and minor repairs: $200 to $400

- Clean eavestroughs and downspouts, twice per year: $0 to $500

- Repair gutters, fascia and soffits, once every two years: $200 to $500

Total Annual Cost: $550 to $2,400

Per Square Foot Cost: $0.36 to $1.60

Amortized Strategic Updates: The Roof

If you end up owning property for more than a decade of your life, chances are you'll end up paying to replace one or all of your roof's components. This can often be expensive. To give you an accurate picture of the cost of each component, I've separated them in the list (under Amortized Strategic Update Costs). But quite often, the same company can do all of this work for you. (Or, at the very least, one company will reshingle and another will complete the replacements of all the other components.)

VALUE OF A NEW ROOF

A roof replacement or upgrade will rarely add perceived value to your home. Very few potential buyers will value a home more just because a roof has been updated or replaced. If anything, not replacing, updating (or even maintaining) your roof and its complementary support network (like the eavestroughs and gutters) will hurt resale value. This is particularly true if the neglect has gone on long enough that other problems, like rot or mould, have emerged.

Still, your home's roof is arguably the most important component of your home, and aside from its role in structural integrity, it also makes or breaks your home's curb appeal.

Metal roofs last the longest but are also the most expensive, with the average installation cost between $35,000 and $50,000 for a standard roof on a 2,300-square-foot home. Asphalt shingles don't last as long but are far more cost-effective, with the average installation cost between $10,000 and $15,000.

When selecting materials, opt for a longer warranty, such as 25 or 30 years. It adds about $300 to $500 to your total cost but provides more peace of mind.

Also, when updating your roof, pay to strip away the old roof. It costs a bit more but will prolong the life of your new shingles.

Finally, those with flat roofs should be prepared for sticker shock. Repair and replacement of flat roofs are expensive—costing you three to five times what your peaked-roof neighbours will pay. In part, it's the expertise required to do this work. Flat roofs must be installed correctly to prevent water damage and to prevent condensation or pooling. There's quite a bit of math, angles and calculation involved, as well as layers of work required to complete the job. Expect to pay between $10,000 and $50,000 for a roof replacement; the average ROI on this cost is 61% to 66%.

As a tip, if you are replacing your gutters, consider upgrading from the standard builder's 4-inch gutter to a 5- or 6-inch gutter. It's a nominal cost, and the extra size will help move water away from your house quickly and efficiently, while also preventing damage from debris build-up or the potential for ice dams.

I've also included the cost of insulating your attic. Your attic is the space directly below a pitched roof (so flat-roof houses won't have an attic). Although some homeowners may convert attic space to an office or an additional bedroom, most use it for storage or don't use it at all. But that doesn't detract from the purpose of your attic: to regulate the temperature inside your home. Since uninsulated attics account for 15% of the total energy loss in an average house, most homeowners end up insulating this space.

Standard insulation—fibreglass battens that are inserted between rafters—typically lasts for 15 years before it starts to degrade. Spray foam insulation can last about 20 years, while loose-fill or rock-wool insulation can last up to 100 years (depending on weather, critters and overall attention paid to your home). To determine if your attic insulation needs to be replaced, look for these signs:

- Increased use of heating and cooling to regulate the home's temperature

- Cool drafts within your home

- Consistently damp insulation

- Mould on the insulation

- Very, very dirty insulation

To calculate the size of your attic, measure the length and width to find the room's square footage, then purchase replacement insulation based on manufacturer directions. The goal is to increase the R-value of the attic. The higher the R-value, the better the insulation is at preventing heat from leaving your home. Different insulation types will have various R-values, and insulation will have a better R-value if more is applied to the same space.

Amortized Strategic Update Costs: The Roof

- Remove and reshingle asphalt shingle roof every 20 to 30 years ($4,500 to $13,500): $180 to $540

- Re-insulate attic every 15 years ($1,600 to $4,350): $67 to $290

- Add a roof vent, one-time cost ($30 to $700): $1.20 to $28

- Replace or install attic fan, every 15 to 25 years ($200 to $800): $10 to $40

- Replace soffits & fascia every 20 to 25 years ($3,500 to $6,000): $156 to $267

- Replace gutters every 20 to 40 years ($1,000 to $5,000): $110 to $350

- Install an ice-dam barrier, one-time cost ($140 to $800): $2.80 to $16

- Replace or repair chimney, one-time cost ($1,000 to $4,000): $20 to $80

Total Amortization Cost per Year: $547 to $1,611

Per Square Foot Cost: $0.27 to $0.81

Expense 3: Landscaping and Grading

With the roof secure, it's time to turn your attention to the home's drainage and foundation.

Although a lovely garden can add as much as 20% to the value of your house, even the prettiest patch won't stop the structure from sinking. For that reason, each landscaping, garden and curb appeal project needs to make water drainage its primary goal.

Annual Maintenance Tasks: Landscaping and Grading

Here's a list of the tasks you should accomplish on an annual basis when it comes to drainage and landscaping around your home:

1. Replace mulch around plants and under trees to help the soil hold moisture and wick it away from your home.

2. Examine the ground abutting your home or pour a glass of water on the ground close to your foundation walls. Does it roll away from the home? Does it pool in one area? Worse yet, does it roll towards the home and then pool there, waiting to be absorbed? The minimum standard for grading is one inch for every foot, with at least eight feet of sloping downward grade away from your home, starting at your foundation wall. Any grade that doesn't move water away from your home should be corrected immediately. If not, you could end up paying

for expensive waterproofing remediation—one of the most avoidable, yet costliest repairs to any home.

3. Next, visually inspect the grade of your walkways and driveways. Once again, the slope needs to be sufficient enough to move water away from your home and to avoid pooling or ice-damming.

4. Look for splits or breaks in your paths and driveways, as these cracks can allow water to seep in, which can over-saturate your lawn, promote soil erosion and prevent the garden from keeping water away from your property.

Annual Maintenance Costs: Landscaping and Grading

- Inspect and patch 10' x 12' driveway: $30 to $100

- Add mulch under trees: $30 to $50

Total Annual Cost: $60 to $150

Per Square Foot Cost: $0.03 to $0.08

Amortized Strategic Updates: Landscaping and Grading

If you find that there are grading issues around your home, your best bet is to get this fixed soon. Hopefully, any work to the walkway and driveway can be done in conjunction to ensure that these components are also properly sloping away from your home.

Keep in mind that some companies will break up, regrade and reinstall a driveway all at the same time, while other companies will only install a driveway, meaning you'll need to find another contractor to remove and regrade. Cost out both options to find one that fits your budget and timeline.

Aside from the typical replacement costs, homeowners with older homes that have boxed planters built right against the house—so that soil is touching the home—should consider the removal of these planters. Excess water in these planters has nowhere to go but into your foundation.

- Regrade property around the foundation, one-time cost ($0 to $5,000): $0 to $200

- Repave 120 square feet of a driveway with a new base + regrade, once every 15 to 30 years ($500 to $3,000): $22 to $133

- Repave pathway with new base + regrade, once every 15 to 30 years ($300 to $2,600): $13 to $116

Total Amortization Cost per Year: $35 to $449

Per Square Foot Cost: $0.02 to $0.22

Expense 4: Foundation

Have you ever seen a house that leans to one side? Typically, this is caused by a problematic foundation, and more often than not, these problems are caused by homeowner neglect.

Maintaining your foundation is an easy way to avoid *very* costly repairs—as one homeowner I spoke to found out the hard way. Rather than spend $130 to repair the crack that developed where her driveway meets her home foundation, she ignored the problem. Five years later, she ended up paying just over $10,000 to excavate and waterproof the damaged foundation.

Annual Maintenance Tasks: Foundation

1. The best way to stay on top of foundation issues is by visually inspecting your home at the start of each season.

2. Don't just look for cracks; examine the type of crack. For example, a crack that grows in width from year to year is an indication of larger foundation problems, while a small fissure can simply be a sign of a home settling over time. Crack repair, where hydraulic cement or epoxy is injected into the crack, costs between $50 and $650, depending on the size and location of the crack.

3. Be diligent about snow and debris removal. Snow can melt and cause water damming and damage. Debris can invite pests, as many east-end residents in Toronto learned in the 1940s and again in the 1980s when discarded wood beside homes prompted termite infestations.

4. Inspect the base of your home and your basement for mould and mildew. Use your nose and a flashlight to

look inside closets, behind stored contents and around semi-permanent fixtures, such as the hot water tank.

5. If you find mould, quickly remove it. Then examine the cause. Yes, this may mean a larger-than-anticipated repair bill, but it's nothing compared to ignoring the problem. (For more see Chapter 3, "The Right Way to Remove Mould")

Annual Maintenance Costs: Foundation

- Fill cracks: $100 to $1,000

- Clean up mild mould and mildew: approximately $20

Total Annual Cost: $120 to $1,020

Per Square Foot Cost: $0.06 to $0.51

Amortized Strategic Updates: Foundation

Truth be told, there are few replacement costs to incur when it comes to your foundation, as long as you take care of your home. Seal cracks, grade soil and walkways away from the home, and maintain the roof and gutters, and your foundation should last for 50 years or more. (However, there are some exceptions. See *How Long Will Your Home's Foundation Last?*)

HOW LONG WILL YOUR HOME'S FOUNDATION LAST?

TYPE OF FOUNDATION	LIFE EXPECTANCY IN YEARS
Baseboard waterproofing system	50
Bituminous-coating waterproofing	10
Concrete block	100+
Insulated concrete forms (ICFs)	100
Permanent wood foundation (PWF, treated)	75
Post and pier	20 to 65
Post and tensioned slab on grade	100+
Poured-concrete footings and foundation	100+
Slab on grade (concrete)	100
Wood foundation	5 to 40

Still, not all homeowners address maintenance issues, meaning that somewhere along the way you may need to pay for repairs and upgrades. What you do will depend largely on your specific home. For instance, if you are experiencing persistent basement leaks and, after investigating, realize you have to waterproof your basement, you have two options: an external French drain or internal waterproofing. At first, most homeowners prefer the price point of internal work. However, this doesn't take into consideration the cost of repairing and renovating a basement that was ripped apart to enable the completion of the waterproofing.

HOW TO PROPERLY WATERPROOF YOUR HOME'S FOUNDATION (AND WHY YOU SHOULD CARE)

TYPES OF WATERPROOFING DRAINAGE SYSTEMS	AVERAGE PRO PRICES (Based on 150 linear feet)
1. Interior basement French drain with sump pump and basin: Relies on gravity. Consists of a ditch filled with gravel and perforated pipe, which guides water away. This solution makes sense if the water problem is due to high water table (putting the issue underneath your foundation).	
Typical Linear Foot Cost in the United States: $45 to $105	$6,750 to $15,500
Typical Linear Foot Cost in Canada: $50 to $200	$7,500 to $30,000
2. Exterior French drain: Same as internal but around the outside perimeter of your home. Often cheaper but restricted in its ability to deal with hydrostatic pressure—the pressure caused by a build-up of fluid. For internal and external French drains, the trench is typically dug at least four feet below the foundation.	
Typical Linear Foot Cost in the United States: $20 to $40	$3,000 to $6,000
Typical Linear Foot Cost in Canada: $50 to $300	$7,500 to $45,000
3. Installation or replacement of perimeter or weeping tile systems: Most new builds in North America require this type of drainage as part of the standard build. As a method for waterproofing, this system uses trenches, gravel and perforated piping (or in very old homes, clay pipes) that run along the perimeter of your home at the level of the footings. This is considered standard for home building because it is the most effective way to keep water away from your home's foundation.	
Typical Linear Foot Cost: $35 to $100	$10,500 to $30,000
4. Curtain drain: This is essentially a French drain, but the trench is shallower. At a depth of only two feet, these drains are primarily used where surface wetness is the primary issue.	
Typical Linear Foot Cost: $3.50 to $12	$1,050 to $3,600
5. Yard drainage pipes: This solution involves small catch basins with grates on top. The catch basins are connected to pipes, which move the water away from your home.	

Typical Linear Foot Cost: $13.50 to $40	$2,025 to $6,000
6. Trench or channel: Great option if you need to remove water from areas where puddles form or standing water sits. Involves digging a trough or channel that funnels water to a flush grate that's placed at the low point in the trench. Ideal for driveways or other paved expanses.	
Typical Linear Foot Cost: $30 to $150	$9,000 to $45,000
7. Catch basin or storm drain: A basin that's dug in order to catch the water that builds up during a storm. A grate is usually put over the basin to filter out debris. Best for areas where water could stand, prompting landscape or foundation problems.	
Typical Cost for 10 x 10 Basin: $60 Typical Cost for 12 x 12 Basin: $100 Typical Cost for 20 x 20 Basin: $350	$750 to $3,500
8. Window wells: Although most homeowners consider window wells as a way to install basement windows, these basins also help funnel water away from potential entry points, such as windows. Window wells should have a gravel pit at the bottom that acts as a drain.	
Cost for installation in the United States: $500 to $2,000 Cost for installation in Canada: $800 to $3,500	$500 to $3,500

Amortized Strategic Update Costs: Foundation

Here are the more common foundation replacement jobs and costs you may come across:

- Mould testing and remediation of 200 square foot area, one-time cost ($3,000 to $6,000): $120 to $240

- Waterproofing of 200 linear foot basement foundation, one-time cost ($6,000 to $8,000): $240 to $320

Total Amortization Cost per Year: $360 to $560

Per Square Foot Cost: $0.18 to $0.28

YOUR HOME'S INTERIOR

Now that your home's external structure is taken care of, it's time to move to the interior.

To keep the focus solely on the tasks of maintaining the integrity of the structure and keeping the home running efficiently and effectively, we focus on three main components:

1. Heating, ventilation and air conditioning (known as HVAC)

2. Electrical

3. Plumbing

5 TIPS TO KEEP PESTS AND VERMIN OUT OF YOUR HOME!

If your home is damaged by squirrels, littered with mice, over-run with raccoons or infested with cockroaches, silverfish, ants or other vermin, you are responsible.

Don't consider this a name-and-shame exercise. I've lived in my fair share of apartments with cockroaches, mice or silverfish, and I bought a home that housed five raccoons! Rather, this is about avoiding costly repairs. It's all about the money, honey.

Unfortunately, too many homeowners find out the hard way that damage caused by pests is not covered by home insurance. According to insurance providers, vermin infestations are 100% preventable—through proper maintenance. This means you are responsible for getting rid of pests in your home as well as preventing them from taking up residence in the future.

To stop critters from making your home their home, follow these five tips:

1. Inspect the interior and exterior of your home for gaps, holes and cracks. Some rodents can squeeze into the smallest spots. For example, a mouse can fit into a hole the size of a dime, and squirrels need a gap only an inch wide!

2. Fix the holes and remove water sources. Whether it's caulking, sealant or steel wool, plug up or seal every single hole. Let's say that again: Every. Single. Hole. You will also want to remove all sources of water. Inside the home, that means fixing any leaks. (Did you know cockroaches gather in the well of your dishwasher when you're not looking?) Outside of your home, it also means consistently dumping stagnant water.

3. Once all the holes in your home have been filled, examine other points of entry. For example, squirrels love holes in siding and will use ventilation systems to get into your home. Cats, mice and other vermin find ways through basement window wells and under porches or decks.

4. Install one-way trap doors where rodents are nesting, such as in the attic. These doors allow the squirrels or

other vermin to get outside but lock and prevent them from getting back inside.

5. Get rid of all food. For spiders, this means getting rid of dead bug debris. For raccoons, cats and squirrels, this means sheltering your food waste receptacles (either by bringing them inside or using a lidded bin) and storing food in your kitchen in pest-free containers (plastic or glass jars with lids). Also, rotate loose stored goods, such as cans or bottles in your pantry, as well as linens and towels in your closets.

If you want to use natural or chemical-free deterrents, here's a good list:

- For mice, use steel wool to plug up holes bigger than a dime.

- Ants won't cross an unbroken line of cayenne or black pepper. (Keep in mind that children and dogs can hurt themselves if they ingest too much.)

- Ants dislike strong smells. Wipe down entry spots with oil of cloves or eucalyptus.

- Use a natural powder, such as diatomaceous earth, around baseboards and window frames/wells. It adheres to the shell of insects and slowly dehydrates them. It's safe for pets and humans, but be careful not to ingest it, and wear a paper mask when applying.

- Peanut butter is great at attracting raccoons and mice to traps. These critters love sugar-loaded foods.

Some companies attest to the power of predator urine, mothballs, ammonia-soaked rags or ultrasonic emitters, but this is just the vermin equivalent of snake oil. They don't work. The only way to take care of a vermin problem is to trap and remove (or kill, depending on local laws and your principles). Follow the five steps above, consistently and repeatedly, and your vermin problems will go away. For more on insect infestation, go online to www.zolo.ca/house-poor-no-more.

Expense 5: Heating, Ventilation and Air Conditioning

Your home's heating, ventilation and air conditioning systems (known together as HVAC) are what make your residence comfortable in all seasons—at a price. These systems, together, can easily consume half of a household's energy bill. It makes sense, then, to regularly maintain and check your furnace, ductwork, A/C unit and heat recovery unit and to look for ways to save.

Annual Maintenance Tasks: HVAC

1. Schedule an annual inspection and cleaning of your furnace by early fall, before the cold season.

If you've read the furnace manual, then you know that this annual inspection is required to keep your warranty in place. However, many heating specialists confess that any furnace less than 10 years old probably only needs inspection once every two years.

Don't skip the inspection completely as big, expensive problems can often be avoided with preventative maintenance.

Although there are competent do-it-yourselfers who can tackle furnace or A/C repairs, most homeowners will want to call in the professionals.

2. The same diligence doesn't apply to your central A/C unit, as long as you clean out leaves and debris before you run it.

3. The easiest and possibly the most important task is replacing your furnace filter every three months.

"Imagine breathing through a straw. That's what your furnace is doing when you leave a dirty filter in for too long," my husband explained to me. By regularly changing the filter, you're improving not only air quality but also the efficiency of your furnace.

4. Vacuum air grates or electric baseboard heaters to remove dirt and debris.

5. Cover your A/C unit with a breathable, flexible cover to keep out dirt and leaves.

(Don't wrap the cover too tightly across the unit, as you could damage its coils.)

6. Clean out lint traps, hood vents and grates.

Ideally, these vents and grates should be cleaned once per week, but if that's not possible, consider scheduling a cleaning at least once per month. Don't forget to confirm that outside vents are not clogged and are working correctly.

Annual Maintenance Costs: HVAC

- Fill cracks: $100 to $1,000

- Clean up mild mould and mildew: $20

- Replace furnace filters every three months (annual cost): $20 to $160

- Annual furnace inspection and cleaning by a licensed technician: $80 to $300

- Cover (but don't wrap) A/C and clear leaves before use: $0

- Clear out lint traps, hood vents above the stove and in the bathroom: $0

Total Annual Cost: $220 to $1,480

Per Square Foot Cost: $0.11 to $0.74

Amortized Strategic Update Costs: HVAC

Consider getting professional duct cleaning, but only if the furnace is over 10 years old, or you recently underwent major renovations. Studies show that cleaning the ductwork annually or biannually does little to contribute to your health or the HVAC's efficiency unless the units are old or stressed due to increased irritants (such as dust and drywall particles from a renovation).

- Replace gas furnace with a high-efficiency gas furnace, every 15 to 25 years ($2,000 to $6,000): $100 to $300

- Replace central A/C unit every 7 to 10 years ($3,000 to $6,000): $353 to $706

- Professional duct cleaning (only if home underwent major renovations or furnace is over 10 years old), one time cost ($120 to $600): $4.80 to $24

- Buy A/C cover, once every 5 years ($30 to $100): $6 to $20

- Replace thermostat, every 25 years ($15 to $500): $0.60 to $20

- Replace gas fireplace, every 15 to 25 years ($200 to $3,000): $10 to $150

- Replace ductwork, every 60 to 100 years ($1,000 to $5,000): $12.50 to $62.50

- Replace (or add) heat exchange or pump, every 10 to 15 years ($600 to $8,000): $48 to $640

Total Amortization Cost per Year: $535 to $1,923

Per Square Foot Cost: $0.28 to $0.96

WHEN SHOULD YOU REPLACE A FURNACE?

To quickly ascertain if there's still life in your old furnace, or if you should be shopping for a newer, more efficient model, you'll need to examine the following four factors:

AGE MATTERS

A well-maintained furnace can live up to 25 years. But like everything, the older your furnace gets, the harder it has to work to do the same ol' thing. When considering a replacement, consider the age of your current unit. If it's older than 15 years, it's time to start thinking about an upgrade.

EFFICIENCY MATTERS

Old natural gas furnaces were only about 50% to 60% efficient. Newer, high-efficiency furnaces are 80% to 98% efficient. What does this mean? If the efficiency is 90%, that means 90% of the energy from the fuel will become heat, which warms your home, while the other 10% escapes up the chimney and out through the cracks in your house.

If your furnace is less than 80% efficient, it's a strong reason to consider a replacement.

MAINTENANCE MATTERS

Regular maintenance means changing the filters at least once per season, if not more. It also means paying for semi-annual or annual inspections and personally inspecting and cleaning the furnace's different components (such as fan and blower) regularly. Do all this, and your furnace could easily last 25 years. Neglect this work, and you may get only 10 to 15 years, give or take.

COST OF REPAIRS MATTERS

We typically don't consider replacing a furnace until it breaks. This is when you'll need to decide: pay to repair or pay to upgrade?

Side by side, fixing is always dollar-for-dollar cheaper—a broken fan costs about $600 to replace, while a new high-efficiency furnace can cost $5,000, or more, to install.

But like an old car, you need to factor in all the current and future repairs and replacements to determine if it's time to retire the old beast. Here are some signs to look for that indicate you should consider replacing your furnace:

- Big temperature differences in different rooms (and it's not an insulation issue).

- Your furnace frequently turns on and off.

- Hearing an annoying hum.

- Excessive dust in your house or on your furniture.

- Your furnace doesn't turn on.

- Suggested repairs will cost you $1,000 or more (or about 20% of a new high-efficiency furnace plus installation).

Expense 6: Electrical

Electrical preventive maintenance and testing are some of the most important ways to maintain the reliability and integrity of your home. The statement sounds stuffy, but it's so true.

Out-of-date wiring is dangerous. According to a 2009 National Fire Prevention Association study, faulty wiring is the primary cause of residential fires. Plus, maintaining and updating your electrical system is an essential way to add value to your home.

The problem for most homeowners is that electrical wiring is typically out of sight, meaning it's easy to forget about it and its routine maintenance. Over time, however, electrical wires suffer wear and tear, and this deterioration can impact appliances and equipment that operate on your home's electrical circuit board (that grey box, usually located in the basement room where your furnace sits, that all the wires run to).

If you neglect your home's electrical system, you'll eventually have to deal with problems. The best way to avoid complications is to perform routine inspections and standard maintenance and, when appropriate, hire a professional.

The hardest part of electrical maintenance is learning the process. As with HVAC, it's best to hire professionals when a task is outside of your comfort bubble or beyond your capabilities—electrical mistakes can result in mild or severe injury.

Still, there are routine tasks every homeowner can do to keep their home's electrical system operating efficiently.

Annual Maintenance Tasks: Electrical

1. Make sure all outlets and cords—particularly those kept outside—aren't damaged. Replace or repair frayed wires and plug heads.

2. Although some smoke alarms, carbon monoxide detectors and radon detectors are operated by batteries, some are hardwired into your home. Regardless of the type, make sure you test each alarm at least once per year (preferably twice); if operated by battery, change the batteries twice each year.

3. Make sure each light fixture is fitted with the proper bulb wattage. A stronger wattage can shorten the life of the bulb and light fixture.

4. Check your ground fault outlets, known as GFI plugs, by pushing the test/reset buttons.

5. If you need to replace a part, make sure you replace old and damaged wiring with high-quality electrical parts. Pay for quality when it comes to electrical components. (The same principle applies to plumbing parts.) Although it may cost a bit more up front, quality parts have fewer instances of deterioration and failure and last longer, which helps amortize the cost over a longer period of time.

6. Check all your electrical outlets with a circuit tester.

7. Check plug covers. Look for water damage and discolouration around the outlet due to heat. If you notice these problems, you probably need to call a professional to diagnose the problem.

8. Check for possible circuit overloading. Overloading can cause power outages and severe damage to equipment and appliances and can trigger house fires. Typically, a short circuit is caused by weak or loose wiring, so the key here is to look for potential overloading points. Walk around your house and look for areas where you rely heavily on extension cords or multiple plugs, as well as locations in the home that rely heavily on space heaters. Look for worn-out light fixtures, burns or scorch marks on electrical appliances, or locations or appliances that smell burnt. These are all situations and areas where an electrician could help create a safer environment. This solution will cost money, but it could drastically reduce potential problems.

Home electrical maintenance is about staying on top of potential issues and fixing them before they become large repairs or replacements.

Annual Maintenance Costs: Electrical

- Check bulbs, outlets and cords: $0

- Replace bulbs with LED (for energy and cost savings): $25 to $35

- Replace batteries and check all detectors: $30

- Check all electrical outlets using a tester (one-time cost to buy the tester): $15

Total Annual Cost: $70 to $80

Per Square Foot Cost: $0.04 to $0.04

Amortized Strategic Updates: Electrical

Some homeowners want peace of mind and hire a professional or licensed electrician to complete an annual maintenance check on the home's electrical system. For most homeowners, however, this routine expense is not necessary. Instead, you can complete the annual routine maintenance checks, and if you spot problems, call a professional. Keep in mind, you should call a professional—regardless of where you are in your regular maintenance routine—if you notice the following:

- Sparking and loose wires. These are definite signs of problems with your home's circuit breaker. Even if you don't see active sparks, any scorch or burn marks in or on the panel or breaker need to be examined carefully and quickly by a licensed professional.

- Persistent flickering lights can be an indication that something is wrong with your home's electrical system. So are very dim lights.

- Frequent tripping of a circuit breaker is a sign of issues with your home's electrical system.

- Buzzing sounds from power outlets when they are in use are also a problem, as is a slight tingle or a hot-to-the-touch appliance or outlet. If you feel that tingle, it means the plug or appliance is not grounded. This puts your home at greater risk of fire and you and your family at greater risk of injury. If the appliance or outlet is hot to the touch, it's overheating and you run the risk of damaging whatever is using the outlet.

Even though every homeowner strives to avoid electrical issues, chances are you'll run into one or more problem areas during the lifetime of homeownership. One home may offer no problems, while another may offer nothing but problems. Remember, too, that fixer-upper homes typically don't have updated electrical systems or panels. If the wiring in your home is more than a few decades old, it may require a complete update. The more common upgrades and replacements to consider are listed below.

Amortized Strategic Update Costs: Electrical

- Upgrading your electrical service, from 60-amp (in old homes) to 100-amp/200-amp/400-amp service, one-time cost ($1,000 to $5,000): $40 to $200

- Rewire entire house and update existing panel, one-time cost ($5,500 to $15,000): $220 to $600

- Replace smoke, carbon monoxide and radon detectors every 10 years, assumes four detectors, and range is for DIY and pro costs ($60 to $600): $6 to $60

- Add an outlet where none exists (doesn't include the cost to repair walls), one-time cost ($100 to $250): $4 to $10

- Repair or replace an outlet receptacle or switch, DIY and pro cost options, one-time cost ($10 to $150): $0.40 to $6

- Replace a standard outlet with a ground fault circuit interrupter (GFCI) outlet, DIY and pro cost options, one-time cost ($15 to $300): $0.60 to $12

- Install a 220/240-volt outlet for an electric dryer or range, one-time cost ($250 to $500): $10 to $20

- Install three-way switches, one-time cost ($150 to $500): $6 to $20

- Replace circuit breaker (no changes), DIY and pro cost options, one-time cost ($50 to $300): $2 to $12

Total Amortization Cost per Year: $289 to $940

Per Square Foot Cost: $0.15 to $0.47

SHOULD YOU UPGRADE YOUR HOME'S ELECTRICAL SYSTEM?

Like many expensive home upgrades, updating your electrical system rarely increases the perceived value of your home. Don't expect buyers to value these upgrades as most consider this work, and the associated costs, to be a part of regular maintenance. This also means that ignoring these home upgrades can certainly hurt your home's resale value. (Leave it too long, and it will even cost you, with higher insurance rates and costlier repairs.)

The good news is that the completion of this home improvement job should help you add other cost-saving mechanisms, such as smart home appliances or tools.

Remember, saving money is not a sufficient reason for doing your own electrical repairs. Only undertake electrical repairs or upgrades if you are knowledgeable and comfortable with your skills. Electricity behaves in a very logical fashion that becomes easy to understand with experience, but it can and does kill people who make mistakes.

Expense 7: Plumbing

Chances are, you probably don't spend too much time thinking about the network of water and sewer pipes inside your walls. You turn taps, hot and cold water is delivered relatively on-demand and your waste is easily evacuated and eliminated from your home. Out of sight, out of mind, right? But like other home maintenance tasks, taking a proactive approach to your home's plumbing can offer significant savings and benefits.

For instance, did you know that a tap that leaks only one drop of water per second adds up to 10,000 litres of water waste over a year—that's the equivalent of 70 baths! Although this wasted water won't cost you too much—about $30 per year—it's not good for your home or the earth. Then there are hidden leaks, such as a toilet that continues to run after being flushed. Just one running toilet will waste 200,000 litres per year. That's the equivalent of 1,400 baths, at a cost of almost $600 per year! It's not just the cost of the water and the waste of a valuable resource, but this prolonged overuse can be corrosive to pipes and fixtures, which requires you to fix, repair or replace these components sooner rather than later.

HOW TO TELL IF YOUR HOME HAS LEAD PIPES

There is no safe level of lead exposure. That's a full-stop sentence. As a result, more buyers and homeowners have become quite concerned with whether a home has lead piping.

Before calling in a plumber for an inspection, it pays to do your investigation. First, go to your home's service line—the line that leads from the municipality's main water line into your house. Typically, this will be found in your basement or, if you don't have a basement, in the lowest section of your home. This pipe will be sticking up from the floor and have a variety of other plumbing pipes sprouting off from it.

If the pipe coming into your home is a dark matte grey colour, chances are your home is being supplied with a lead service line. To be sure, scrape the pipe with a screwdriver. If the metal is soft and turns shiny, you have a lead service line coming into your home.

Not good.

If you see copper, steel or plastic, chances are there is no lead in your water, but that's not a guarantee. Sometimes cities update only a portion of water mains and leave older sections for another year.

To verify if service lines in your area have been updated, call the city.

Then there's trace lead. At some point, builders stopped using lead and started using copper pipes. However, it wasn't until 1986 that North American regulators banned lead from being used in solder for pipes. Up until then, plumbers could use a 50-50 solder—50% tin and 50% lead.

To confirm that there is no lead in the solder joints, use a screwdriver to scrape the metal. If it becomes shiny, chances are the plumber who installed your home's copper pipes used a lead mix.

If you suspect lead in your pipes, here are some precautions to take:

1. **Flush the water.** Always allow your tap to run to flush the standing water (which collects more lead due to prolonged exposure). A good rule of thumb is to run your water for a minimum of two minutes.

2. **Replace plumbing components.** This includes replacing pipes (very expensive), re-soldering joints and replacing faucets and fixtures that were built with lead.

3. **Buy a water filter.** Proper filtration systems that attach to your drinking faucets are very effective at removing lead. Just look for cer ication.

The good news is that many expensive plumbing problems can be avoided. Although some homeowners can handle a few home plumbing tasks on their own, most of us need a professional contractor.

Annual Maintenance Tasks: Plumbing

Thankfully, a few simple maintenance steps when it comes to your home's plumbing system can go a long way.

1. Test all faucets and check for leaks. Look under sinks or inside cabinets for moisture or puddles of water (indications of a leak). Use your eyes and your nose, as a musty smell or mould growth are also indications of a leak.

2. Swap out old washers (the thin ring or disk-shaped plate) that are inserted between two points of a thread, such as a bolt or a nut, to distribute the load between both ends and ensure a more secure fitting.

3. Once a year, top up floor-drains with water to prevent sewer gases from entering your home. A properly installed drain should have a trap—a U-shaped pipe that holds water and prevents sewer gas, such as methane, from seeping into your home. Over time this water can evaporate, particularly in drains that are infrequently used. An old plumber's trick is to pour a quarter cup of mineral oil down the drain. The mineral oil sits on the water barrier and slows down the rate of evaporation.

4. For all other drains, pour a gallon (about 4 litres) of water and watch how quickly the water drains. If it's slow, you will need to snake the drain.

5. If you find there is an excessive amount of condensation in one area or room of your house, run a dehumidifier.

6. In the fall, disconnect water hoses from outdoor faucets (also known as spigots). If left connected, the hose can freeze, expand and cause the indoor pipes attached to that spigot to burst.

7. Once a year, check the pressure valve in your water heater. For most units, simply lift the lever and allow it to snap back into place. If you're unsure, you can probably find your model and tips for checking the pressure valve through an online search.

8. Check the water heater's temperature. For optimal performance, keep the water heater at a temperature of 120°F/48.9°C.

9. Once a year, check your toilet bowl and toilet tank for leaks. Add a few drops of food colouring to the toilet tank. If you notice the colour in the toilet bowl within 30 minutes, there's a leak.

10. Once a year, check all appliances that are connected to your plumbing system, such as your dishwasher, washing machine and water-on-demand refrigerators. Confirm that hoses are not cracked, bulging or torn. Even if the hoses are good, consider replacing worn

hoses to prevent future leaks. Check seals and replace damaged or worn seals. (This simple rubberized component keeps the water inside the appliance, where it's supposed to be.)

11. If you have a sump pump, make sure you inspect and clean this device at least once per year. Visually inspect the float switch for build-up or debris as this build-up can prevent the switch from operating properly and cause sewer backups. Once you've cleared the debris, reassemble the sump pump and pour water into the drain. You want to hear the water hammer sound to confirm that the pump is fully operational. Sump pump maintenance isn't always an easy task, so you may want to consider professional help.

12. If you are on a septic system, keep up to date with pumping and inspections. Installing and fixing a septic system can be costly—as high as $10,000 to $30,000! This means the ongoing tasks to keep it running effectively are worth it.

To avoid a frozen bib (outside tap), replace all external taps with an anti-freeze model. This do-it-yourself replacement piece costs about $30, plus a bit of time to replace. Expect to pay a few hundred dollars if you hire a professional to swap out this fixture. No matter which option you choose, the cost is worth it, since it will help you avoid a frozen tap, which can lead to frozen and potentially burst internal pipes, which can cause thousands of dollars in damage to your home.

Annual Maintenance Costs: Plumbing

- Test all faucets for drips, change washers as needed: $10 to $150

- Remove leaves and debris from all outside drains, top up water in drains, locate and test main shut-off valve: $0

- Check all water-dependent appliances, including hot water tank: $0

- Check toilet bowl with food dye + top up floor-drains with water and mineral oil: $5

- Inspect and maintain sump pump: $0 to $800

- Inspect outside garden hoses and bleed outside faucets: $0

- Inspect and replace worn caulking around toilets, sinks and bathtubs: $20 to $100

- If you don't use a strainer on drains, clean hair and debris from drains, at least once per month: $0

Total Annual Cost: $35 to $1,055

Per Square Foot Cost: $0.02 to $0.53

Amortized Strategic Updates: Plumbing

If you (and hopefully the previous owners) are good about maintaining your home's plumbing, this system should last a very long time. Still, there are always issues as property ages and conditions change.

SHOULD YOU UPGRADE YOUR HOME'S PLUMBING?

Although you may have paid thousands to install new copper or cross-linked polyethylene (PEX) plumbing in your home, or tens of thousands to replace sewer lines or septic systems, the tough truth is that this upgrade rarely attracts more dollars when you resell your home.

That doesn't mean you shouldn't upgrade your plumbing. Anyone who has lived in an older home will tell you how frustrating it is to find a trickle of water coming from a tap because pipes are clogged and rusty. Then there are health concerns. There's a massive body of scientific evidence that shows repeated exposure to lead—from water running through lead pipes—can have serious health consequences, harming your nervous system, cardiovascular system, neurodevelopment, kidneys and reproductive organs.

Although the aim is to complete home improvement jobs that add value, not upgrading your plumbing can have the reverse effect: devaluing your property in the eyes of potential buyers.

One advantage to upgrading your plumbing is that you can add in more recent technology that can help save energy and cut down utility costs. Here are four plumbing additions to consider:

1. **Install a pressure-reducing valve.** Many households use more water than they need because there's simply too much water pressure in their pipes. Install a pressure-reducing valve to automatically control the amount of pres-

sure that flows into your pipe system, typically dropping it from 70 pressure per square inch (psi) to 35 psi.

2. **Install high-efficiency toilets.** If your toilet bowl is an older model, you're probably flushing about 3.5 gallons of water down the drain with each flush. To reduce your usage, install a high-efficiency toilet. Sometimes known as dual flush, these toilets use as little as 1.3 gallons per flush. With this simple swap, you can save thousands of gallons per year and slash your water bills considerably.

3. **Use low-flow showerheads or faucet aerators.** Showering uses up to 2.5 gallons of water per minute, which translates into 20% of a typical household's water consumption. Installing a low-flow showerhead can reduce your water usage by as much as 70%. For other plumbing fixtures, consider adding faucet aerators, which increase water pressure and reduce usage at the source.

4. **Upgrade your water heater.** You can save on hydro- and water consumption costs by upgrading an old water heater.

Although upgrading your home's plumbing is a significant up-front cost, neglecting this ongoing maintenance or ignoring outdated plumbing systems can seriously detract from your property's value. To help sweeten this bitter expense, calculate how much you will save on utility bills after finishing the upgrades; also, be sure to shop sales and research rebates (from manufacturers as well as from utility companies and various government agencies). For more on rebates and savings, see Chapter 5.

For instance, a small but important maintenance tip is to buy foam pipe insulation and wrap it around your uninsulated water pipes. This $150 fix can save you $10,000 or more since it prevents condensation from building up, dripping and potentially damaging your home's structure or foundation. If these exposed pipes are prone to freezing, wrap them in heat tape.

If water in the basement is an issue, you'll need to consider each possible cause. For instance, if the water table—where soil and gravel are completely saturated with water—is high where your home's foundation sits, you may need to install a pit and sump to help move the water away from your home's foundation or risk water seeping into the basement. If a sump pump is required, seriously consider adding an electronic float switch—an alarm that is triggered once the water level is too high. This $90 switch alerts you when the sump isn't working properly or when the water is rising too quickly for the pump to remove. Once alerted, you can then avoid a dirty sewer backup by manually pumping excess water.

If you have a persistent basement leak, you may need to examine your home's weeping tile system.

Sadly, my wonderful (former) climbing partner, Suzie, found this out the hard way. Over a decade ago, she and her now ex-husband purchased a semi-detached house (known as a duplex on the west coast) in Toronto's bustling west end. About a month into living there, the kids stepped onto the front lawn only to sink two to three inches into the dirt. It had not rained in months. Suzie quickly realized this was a sign of a big problem. She called a plumbing service to do a drain camera inspection. The company inserted this small, waterproof video camera, which is attached to an industrial plumber's snake, into the sewer pipes. What they saw was startling. The service pipe from the city to Suzie's house had collapsed. The roots from the lovely, decades-old maple tree in the home's front yard had grown around and through the clay pipe—completely destroying this portion of the home's weeping system. As a result, a significant portion of the water pumped from the city to Suzie's home was being lost to seepage in the front yard. It cost Suzie and her family $10,000 to fix (not including landscaping to replace the dug-up front yard).

Of course, each city and district has its regulations around who can remove a tree and when, so check your area's bylaws. Also, consider if there is another way to handle potential root damage. By paying for a sewer camera inspection and talking with a plumber, you may find that there are options to create a well-functioning plumbing system without destroying the beauty of nature. Better still, a camera inspection may highlight unseen leaks and concerns in your home's plumbing system. If caught early, these problems can cost much less to fix (and prevent damage to your home's structure).

Amortized Strategic Update Costs: Plumbing

- Update all pipes (cost for upgrade, not to repair holes), one-time cost ($8,000 to $12,000): $320 to $480

- Replace hot water heater, every 8 to 12 years for gas and 10 to 15 years for electric (DIY: $280 to $650, or supplied and installed: $650 to $1,500): $31 to $167

- Drain camera sewer pipe inspection, one-time cost ($100 to $800): $4 to $32

- Install or replace sump pump, every 4 to 6 years ($300 to $1,600): $60 to $320

- Insulate cold and hot water pipes, one-time cost ($6 to $150): $0.24 to $6

- Add an electronic float switch to a sump pump, one-time cost ($90 to $500): $3.60 to $20

- Unclog a drain or toilet (mainline clogs are more expensive than secondary lines), one-time cost ($20 to $500): $0.80 to $20

- Emergency plumbing repair or fix (example: rapid water supply line leak or no water flowing throughout the house), one-time cost ($150 to $2,000+): $6 to $80

- Septic inspection, once every 3 to 5 years ($150 to $600): $37.50 to $150

- Septic pumping, once every 3 to 5 years ($100 to $800): $25 to $200

Total Amortization Cost per Year: $488 to $1,475

Per Square Foot Cost: $0.24 to $0.74

COMMON SEWER AND DRAIN PROBLEMS

Anyone who has purchased a resale home that is older than 10 or 20 years should seriously consider paying for a camera sewer inspection. Even though most sewer and drain problems don't show up for decades, it's still better to spend a few hundred on preventative diagnosis than a few thousand on remediation and fixes.

Here are the most common problems found in sewer lines and drains in North America:

Fractured or Cracked Pipes. A pipe will crack for a variety of reasons, from environmental to man-made strain, such as continually driving over the part of your lawn where your pipes are located.

Collapsed Sewer or Drain Pipes. Very old sewer pipes, or drains that are installed incorrectly, can collapse, either partially or completely. Unfortunately, this is a very serious issue that must be dealt with immediately.

Root Infestation. Not surprisingly, trees are very effective at finding water in the ground, which is why some homeowners learn that a tree's root system has infiltrated the sewer pipe. Over time, the pipe will become more and more clogged, which will cause cracks. This causes additional material deposited into the pipe, which causes even more clogs.

Bellied or Settled Pipes. This is when a portion of a pipe settles into the ground, creating a depressed area (known as a belly) where water can collect. Over time, this excess water will attract insects, roots and even animals looking for easy sources of water.

One reason for proactively paying for a drain camera inspection, particularly in a resale home, is to assess how effectively the pipes and ground are moving the water away from your home. Quite often, substantial basement leaks are caused by external pipes that cracked or collapsed years ago and were never fixed.

REPLACE (OR REPAIR) WEEPING TILE SYSTEM

One of the most important household drains is located outside your home. Known as a perimeter drain—or weeping tile system—it's an integral part of moving water away from your home to prevent leaks, floods, cracked foundations and a host of other problems.

Despite its importance, most homeowners, buyers and sellers rarely pay attention to the weeping tile system—that is, until there is an issue. Catch the issue too late, and you can anticipate paying thousands and even tens of thousands in repair and replacement costs. Sounds scary? It should!

There is a lot to know about your home's weeping tile system, but the main idea is that pipes with pre-drilled holes are used to create a "path of least resistance" for water near your home. Water will travel along this path, away from your home, rather than seeping into the foundation.

What's scary is that most homes built before 1960 don't have a perimeter drainage system installed. Homes built between 1960 and the 1980s primarily use clay pipes, which work well but decay and crumble over time.

These days, the best systems are plastic or PVC perforated pipe, installed underground around the perimeter of your house using a mesh sock system (a small, mesh wire that prevents rocks and debris from clogging the pipe).

If you suspect an issue—or just want to be extra-cautious— hire a drain specialist or plumber who uses a drain snake camera. They'll use the camera as a scope in your drains to find out if there are problems.

If there are problems, you will need to consider an external or internal solution. An exterior solution is to dig up and remove the old weeping tile and bury the new pipe. This system focuses on removing water away from your home before it enters your foundation. An interior solution runs along the floor at the lowest points of the basement and focuses on collecting and safely removing water that has already passed through the home's foundation and now needs a place to go. (For tips on finding the right option, see "How to Properly Waterproof Your Home's Foundation" earlier in this chapter.)

Keep in mind that both work by helping to relieve hydrostatic pressure; this is the pressure that builds up against your walls due to groundwater and insufficient drainage. The danger with hydrostatic pressure is that it can crack and damage your foundation and, if not given a way to escape, can penetrate other areas of the home, such as the wood frame, insulation and drywall.

If you don't need to replace but want to be sure to keep your weeping tile system in optimal condition, consider the following:

- **Install a clean-out port.** If replacing the system, ask your contractor to include a clean-out port. This type of port can be accessed from the surface, which eliminates the expensive process of digging up your yard to solve a future problem.

- **Disconnect the weeping tile from the sewer system.** Older homes were often constructed so that water from downspouts and weeping tiles went directly to the sewer system—a system that was never designed to handle such large volumes of runoff. To reduce the risk of sewer backups, disconnect your home's drainage from the sewer system. (In some municipalities, this upgrade is considered mandatory.)

- **Clean and service your drains on a routine basis.** Typically, this means paying for a camera drainage inspection and any repairs unearthed from this inspection. Older drains (using clay or concrete) should be inspected every year or two; newer PVC drains should be inspected once every three to five years. Keep in mind that even if you have your drains cleaned every year, you still need to inspect the drains regularly to identify potential or current problems.

- **Install a backflow valve.** These valves prevent backflow from the storm drain from washing back into your home when the city's storm drains are overloaded (say during a big storm or when all the snow and ice melts in the spring). Many insurance companies now require this valve if you want coverage (or enhanced coverage) for water damage to your basement.

Here's the bad news: there is little to no return on the money you spend on repairing or replacing your weeping tile—a cost that can range from $1,000 to over $50,000 (with an ROI of 10% if you're lucky). It's a maintenance issue; however, ignore the work required to keep this drainage tool working properly, and you could end up with expensive home repairs or replacements (or lower-than-anticipated market value).

The only bright spot is that virtually all resale homes built before the 1990s will need to address their weeping tile system. If you aren't already a homeowner, this is a cost you need to consider with any older resale home—and an element that should be considered in your homeowner budget and when negotiating the purchase of a home.

TOTAL AVERAGE HOME MAINTENANCE COSTS

Each year, on average, it **costs between $1,230 and $7,070 to** *maintain* **a home**.

The low end reflects the costs of a very well-maintained home with all of the work completed by a handy homeowner; the top end reflects a completely hands-off, pay-someone-to-do-just-about-everything homeowner living in an older or seriously neglected home.

But maintenance work doesn't factor in the upgrades required to keep a home working optimally. A new furnace, new roof, new windows and new paint are more than updates for resale—these are strategic updates required to keep your home operating at its highest and best use. Of course, it's hard to account for these larger, more expensive costs since these upgrades can either happen suddenly—the furnace stops working—or over a long period of time. To account for these costs, the largest and most prevalent updates virtually every homeowner will face at least once in their lifetime of owner-ship, were calculated.

The **cost of these larger repairs and upgrades** on an annual basis will range between **$3,526 and $11,166 per year**!

The lower end is for the DIY homeowner, and the upper end reflects the hands-off, pay-the-pros homeowner faced with completing *all* the typical major upgrades as outlined in this chapter. This extreme scenario is highly unlikely unless you bought a true fixer-upper that faced decades of neglect.

Still, these maintenance and annualized upgrade costs can now help you make better, more informed decisions when it comes to saving and spending on home costs.

WHEN TO COMPLETE THESE MAINTENANCE TASKS

Great. Now that you've got a realistic budget, our work here is done, right? Not quite.

First, you need to set up a regular maintenance schedule. Grouping tasks by season helps you do the bulk of the upkeep work when it's most needed—making it an efficient use of your time and money. That's smart homeownership!

To help with this, I've created seasonal maintenance to-do lists broken out into the tasks to complete for each of your home's seven housing components. Find them for free online at www.zolo.ca/house-poor-no-more.

For those who need a more interactive method of creating their household expense budget, use the interactive Excel (or Google) spreadsheet found online (at www.zolo.ca/house-poor-no-more). This budget template breaks housing expenses into four categories:

1. **Direct Expenses** (such as mortgage payment, hydro, heat and property taxes, etc.)

2. **Maintenance Expenses** (such as snow removal costs, gutter and eavestrough cleaning, lawn care, etc.)

3. **Indirect Expenses** (such as cleaning supplies, light bulbs, pest control, etc.)

4. **Discretionary Expenses** (such as cable TV, internet and subscription costs like Netflix or Spotify, etc.)

If you choose to add your income, you can see a great break-out of how much of your monthly earnings go towards direct and indirect housing costs. Also, if you are unsure of how much a service or task will cost, the spreadsheet offers bench-marks—average or standard costs that homeowners pay for these services. These benchmark costs reflect both American average homeowner expenses and Canadian average home-owner expenses (just be sure to select the right location). You can also compare what you spend with the benchmark expenses of other homeowners.

SUM IT UP

Based on these calculations, homeowners can expect to pay:

Annual **maintenance** costs range between: $1,230 to $7,070

+ Annual **amortized strategic update** costs range between: $3,526 and $11,166

= Total annual **maintenance + strategic update** costs that range between: $4,756 and $18,236

Using the per square foot costs—based on the Per Square Foot Contractor (PSFC) method of budgeting)—you can expect to budget between $0.71/ft and $3.94/sf for regular maintenance, plus between $1.78/sf and $5.62/sf for amortized upgrades.

**To create a home maintenance budget using PSFC, multiply
your home's square footage by total annual costs—$2.49/sf
on the low end, up to $9.56/sf.**

That means a family living in a 1,500-square-foot bungalow should budget between $3,735 and $14,340 per year on
home maintenance and upgrades—depending on their level
of involvement and the home's general condition (the factors
mentioned in Chapter 3, "How Much Should You Budget for
Home Maintenance?"). A family living in a 4,000-square-
foot home could expect to pay between $9,960 and $38,240—
again, depending on their level of involvement and the home's
general condition.

The big takeaway: owning a home is a *big* financial obligation.
The good news is that the costs associated with home maintenance, along with repair and remediation costs, don't need to be
a shock and don't have to blow a hole through your budget.

And by using the PSFC method of creating a home maintenance
budget, you don't tie up money unnecessarily—money that can
be put to work growing your net worth.

Here's what I mean, based on a 2,000-square-foot home valued at
$750,000 and assuming a five-year timeframe:

	DIY ANNUAL BUDGET	PAY-THE-PROS ANNUAL BUDGET
1% to 5% Rule	$37,500	$187,500
PSFC method	$21,900	$95,600
Money you save (and *could* invest)	$15,600	$91,900

Using the PSFC method, a smart homeowner can create a realistic budget that includes the cost of known maintenance tasks while building a slush fund in anticipation of bigger, unexpected repairs. The best part is that you won't be over-allocating funds to your home—funds that should be used to achieve other financial goals, such as saving up for a child's education or lining the retirement nest egg.

Sure, home maintenance is expensive. But neglecting or ignoring these tasks only puts your structure's integrity at risk and devalues a very expensive asset—and powerful tool—in your personal portfolio.

TAKEAWAYS

Invest in Your Future. The key to getting your financial life under control is making a budget. That is the first step for all financial decisions, including the decision to become a homeowner. Invest the time to create a budget. Don't worry if it's not 100% accurate. The aim is to start paying attention and modify as you go. The goal is to make smarter decisions for each dollar you earn, save and spend—including the money allocated to home maintenance.

Don't Be an Ostrich. Homeownership is expensive—plan for it.

Cash Isn't King. Cash is good for current expenses and emergencies—nothing more. Holding too much cash—either in a bank account, a piggy bank, or sitting untapped in an asset—means you're losing long-term value.

Spend a Penny, Keep a Pound. There's an old cliché that a penny spent on prevention is worth a (sterling) pound spent on a cure. As a homeowner, expenses can quickly add up and blow a hole through your budget. To prevent this from happening, you need to keep your high-priced wealth-building tool—your home—in good operating condition. Spend the time getting to know the property; learn how to maintain it and all its components; complete tasks as they arise. Yes, it will cost you, but you'll spend much less with consistent maintenance than with a neglect-and-pray strategy.

4

MAKING STRATEGIC HOME IMPROVEMENTS

ACHIEVE YOUR GOALS WITH STRATEGIC SPENDING ON UPGRADES, UPDATES AND RENOVATIONS

The home renovation industry is big business—and it's easy to understand why when you look at how much we spend on home improvement and upgrades.

In Canada, homeowners spent just over $6.8 billion on home renovations by mid-2019, up from $5.3 billion spent in 2018 (based on Statistics Canada data).

In America, these numbers are even more staggering. According to the Joint Center for Housing Studies at Harvard University, Americans spend more than $400 billion USD a year on residential renovations and repairs.

Quite often, the justification for renovation spending is the ever-constant increase in home prices.

To put this in perspective, in the year 2000, the average price of an American home was $126,000 USD. In the year 2020, the average home value jumped to $259,000 USD—a record high and an increase of 106% in just two decades.

Of course, the path from price A to price B was anything but linear! During that time, home shoppers faced a financial crisis, the Great Recession, a couple of housing bubbles and, at present, economic and health fallout from the COVID-19 pandemic.

Still, the urge to buy a home and renovate continues. And the justification that a renovation can be beneficial is not without merit.

According to the Appraisal Institute of Canada (AIC), renovating your home has three primary benefits:

- Maintain a home's value

- Increase the homeowner's enjoyment

- Increase the property's selling price

Unfortunately, most people use the third reason—increased sale price—as a way to justify the expense of a reno. Sure, you spend money renovating but you gain value, and this return on investment (ROI) justifies the cost of the upgrade or remodel.

There are problems with this logic. The first problem is the use of ROI.

In personal finance terms, ROI measures the value of an investment by comparing the amount of a return relative to the investment's cost.

The basic ROI formula is:

ROI = (Current Value of Investment minus Cost of Investment)
    / Cost of Investment

In absolute terms, spending to renovate a home fits with the basic ROI investment formula. However, the money spent on a home renovation isn't the same as money used to buy a bond, stock, fund (such as an exchange-traded fund [ETF]) or other financial assets. That's because the money spent on a renovation **may not** provide a return—and if it does, it's certainly not dollar for dollar.

What do I mean?

Let's assume you have $15,000 to invest and let's say the first option is to invest in an index ETF with a projected annualized return of 4%.

An **ETF** is a type of security that holds or tracks an index, sector or commodity. As a diversified basket of holdings investors can purchase or sell an ETF on a stock exchange, just like regular stock shares.

An **annualized rate of return** is calculated as the equivalent annual return an investor receives over a given period. It's expressed as a percentage and differs from the annual performance of an investment, which can vary considerably from year to year.

If you held that ETF for five years and then sold it, you would have just under $18,250. Not bad.

Now, what if you invested in a bathroom renovation. Why not? Chocolate brown bathroom tiles are never coming back in style and the reno will only add value to your home, right? Assuming the return on this reno investment equals the industry standard of 64% (more on that in a bit), that means after five years, this bathroom upgrade will add $9,600 to the sale price of your home.

Now, using a simplified apples-to-apples approach (hard to do, but...), let's see how these two investments stack up:

	PURCHASE PRICE	RETURN	TOTAL CASH IN HAND
ETF	$15,000	$3,250	$18,250
Bathroom reno	$15,000	$9,600	−$5,400

Does the math feel a bit wonky? It will until you realize that with an investment gain you also get your initial investment sum back; that's not the case with the money spent on that bathroom upgrade.

For a home renovation to qualify as a "good investment"—an investment that makes you money—it would need to give a return of 100%, or more, and that's virtually impossible.

To back up this claim, I turned to data collected by *Remodeling* magazine, an American publication that has spent more than a decade collecting data on the cost of home renovation projects and how much these projects add to the value of a home.

Here is the average ROI of a select number of common renovation projects (all costs are in USD):

Making Strategic Home Improvements

PROJECT	JOB COST	RESALE VALUE	% OF COST-RECOUPED
Master Suite Addition—Upscale	$282,062	$145,486	51.6%
Master Suite Addition—Mid-range	$136,739	$80,029	58.5%
Major Kitchen Remodel—Upscale	$135,547	$72,993	53.9%
Major Kitchen Remodel—Mid-range	$68,490	$40,127	58.6%
Minor Kitchen Remodel—Mid-range	$23,452	$18,206	77.6%
Bathroom Addition—Upscale	$91,287	$49,961	54.7%
Bathroom Addition—Mid-range	$49,598	$26,807	54.0%
Bathroom Remodel—Universal Design	$34,643	$21,463	62.0%
Bathroom Remodel—Mid-range	$21,377	$13,688	64.0%
Roof Replacement—Metal	$40,318	$24,682	61.2%
Roof Replacement—Asphalt Shingles	$24,700	$16,287	65.9%
Window Replacement—Wood	$21,495	$14,804	68.9%
Deck Addition—Composite	$19,856	$13,257	66.8%
Deck Addition—Wood	$14,360	$10,355	72.1%
Siding Replacement—Fiber-cement	$17,008	$13,195	77.6%
Siding Replacement—Vinyl	$14,359	$10,731	74.7%
Manufactured Stone Veneer	$9,357	$8,943	95.6%
Grand Entrance—Fiberglass	$9,254	$4,930	53.3%
Entry Door Replacement—Steel	$1,881	$1,294	68.8%
Entry Door Replacement—Fiberglass	$2,926	$2,107	72.0%**
Garage Door Replacement	$3,695	$3,491	94.5%
Attic Insulation—Replace Fiberglass	$1,343	$1,446	107.7%*
Basement Remodel	$71,115	$49,768	70.0%*
Family Room Addition	$89,566	$62,055	69.3%*
Two-storey Addition	$161,925	$103,848	64.1%
Attic bedroom Addition	$51,696	$39,908	77.2%**

Note: Costs and dollar value of returns based on 2020 report, except where indicated. All dollar figures in USD.

*Data collected in 2017 by Remodeling magazine

**Data collected in 2015 by Remodeling magazine

151

These averages are based on US national averages, and although material, labour and housing costs vary significantly between Canada and the United States, these dollar figures still offer insight into what Canadian homeowners can expect. The bottom line: a dollar spent is **not** a dollar earned when it comes to home renovations.

But what about that house that sold way above asking? You know, the one that was renovated and professionally staged? The home that sold for way more than a similar unrenovated home on the same street?

This is not an atypical question. Whether people say it or just think it, there's often a disconnect between the value renovations add to a home and the fact that they are not investments. The difficulty is in the language.

Value means that some asset we own or want is deemed to be important and have worth. As such, we see the action of increasing the market value of a home as an investment, since it theoretically gives us more money.

But an investment means using money to earn more money—and that's not what we do when we pay to renovate our homes.

To illustrate, let's look at the example of two comparable homes on the same street. Both are for sale. House A is updated. House B is not. As we know, the updated home sells for a much higher price. This is where we get the rationalization that money spent on home improvement increases the value of the home—making the reno a good investment.

To understand why this isn't accurate, let's look at the numbers. Let's assume that both homes were bought 10 years ago, each for

$200,000. Over the years, Home A's homeowner spends $75,000 on home renovations and upgrades and eventually sells their home for $357,500. In that same time frame, Home B's home-owner spends nothing on upgrades and sells the unrenovated home for $280,000.

Based on the math, Home A's owners earned a 30% return on their "investment" (home price + reno costs). Pretty good. The owners of the outdated house, however, earned a 40% return on their "investment" (home price). An even better return.

This example omits some big mitigating factors like the cost of mortgage debt, annual property taxes, price appreciation and increase in maintenance costs due to a lack of upgrades and improvements. But based purely on the math, the home-owner who chose not to spend on renovations earned more profit.

WHY HOME RENOVATIONS *ARE* INVESTMENTS

I want to be crystal clear about the fact that **home renovations are not typical investments**.

If I were a personal finance purist (or a trained economist), I'd take this a step further and state that home improvement projects or renovation upgrades do not qualify as investments. In finance geek terms, an investment is defined as "the action or process of investing money for profit or material result."

Because money spent on a home reno is not purely to earn a profit—except flippers or real estate investors—this makes it an expenditure, not an investment.

A quick word to the flippers (individuals and businesses that buy homes, renovate and sell for a profit): You can still make money on a flip depending on your sweat equity, market conditions and knowledge about what sells. Flipping is part investment, part due diligence and part speculation. Know this before you start a project and build in contingencies.

But I'm not a purist. I truly believe home renos can and do add value, some of which is captured financially. So, rather than see renovations as a consumer spending luxury (or a justification to spend), I tend to consider home upgrades as a process of choosing the best option or scenario along a spectrum of outcomes. At one end is a depreciating asset (sitting on valuable land); at the other end is a high-value asset (land) that consistently appreciates over time and can be optimized with continual updates to achieve the best and highest use.

Remember, if our ultimate goal is to grow our net worth, then any action we take to maintain or grow the value of our property will move us towards that goal. That means learning to spend money on smart home renovations.

HOW TO INCREASE THE VALUE OF YOUR HOME WITH RENOVATIONS

Since home renovations can be both an expense and an investment, we need to figure out how to be smart about our upgrade and home improvement decisions. This requires discipline, due diligence and the equivalent of a metric tonne of research.

It's not enough to blindly follow current design trends or stick to cliché reno rules, such as focusing on bathroom or kitchen updates. Smart renovations take into consideration the entire picture of a home, not just a fragment. Smart renovations also focus on fixing a problem, not just updating a design choice or personal style.

To stay on track with the overall strategy of using the home as a tool for wealth accumulation, each home reno project needs to be critically assessed to determine if it's a "smart renovation":

1. Does it increase your home's functionality (and/or desirability)?

2. Will you have to take on expensive debt?

3. Does it meet your family's current needs and goals?

4. Does it have a strong possibility of meeting your family's future needs and goals?

HOW TO DETERMINE IF YOUR PROJECT IS A SMART HOME RENOVATION

Answering these questions is not easy, particularly when circumstances change. I should know.

In 2014, my husband and I felt very fortunate when we purchased our "forever home" in a fantastic inner suburban Toronto neighbourhood. It was a dilapidated rancher whose former occupants were a shut-in hoarder and five raccoons. (I wish I was making this up!) And we weren't the only ones who saw potential. We got into a bidding war and paid $60,000 more than we wanted to! This premium on the sale price was worth it for us since the house met our current needs and our future goals and, most importantly, we were confident of the strong potential for future price growth.

So we threw ourselves into the job of renovating the property. We added old-growth, reclaimed barn wood floors, and framed, drywalled, taped and painted every inch of the home. We gutted and rebuilt the kitchen and completely remodelled all the bathrooms. Nothing in that home was left untouched.

Fast-forward three years and our family was living out of cardboard boxes in a soon-to-be-torn-down (and very dated) townhouse rental in North Vancouver, BC. We'd found our dream house and renovated it to last forever, but our plans, goals and needs changed; as a result, we sold that house and moved to meet those needs.

To be clear, things turned out pretty good for us, but we have an edge: I'm considered a personal finance and real estate expert and my husband is a master carpenter and residential contractor. The vast majority of homeowners don't have this knowledge or skillset at their disposal. This doesn't mean the vast majority of homeowners can't make smart and strategic home renovation decisions. (If I believed that, I would never have written this book!)

All homeowners can make smart reno decisions as long as they understand what they are trying to achieve. In general, there are four categories of home renovations and upgrades:

1. **The basics:** Renos that ensure a solid, water-repellant structure and include everything that goes into keeping your home in solid shape. Examples include capital

upgrades, such as replacing the roof or updating the plumbing.

2. **Curb appeal:** All projects that increase the home's appearance and perceived desirability, such as a well-manicured lawn, low-cost landscaping, fresh paint inside and out, cleaned carpets and new fixtures.

3. **Value-added:** Includes all upgrades that potential buyers would find attractive (because it's new, it looks better or it offers better functionality or use of the home), such as new siding, kitchen renovations, and new windows.

4. **Personal preference:** Any project that you and your family want, even if it adds nothing to the home's value. This includes a massive master en suite, swimming pools, hot tubs, wine cellars, basement game rooms and ponds, to name a few.

Regardless of which category the home renovation project falls into, if it solves a problem, it will add value. The more universal the problem, the more valuable the solution and the smarter the reno.

Anecdotally, I know this is true because our Toronto home attracted the second-highest sale price, on record, for that style of home in that community.

Don't trust personal anecdotes? Not to worry. Data backs me up. Take, for instance, the three biggest home-related annoyances, according to a recent survey from mortgage broker HSH. If you were to brainstorm the potential solutions to these homeowner problems, you might be surprised by the ROI on the upgrades.

- ❏ 67% of homeowners report lack of storage as their number one problem

  - → Potential Solution: Basement remodel

    - ✔ 70% ROI

- ❏ 66% of homeowners report that too much maintenance is their biggest grievance

  - → Potential Solution: Replace attic insulation (create a more climate-controlled home)

    - ✔ 108% ROI

- ❏ 52% of homeowners complain that their home is too small

  - → Potential Solution: Family room addition/second storey addition

    - ✔ 65% ROI

Obviously, there are many other solutions to the above problems, but the takeaway is that any home improvement project that can fix or minimize a perceived problem has a strong chance of increasing the value of a property.

Take the time to answer the above questions, and it will be much easier to develop a list of updates and upgrades for your home that will help you move a step closer to the ultimate goal of customizing a home to suit your needs *and* increasing your overall net worth by increasing the market value of your property.

Don't be fooled: this process is much harder than it appears, even for veteran flippers and real estate investors.

To get comfortable with the process of determining whether a home renovation is a smart one, I've listed a few of the more common North American homeowner problems along with potential solutions.

These solutions focus on a simple formula: spend the least amount to add the most value.

Value is determined by how well the solution—the specific upgrade, remodel or renovation—solves a problem. The more functional and desirable the solution, the more value it adds to your home.

(This doesn't mean you can't remodel or upgrade to suit your style or desires. Even personal preference renos are justified if the cost of this desire suits your financial goals and fits into your financial plan.)

This is not a definitive list. You will have to do your own investigative work to determine the most cost-effective smart renovation, but it is a good place to start. When assessing any solution, always remember to clearly define what category the reno falls into (basics, curb appeal, value-added or personal preference) and be honest as to whether it solves a problem, forces you to take on expensive debt, and meets your current needs and goals with the potential of meeting future needs and goals.

Again, the overall aim is to find a solution that costs the least but adds the most value. This isn't code for cheap. There are times when a good solution costs more than a cheap alternative.

Instead, focus on solving problems. If the update, remodel or renovation increases your home's functionality and desirability, this should translate into higher market value, even if the book value of property in your area is stagnant or declining.

SOLVING PROBLEMS WITH SMART RENOVATIONS

Problem: Not Enough Home Storage

67% of homeowners complain about their home's lack of storage

---

Over a decade ago, as I watched my belly grow because of the little human inside, I realized that the urban rowhouse that my husband and I called home was not well suited for new-baby life.

The century-old rowhouse was built much like a large townhouse, which meant stacked living and lots of stairs. Plus, it had the added problems of insufficient storage space, which wasn't surprising since it was originally built as temporary housing for immigrant bricklayers and labourers, who helped build the city of Toronto.

Our dilemma wasn't unique. Many couples find themselves house hunting to find a more family-friendly home. But with space at a premium in North America's largest cities, this desire for more square footage can certainly come with a hefty price tag.

Turns out, not enough storage space is the number one pet peeve for current homeowners, which is why any improvement to your home's organization and storage capacity will add to your property's current market value.

Thankfully, the problem of finding more space doesn't require a one-size-fits-all solution. All homeowners in all property types can use smart renos to add storage and increase the value of their home. Here are a couple of options to start the process.

Solution: Declutter

When you've got a small budget, updating your home or finding more space seems almost impossible. Decor updates will change the image of your home, but decluttering (and organizing) will change the functionality. The best part is that decluttering is the easiest, most cost-effective and least intrusive way to reclaim precious square footage and *add value*.

Every box of clutter removed from your home adds, on average, about $500 to the value of your property. This is based on more than a decade of observations and data from professional organizers and stagers who monitor, track and report on the sale prices of homes.

- **Average Budget:** $1,000 or less

- **Average ROI:** 100% to 300% of project cost

Solution: Off-the-Shelf or Custom Storage Solutions

Spend a bit more and develop unique-to-your-home storage solutions. This can mean custom storage—such as built-in cabinets—or off-the-shelf solutions that adapt to your needs.

The goal of this solution is to maximize the use of walls, stairwells, doorways, tight corners or any other underutilized space in your home.

If you're not handy or have difficulty with conceptualizing space, pay for a storage consultation. The typical cost is $150 per hour, but expect to pay between $150 and $500 for a complete set of custom storage plans for your home. Don't underestimate the value of having a trained professional, such as a professional organizer, closet manufacturer, interior designer (with experience in custom storage) or carpenter who specializes in space-saving cabinetry review and create these plans. These space-utilization experts will see possibilities you don't and help recapture underused or unused space.

Some companies will absorb the consultation cost as long as you hire them for the project—just be sure this is the direction you want to go. Even though it's hard to justify spending $200 on just a concept, if it saves you $1,000 on the execution, it could be well worth the cost.

Keep in mind, though, that cheaper isn't always better as corners need to be cut somewhere. For example, many off-the-shelf closet systems found in big-box or home reno stores will use 12-inch deep shelves. Turns out, most adult clothing, when folded, needs a 14-inch shelf to prevent the clothes from hanging over the edge.

Whether you go custom or off-the-shelf, the key is to put every nook and cranny to work so you can reclaim all the underused space in your home.

Average Budget: $600 to $10,000

Average ROI: 53% to 75% of project cost

Problem: House Is Too Small

52% of homeowners regret not buying a bigger home

It's hard to get into the housing market. Quite often, that difficulty leads to compromises. To find the right solution, you need to figure out the precise problem.

For some, space is the issue. For example, my friends Nancy and Pat ended up buying a lovely two-bedroom semi-detached home before the birth of their son. By the time their baby girl was born, they were feeling the pinch.

For others, the problem is more perceptual. You don't need an extra bedroom if all you want to use it for is a place to store hobbies. Before you say "But...," from a personal finance perspective, spending on better clutter control (even custom storage) is a lot cheaper than buying a bigger home or paying to add more space.

To find the right solution at the right price point, first determine if what you need is more space or the idea of more space. If the problem is more about design and decor, consider the first two solutions below. If the problem requires a more permanent solution, consider the last four.

Solution: Remove a Wall to Create an Open Concept

Removing an interior wall is one of the easiest and most dramatic ways to add space or change the use of space in your home. In that home decor show, tearing out a wall is that pinnacle moment—

the symbolic moment that signifies the "out with the old" and "good things are coming" attitudes that make the stress of home renos worthwhile.

By removing a wall, you create a wide-open space that can accommodate growing families and multiple needs. It's why the "open concept" design became so popular pre-2020 pandemic.

Any wall you remove may open up your space, but this solution doesn't always add value to your home. For example, the removal of a wall between two small bedrooms—effectively taking a four-bedroom home and turning it into a three-bedroom home—will more than likely hurt the resale value of your home.

To make sure removing a wall is the right solution, ask yourself the following five questions:

1. **What problem is this trying to solve?** Take a step back and decide if wall removal is the right answer. Is it that you want your space to look larger? Or do you want to be able to keep an eye on your kids while you cook dinner?

2. **Is this a load-bearing wall?** Load-bearing walls hold up your home's structure. This doesn't mean you can't remove an interior load-bearing wall, but you will need a plan to replace the structural role this wall played in your home. It also means you will need permits and, very likely, experts to help you.

3. **What will my home and family lose when this wall is removed?** You dream of wide-open space, but you need to know that there's a tradeoff. Removing a wall can mean less privacy and more noise. It can also be harder to hide messes and effectively heat or cool the space.

4. **What's inside the wall?** That wall may be hiding more than just the bones of your house. There may be electric lines, plumbing, HVAC or even old gas lines! Proceed with caution, and make a plan for dealing with what's hidden in the walls.

5. **What will this mean for the home's resale value?** It can be tempting to combine two smaller bedrooms into one. However, evidence shows that buyers are usually willing to pay more for a property with more bedrooms, regardless of size. To find out whether a wall removal will increase or decrease the value of your home, it's a good idea to hire a home appraiser or speak to a real estate agent.

Average Budget: $2,000 to $15,000

Average ROI: 55% to 75% of project cost

Solution: Convert Underused or Unfinished Rooms to Living Space

Nothing will increase your living space as dramatically as renovating your attic or basement.

On a small budget, you won't be able to do large, room-altering changes such as dropping the basement floor (known as benching or underpinning), but even a smaller budget, say between $15,000 and $60,000, can turn an already roughed-in basement into quality living space. Costs typically go up for older homes or if you need significant upgrades such as structural changes that require permits and inspections, plumbing, electrical or ductwork repositioning.

In older homes where the basement ceiling height is too short, you may need to pay an additional cost to bench or under-pin your home's foundation. This is a labour-intensive job that will add time and money to the basement conversion costs. For example, dropping your 1,000-square-foot basement floor eight inches will cost you $25,000 or more. And that doesn't include the $60,000 or so you'll need to renovate.

But the bigger job will cost you. A basic 800-square-foot basement that requires insulation, a vapour barrier and a complete bolts-to-nuts finishing job will cost you $30,000 to $40,000. Add in bathrooms and/or other "specialized options," and that number starts to climb to $50,000 to $75,000 or more. And all of this assumes mid-grade finishes. Still, this cost is relatively inexpensive when you consider the amount of living space this upgrade adds to your home.

Average Budget: $10,000 to $75,000

Average ROI: 69% to 77% of project cost

Solution: Small-Scale Addition

If your family is growing or you just need a bigger kitchen to accommodate your crew, the best option is to take on a small-scale addition, such as a 12-foot by 12-foot addition at the back of the house.

Just be prepared since a job of this scale takes time. A typical 12-foot by 12-foot addition that includes foundation, excavation, new footings, wooden frame, electrical wiring and climate control (i.e., heating) can take up to four months to complete. Plus, you'll need to check with your municipality to learn what permits and drawings are required.

If your four-season addition is above ground, it may cost as little as $50,000. If you opt to dig deeper than the footings and add additional below-grade space like another room in the basement, the cost will increase to $75,000 or more.

Of course, every major reno has unexpected costs. To keep your budget from spiralling out of control, limit changes once the build has started. Also, ask to be invoiced as soon as extras crop up so unanticipated costs don't snowball. Finally, remember to add in contingency costs. A good rule of thumb is to add 10% to 20% of the overall project price to your overall budget. That means, if your budget for the reno is $80,000, plan to spend $100,000—giving you a $20,000 buffer for unexpected costs.

Average Budget: $75,000 to $150,000

Average ROI: 60% to 80% of project cost

Solution: Large Addition

Let's assume you and your partner bought a bungalow 10 years ago that was perfect at the time. You had a bedroom, an office and enough community living space to entertain or just chill out. But three kids later, your family is busting out of the two cramped bedrooms, your office is now any corner of the kitchen table and you have nowhere to chill. This is when you need to add more space to your small home—a lot more space. It's also the right time to consider a second-floor addition or a large expansion.

This project won't be cheap. I've heard some homeowners pay as little as $150,000 for this type of expansion, but most end up paying $200,000 (assuming that the expansion includes at least one bathroom). If you need to double your space—say, turn your 1,200-square-foot bungalow into a 2,400-square-foot two-storey home—budget at least $400,000. If you source the materials yourself or opt for low-to-mid-range finishes, you can cut this price down, sometimes quite significantly.

Average Budget: $200,000+

Average ROI: 70% to 90% of project cost

Solution: Build New

The most expensive "more space" option is to demolish your existing home and build again. Although expensive, this option lets you customize your space without moving away from the neighbourhood you love.

Most contractors can build a family home with good quality mid-priced fixtures and materials for about $250 to $350 per square foot (a more modest home can be built for $150 to $225 per square foot). To demolish a 1,200-square-foot bungalow and build a new 2,400-square-foot two-storey home, the total cost would be between $600,000 and $840,000, including architectural fees, surveying, hydro, landscaping, labour and materials. Adding another floor, upgrading to fine finishes or installing state-of-the-art wiring can push that cost much higher. The cost of building isn't the only factor; you need to find and pay for a place to live while your new home is being built—and this could take 24 months or longer.

Average Budget: $350,000+

Average ROI: variable

Solution: Move

OK, I know this is a book about maximizing your net worth using your single most expensive asset, but I'd be remiss if I didn't mention the final and ultimate solution to the problem of a small home: sell and move.

Quite often, this is the go-to solution for this problem, but to make a smart decision, you need to know the basics. Typically, it will cost you between $200 and $300 per square foot to move house. This price point is the lower end of a custom home build, but the result is a new home, with new surprises on what does and doesn't work.

Most of the time, the option to move rather than renovate or customize boils down to financing. It's easier to qualify for a mortgage on a home purchase than find reasonable financing terms on a custom-built home. I'm not saying it's impossible to get financing. If it were impossible custom homes would never be built—it's just harder.

Average Budget: variable

Average ROI: variable

Problem: Property Is in a Bad Location

8% of homeowners regret their purchase due to a bad location

35% of home buyers want a property close to work

Real estate agents warn against buying a good house in an unde-sirable area, referring to the mantra "Location trumps all." But someone usually ends up buying the property anyway, and more often than not, it's because of the price.

For the most part, less-than-appealing community features, such as major roads, cemeteries, utility structures, landfills or airports, to name a few, usually hurt the home's market value.

Still, there are ways to mitigate the impact of a bad location. The first is to maximize the use and appearance of the home. The better the flow and functionality of the property, the easier it will be to overcome a potential buyer's concerns.

Another option is to find a solution that addresses your primary concern. Don't forget, your problem or pain point will not be unique to you, so finding a solution will go a long way towards increasing the value of your home, even if it is close to unde-sirable areas. For instance, if you don't like the schools in your current community but love everything else, consider registering your children in an out-of-catchment school.

Here are a few solutions to some of the more common prob-lems:

Solution: Build a Fence

When the regret is due to road noise (or unsightly views), a fairly obvious option is to build a fence.

Be sure to check municipal bylaws; they can vary dramatically. For instance, one city may limit residential fence heights to six feet but allow for special exemptions, while another city can have a strict four-foot fence rule. Keep in mind, the type of fence and where it's located will also play a factor.

Fence costs vary and you can expect to pay a professional:

- $2,000 to $4,500 for a wooden tongue-and-groove fence (including fence posts)

- $3,500 to $7,500 for a wooden fence with 100 square feet of mass-loaded vinyl (a noise absorption material)

- $3,100 to $9,000 for a poured concrete wall

- $5,000+ for a fence made of sound barrier panels

- $7,000+ for a brick wall

When choosing the type of fence, keep in mind that potential buyers rarely notice the quality of a fence, but they will notice if the fence offers them privacy in an attractive way. (Think curb appeal.)

Whatever material you select, be sure the fence is built as one continuous barrier. Spaces and holes will let in noise. Also, try and build the fence above your sight line since noise can travel in spaces with a clear line of sight. Finally, remember that material matters. Potential buyers won't see intrinsic value in a fence, but they will appreciate aesthetic appeal and, if they compare other homes on the same street, will then appreciate the value of a noise barrier.

Average Budget: $2,000+

Average ROI: 25% to 100% of project cost

Solution: Carve Out More Parking Spots

Quite often, a location is considered less desirable because it's busy. A home on a major street or a property close to a popular commercial space, such as a grocery store or stadium, can run into a few issues including limited parking. The solution is to add private parking to your property.

For this, you will need to apply and pay for permits, and it will require professional drawings—all of which adds time and expense. Still, if this is the right solution for your problem, you could ease your annoyance for less than $10,000.

Average Budget: $2,000 to $7,500 (basic, asphalt driveway)

Average ROI: 100% to 300% (in large, urban areas)

Problem: Outdated Home Decor (or Design)

69% of homeowners say out-of-date design is their biggest pet peeve

Making Strategic Home Improvements

Despite all our talk about the importance of maintenance and upkeep, the top motivation for the majority of home upgrades and renovations is still **outdated or undesirable design choices**.

The most popular remodels are:

- 31% Kitchen

- 27% Bathroom

- 25% Living/Family room

- 21% Master bathroom

- 18% Entry, foyer or mudroom

This is in line with what the Appraisal Institute of Canada lists as the top five renovations with the highest return:

1. Kitchen (renovate or update)

2. Bathroom (renovate or add)

3. Repainting the interior and/or exterior (choose colours and shades with wide-ranging market appeal)

4. Updating decor (lighting and plumbing fixtures, countertops, replacing worn flooring or refinishing hardwood floors)

5. Decluttering (removing all excess items to showcase the features of your home)

Solution: Scale Your Upgrade and Reno Plans

Design and decor upgrades can and do add value to your home, as long as you are smart about the renovation. Remember, you want to spend the least to get the most. If your home design and decor aren't too dated, consider cheaper, less intrusive updates first. However, if your home is older or really dated, splurging on a complete remodel will definitely give you the biggest ROI bang for your buck.

Here are some general tips to help you make smart choices on design upgrades:

1. **Make modern updates to high-traffic areas.** For the highest possible return, choose finishes that are contemporary and neutral. Just remember that even a well-thought-out remodel can look outdated in 15 or so years. To be smart, choose a design that suits your family's needs but with features that can be easily updated when it comes time to sell.

2. **Don't underestimate the inexpensive remodel plans.** It's easy to focus on the major stuff, like kitchens or bathrooms, particularly when prepping your home to sell. But quite often, it's the smaller, less-expensive upgrades, like painting your home neutral colours or replacing the entry door, that make a difference.

3. **Consider energy efficiency.** The upgrades and renovations that help a home become more energy efficient can often provide the best return *and* give you added savings while you still live in the home.

4. **Always match the upgrade to your area.** The key with any home upgrade or renovation is to add value

that fits in with the surrounding neighbourhood expectations. For example, a $12,000 porcelain sink for your bathroom could be a great addition to a large luxury home but a waste of money if added to a single-family detached home.

Solution: Follow the Four Functional Home Design Rules

If you have the option to completely renovate an entire floor, here are four functional home design rules to follow:

1. **Choose your home layout based on your lifestyle.**
   For example, if your family spends as much time outside as inside, make sure the path from the external door to a bathroom is relatively short and straightforward, as this will promote hand-washing and keep dirt and mud to a minimum.

2. **Position the kitchen near all eating areas.** This may seem obvious since most dining rooms are off the kitchen, but this design rule also applies to decks and patios.

3. **Position the kitchen close to the front or side doors.** If your kitchen is too far from external entry doors, you'll be forced to carry heavy grocery bags a long way through your home.

4. **Pay attention to flow and footpaths.** When you design and build a home with flow and footpaths in mind, it allows family life to flow easily and naturally throughout each room and the entire house.

Inefficient space is a never-ending source of frustration for homeowners. Renovations and upgrades that address functionality not only solve your family's immediate needs but have the potential to offer solutions to future buyers. Keep in mind, your home's most efficient state will change over time. Whereas growing families may need more bedrooms or another bathroom, ageing couples may want to reduce or remove room transitions (and tripping hazards).

To get an idea, here are the most common issues when it comes to outdated design. Consider these the areas that potential buyers see first and value most.

Problem: Outdated or Poorly Laid-Out Kitchen

Remodelling an old, outdated kitchen can be one of the smartest reno jobs a homeowner can undertake.

Planning a kitchen renovation is more than just deciding where the stove goes. You need to consider workflow and traffic patterns within the kitchen, as well as the surrounding spaces. You'll also need to consider materials and choose fixtures for form and function while staying within your budget.

Costing out a kitchen renovation can be daunting. As a general rule of thumb, most experts suggest **spending no more than 15% of your property's total value on a kitchen remodel**. For a $1 million home, that means a budget of $150,000. For a $250,000 house, the budget should be capped at $37,000.

Keep in mind, the return on the money spent on this upgrade is relative. If the kitchen is very dated and poorly laid out, you could see a 100% return on your project costs. If the kitchen is already in good shape, the ROI will be much lower.

Here's a breakdown of some smart kitchen upgrades.

Solution: Add a Kitchen Island

48% of homebuyers would pay extra for a home with a kitchen island

Kitchen islands have gained in popularity over the last decade since they provide a gathering place for friends and family, offer additional room for food prep and can even double as the eat-in kitchen alternative.

Expect to pay about $5,000 for a 24-square-foot semi-custom island with seating on one side, a granite countertop and a bar sink. A much cheaper version, without a sink, is a $500 out-of-the-box rolling island with a wood countertop.

Average Budget: $500 to $7,000

Average ROI: 25%

Solution: New Countertops

55% of homebuyers would pay extra for a home with granite countertops

When it comes to kitchen countertops, there are so many options that it can be tough to choose. The key is to pick something beautiful, affordable and durable that will resist stains, won't show cuts and nicks and won't warp, chip or break. Here are the most popular countertop options on the market right now.

Comparison of Different Countertop Materials

STAINLESS STEEL

Advantages

- Seams can be welded, ground and buffed out to create a seamless look.

- Excellent resistance to heat and stains.

Disadvantages

- Dents and scratches easily.

- Fingerprint smudges are obvious.

BUTCHER'S BLOCK

Advantages

- Maple and teak are the most common, but other woods are available.

- Wooden countertops can double as a cutting board.

- Relatively easy to install and repair.

Disadvantages

- Not great with heat.

- Will visibly show cuts and scrapes.

- Needs to be oiled every few months (or will warp and/
  or crack).

LIMESTONE

Advantages

- Can look high-end and pristine.

- Great for decorative embellishments.

Disadvantages

- Best kept to areas where food preparation is least likely
  to take place.

- Can scratch, chip and stain very easily.

BAMBOO

Advantage

- An eco-friendly option.

Disadvantages

- Can stain easily. Will show scorch marks (so not great with high heat) and will show cuts and scrapes easily.

- Moisture will warp bamboo countertops (and shouldn't be used around the sink).

RECYCLED GLASS

Advantages

- Great option for adding an infusion of colour into your kitchen.

- Resistant to heat, cuts and scratches.

- Can be an eco-friendly option if you opt for a countertop created from recycled glass shards.

Disadvantages

- Can chip easily.

- Resin between the glass pieces can stain easily.

QUARTZ

Advantages

- This engineered product is made from a blend of stone chips and offers a large selection of colours and styles.

- Great at repelling spills.

- Handles heat and knife cuts well.

- Doesn't have to be sealed for stain protection.

- Waterproof.

- Great option if installing an undermount sink.

Disadvantages

- Some patterns can appear too uniform and unnatural.

- Edges and corners are more prone to chipping. To prevent this costly repair, consider paying for rounded corners.

GRANITE

Advantages

- A natural, sought-after product.

- Each slab is unique.

- Excellent option when it comes to dealing with spills, hot pots and knife blades.

Disadvantage

- Does require periodic sealing for stain protection.

LAMINATE

Advantages

- Stain and heat resistant.

Disadvantages

- Quality of laminate in the market can differ dramatically.

- Cheaper options often have a colour layer on top of a core, and this type of construction can let water seep into the seams causing separation and peeling corners.

- Not good at handling knife nicks and scratches.

TILE

Advantages

- Great choice for cost-conscious shoppers.

- Durable and a tile countertop can easily transition into a tile backsplash.

- For intense stain resistance, consider porcelain tiles (which are also easier to clean than most other tile materials).

Disadvantages

- Can chip easily. Consider buying a few extra tiles (cheaper and easier to repair if you have the tile and will help prolong the longevity of the countertop).

- Lighter grout lines can look dirty if not properly cleaned frequently. To avoid, consider using a darker colour grout.

SOAPSTONE

Advantage

- Affordable alternative to granite.

- Natural product.

- Withstands heat well.

Disadvantages

- Doesn't withstand cuts and scrapes well.

- Need to rub with mineral oil on a regular basis.

POLISHED CONCRETE

Advantages

- Modern, clean look.

Disadvantages

- Chips and scratches easily.

- Need to double-seal it with a topical and a penetrating seal in order to get this material heat and stain protection.

MARBLE

Advantages

- Classic (and classy) option.

- Great at withstanding chips and dings (any that do occur can be easily polished out).

Disadvantages

- Need to seal marble to prevent scratches.

- Can show stains even after it is sealed.

One way to save money is to use more expensive material in prominent areas, such as an island, and less expensive material on background countertops. Also, check the remnant pile, as these smaller pieces are ideal for islands, sink counters and breakfast nooks.

Hard corners are the cheapest option, but rounded edges are not that much more and help reduce chipping. Bevelled and bull-nosed edges will add to your cost.

If you are using a professional installer, make sure your contract itemizes the specific material, dimensions, edges, corners and cut-outs. Also, make sure that the cost of removing the old countertop is included in the total install price.

Average Budget: $2,500 to $6,000

Average ROI: 80% to 100%

What a New Countertop Costs

Average countertop space in a standard kitchen: **30 square feet**

Typical queen-size bed: **30 square feet**

The Cost to Replace a Standard Kitchen Countertop

Resistance level
low ●●●○ high

Material	Cost Sq. ft.	Total Pre-Tax Cost (Without installation) for 30 sq. ft.	Stain	Heat	Scratch	Impact
Laminate	$20 - $50	$600 - $1,500	●●●○	●●●○	●○○○	●○○○
Butcher Block	$35 - $200	$1,050 - $6,000	●●●○	●○○○	●○○○	●○○○
Cultured Marble	$40 - $140	$1,200 - $4,200	●●○○	●●●●	●○○○	●●○○
Corian	$42 - $65	$1,260 - $1,950	●○○○	●○○○	●○○○	●●○○
Recycled Glass	$50 - $125	$1,500 - $3,750	●●●○	●●●○	●○○○	●○○○
Carrara Marble	$50 - $150	$1,500 - $4,500	●●○○	●●●●	●○○○	●●○○
Granite	$50 - $100	$1,500 - $3,000	●●○○	●●●●	●●●●	●●●●
Soapstone	$70 - $120	$2,100 - $3,600	●●●●	●●●●	●○○○	●○○○
Concrete	$70 - $150	$2,100 - $4,500	●●●●	●●○○	●○○○	●○○○
Stainless Steel	$75 - $150	$2,250 - $4,500	●●●●	●●●●	●○○○	●○○○
Quartz	$100 - $150	$3,000 - $4,500	●●●●	●●●○	●●●●	●●●●

Remember: Countertop material costs are based on square feet (size of the countertop) and linear feet the (height of the countertop). A linear foot is the equivalent of 12 inches x 12 inches (30.5cm x 30.5cm)

Decades ago, kitchens were tucked away and kept out of sight. Quite often these galley and L-shaped rooms took up little more than 100 to 150 square feet of living space. In contemporary homes, kitchens now average about 300 square feet, providing about 30 square feet of counter space.

Solution: Update Your Cabinets

Cabinets can be your biggest expense, eating up as much as 40% of your kitchen renovation budget. But the cost is justifiable. New cabinets are more than a fresh face for your kitchen. Your cabinetry also serves an integral function. Cabinets create the frame of your kitchen and establish the overall structure of this very active space in your home.

The overall cost of your new kitchen cabinets will depend on a variety of factors including:

- Cabinet construction (whether the cabinetry is off-the-shelf, semi-custom or custom)

- Cabinet material for both the box and the doors

- Style and finish of your cabinets and doors

- Size of the kitchen

- Features included (such as soft-close doors, pullouts, glass doors or recessed lighting)

To keep costs down but get the best value, consider these tips.

Tip #1: Choose stock or semi-custom cabinets.

For the most cost-effective option, head straight to IKEA or your favourite big-box hardware store. Most off-the-shelf or semi-custom cabinets—where you can pick and choose your design from a range of standard-size units—are sold on a per-unit cost, not a per-linear-foot cost, and come in a selection of standard colours.

	COST/LINEAR FOOT	LONGEVITY	TOTAL PRE-TAX COST*
Custom	$500+	50+ years	$13,000
Semi-custom	$200+	50+ years	$5,200
Stock	$60+	10+ years	$1,560

Sample budget based on 26 linear feet

Tip #2: Avoid particle board or melamine and choose MDF or wood for value and longevity.

Mass-market cabinets made of particleboard or melamine tend to break down or swell if repeatedly exposed to moisture or humidity.

Better quality off-the-shelf cabinets are made from a mixture of medium-density fibreboard (MDF) and wood and tend to be more durable and offer a higher degree of customization.

Tip #3: Customize off-the-shelf cabinets for maximum functionality.

Add customization if it can help you optimize. For instance, lower cabinets offer the biggest storage spaces in your kitchen. But the back half of the cabinet is usually wasted—out of sight and out of reach, as they say. Install pull-outs or rollout shelves to reclaim maximum use of that space. These aftermarket add-ons are typically quite cheap, starting at $25 per pullout.

Tip #4: Know the look you want before you select the cabinet material.

Most cabinets will have a finish applied to them. Typically, this is lacquer or urethane, although factory-made semi-custom or off-the-shelf wood cabinets can also have a baked-on finish, called a catalytic conversion varnish. The key is to determine what type of finish is included and whether it offers the look and durability you need. Remember, different materials, and even different woods, stain or take paint differently. You can opt for a natural, non-stain look as well.

Tip #5: Paint is your best option on a very tight budget.

If you are on a very tight budget, skip the low-end options and just repaint your current cabinets instead. Use semi-gloss and a paint sprayer, and you can keep your cabinet update cost to about $30 per linear foot.

Kitchen: Putting It All Together

Whereas some homeowners will update one or two kitchen components, most of us end up gutting and starting again.

On average, Canadians spent just under $25,600 on a kitchen remodel, according to 2018 Homestars data.

Here's an idea of how this update will impact your budget and your home's value:

Mid-range <u>minor</u> kitchen remodel: Not gutting or changing the layout or moving the walls of the existing kitchen. Includes changing cabinet fronts (but keeping the current cabinet boxes), adding new hardware and faucets, upgrading countertops to granite or quartz, installing a new set of matching appliances, repainting, and putting in a new floor.

Average Budget: $20,000 to $50,000

Average ROI: 80% to 90%

Mid-range <u>major</u> kitchen remodel: This upgrade is a complete overhaul of the entire kitchen. You may move walls and rearrange the layout to improve functionality. You might add an island, semi-custom wood cabinets, energy-efficient appliances, a standard stainless-steel sink and new flooring. The final touches might include freshly painted walls, trim and ceiling.

Average Budget: $60,000 to $85,000

Average ROI: 55% to 60%

Upscale <u>major</u> kitchen remodel: You take the same actions as in the mid-range major update, but the finishes are higher quality, such as top-of-the-line custom cabinetry, stone countertops, high-end appliances, imported ceramic or glass tile backsplash, an under-mount sink, a water-filtration faucet and upgraded lighting. The new floor will be tile, wood-look tile or wood.

Average Budget: $100,000 to $150,000

Average ROI: 50% to 55%

If you're redesigning the layout or doing a major remodel, consider whether your current kitchen layout conforms to the "kitchen triangle" design rule. The aim is to maximize the efficiency of the three busiest areas in your kitchen: the sink, the stove and the refrigerator. There should be no obstacles to these three heavy-use spaces; ignore this rule, and your kitchen will feel inefficient, which can severely detract from your kitchen's value and your home's overall value. (It's why galley-kitchen homes tend to sell for less than homes with better kitchen layouts.)

The other consideration is how traffic flows into and out of your kitchen. Remember, you want the easiest, most unobstructed access to indoor and outdoor dining space, as well as quick access to an external door (so you can get heavy grocery bags into your kitchen quickly and easily).

Be mindful that the return on your kitchen upgrade will be much greater if you are improving a very outdated or very inefficient space, or the remodel is part of a larger plan to modernize the home.

Problem: Outdated or Too Few Bathrooms

Bathrooms in a home can influence buyers' decisions. But that doesn't mean you should spend, spend, spend. Experts suggest capping your bathroom upgrade budget to no more than 5% of your home's current value. For instance, if your home's market value is $1 million, you shouldn't spend more than $50,000 updating *all the bathrooms*.

Should You Renovate Your Kitchen before You List Your House for Sale?

Everyone wants a large, spacious kitchen with all-new appliances where they can cook and entertain (or imagine doing this, even if they never do). If your current kitchen already satisfies these desires, then there's probably no need to take on the financial burden of renovating your home for sale.

However, if your kitchen is a little tired or very dated, it may be good to consider your options. It's possible that you can avoid a major renovation with a few minor updates and some fresh touch-ups. Then again, your kitchen may need a complete overhaul.

To get the right answer, answer the following

Do other homes in the area have renovated kitchens?

What do homes with updated kitchens sell for compared to unrenovated kitchens?

Can you accomplish your remodel goal without spending more than 15% of your projected sale price on the kitchen remodel?

If want to update your kitchen without taking on a huge renovation, consider focusing on the following:

Add a fresh coat of paint.

Add and update all the lighting.

Update and refresh the countertops and backsplash

As far as appliances go, buyers still love stainless steel, but even if appliances aren't this finish, be sure that they are in good working condition and appear clean and in a good state. If the oven, dishwasher or range is out of operation—or in awful shape—you will need to replace these appliances just to match competing properties for sale.

Here are some options:

Solution: Cosmetic Changes

Painting, adding new decor and some shelves, and updating faucets, light fixtures and cabinet hardware can all have a dramatic impact.

But not all updates are created equal. Resist the urge to rip out a bathtub just to create a larger walk-in shower and avoid making structural changes like enlarging your bathroom by reclaiming the space used by one of the bedrooms. Fewer bedrooms and a lack of small-child bathing options make a home less appealing to young families.

Instead, focus on creating a "spa-like" atmosphere with a soothing colour palette, clean, modern lines and upscale finishes such as glass shower doors.

Pro tip: Full frameless looks amazing—like floating glass—but you'll pay a premium. Instead, consider a thinner glass door, installed by a pro, as the best compromise between off-the-shelf cheaper products and high-end custom.

- **Average Budget:** $500+

- **Average ROI:** 150% to 200%

Solution: Replace and Update Tile

Tile is expensive to replace, but it can dramatically alter the look and feel of a bathroom. The good news is that bathrooms are usually smaller rooms, so splashing out on a really good, long-lasting tile shouldn't be too cost prohibitive. Plus, there are options in every price band. For instance, if the cost of marble is too outrageous, consider a porcelain tile that can mimic the look of marble but at a fraction of the price.

Factors That Impact Tile Installation Costs

The following factors will impact the cost of tile upgrades:

- Level of installation difficulty

- Condition of subfloor

- Removal of existing floor and other waste materials

- Contractor/expert you are working with + current market demand for this type of upgrade

Here is a sample of average tile costs to help you assess your home reno upgrade:

- Ceramic: $2.50 to $3.00 average square foot cost

- Porcelain: $3.00 to $10.00 average square foot cost

- Natural Stone: $5.00 to $10.00 average square foot cost

- Marble: $12.00+ average square foot cost

Other factors that will add to your total upgrade cost:

- **Setting materials:** $1.50 to $2.00 average square foot cost

- **Floor tile installation:** $6.00 to $10.00 average square foot cost

- **Wall tile installation:** $7.00 to $12.00 average square foot cost

- **Removal of old floor/subfloor remediation:** $1.00 to $3.00 average square foot cost

Pro tip: It pays to hire a pro when it comes to a bathroom upgrade, as long as they're willing to pass on some of their material discounts. For example, the price of one brand of glossy-glass subway tile is $8.25/square foot for DIYers, while accredited pros can get the same tile for less than $2/square foot.

Average Budget: $600 to $5,000

Average ROI: 50% to 300%

Bathroom: Putting It All Together

If your aim is to go beyond cosmetic changes, you'll need to consider a full bathroom remodel or bathroom addition. Here are the benchmark costs and returns for these options.

Mid-range bathroom remodel: Materials will include ceramic tiles, new standard fixtures and faucets, a single-lever shower handle (one that you twist to turn the water on), a standard white toilet and a solid-surface vanity counter. In other words, the finishes are good quality and functional but not top of the line.

Average Budget: $15,000 to $25,000

Average ROI: 70% to 102%

Upscale bathroom remodel: This upgrade is a complete overhaul of the bathroom and may include structural changes to adjust the layout or size of the room. Finishes include ceramic tiles, heated floors, high-end faucets, new lighting and stone countertops with double sinks. Showers may have frameless glass doors, rain shower fixtures, shower niches and tiled shower walls. Freestanding tubs are also found in this type of bathroom remodel.

Average Budget: $50,000 to $75,000

Average ROI: 55% to 60%

Accessible/Age-in-place bathroom remodel: Rather than concentrate on decor, this mid-range bathroom remodel concentrates on making the bathroom accessible. Features include widened doorways, accessible storage, push-button locks, a walk-in shower that's flush with the floor, a fold-down shower seat, a taller toilet, an open-base vanity that can accommodate a wheelchair, and support bars throughout the bathroom.

Average Budget: $15,000 to $50,000

Average ROI: 60% to 70%

Mid-range bathroom addition: This project includes a full-size fibreglass tub and shower combo in a 6-foot by 8-foot bathroom. There will be similar features to the mid-range bathroom remodel, but the cost is significantly higher since you're starting from scratch.

Average Budget: $35,000 to $50,000

Average ROI: 55% to 65%

Upscale bathroom addition: This is a new bathroom that is at least 100 square feet and will follow the same finishes and features as the upscale bathroom remodel but with the added cost of extending electricity, water and HVAC to this room.

Average Budget: $75,000 to $95,000

Average ROI: 50% to 60%

Problem: Outdated Living/Family Room

There are a few updates you can do to modernize the look of your family room. Adding more light is one option; updating the art and decor is another. Additional projects include the following:

Best Paint Colours that add Value to your Home

 Bathroom

Periwinkle Blue / Light Blue with a Gray-Blue tint.

Added value to the home:
$2500 - $3000

 Dining Room

Soft White.

Added value to the home:
$1000 - $1500

 Kitchen

Tuxedo Cabinets (Dark Lowers / Light Uppers) + Light Wall Colour such as White or Warm Gray.

Added value to the home:
$1300 - $1700

 Bedroom

White or White with blue or gray undertones.

Added value to the home:
$500 - $1000

 Family Room / Den / Basement

Soft White or Earth Neutral Tones -Avoid Yellow Undertones

Added value to the home:
$1000 - $1500

On the flip side, the worst options were

 Dining Room

Oat brown, Medium Sandy Brown, Brown with Yellowish Undertones.

Value removed from the home:
$1500 - $1750

 Kitchen

Brick red, Barn Red, Lighter Raspberry Red.

Value removed from the home:
$2000 - $2500

Solution: Remove Popcorn Ceilings

Very few things date a space like popcorn finish on the ceiling. The good news is that this is not a hard update to take on if you're a handy homeowner, but be mindful that it's a laborious, time-consuming job. The three most common methods to get rid of a popcorn ceiling are scrape it off, cover it with drywall or skim coat on a new design.

The only caveat is that you first need to confirm that your popcorn ceilings weren't applied before the late 1980s, since asbestos was often added to the spray-on texture in older homes with this ceiling type.

Pro tip: To find out if your popcorn ceiling is asbestos-free, spray water onto a small portion of the ceiling and remove a sample without scraping. Send this sample to accredited testing company EMSL Analytical Inc. (there are more than 45 locations throughout the United States and Canada). For $130, they'll test your "consumers' samples." You should get results within a week or two. If there is asbestos, you'll need to double or triple your budget.

Average Budget: $1,000 to $4,000

Average ROI: 10%

Solution: Add a Fireplace

Although often overlooked, fireplaces appear to add value to a home. In a 2007 report from the National Association of Realtors, 46% of home buyers indicated they would pay more for a home with at least one fireplace. The potential return on a fireplace ranges from 25% to 90%, depending on where the home is located, the type of fireplace and how well it functions.

If your home has a fireplace, it's worth it to make it functional. If your home doesn't have a fireplace, you can consider adding one. Options run the gamut from new, prefabricated metal gas or wood-burning fireplaces to electric inserts to full-size masonry units.

Average Budget: $1,500 to $5,000

Average ROI: 10% to 67%

Solution: Update or Replace Crown Mouldings

It's hard to put a value on updating your crown moulding since few buyers walk in and *consciously* notice the impact. But crown moulding can visually make or break a room, and most people wouldn't know it other than to feel like "something was missing."

Installing crown moulding can get tricky, so you may want to hire a pro.

Average Budget: $5/linear foot

Average ROI: 25% to 50%

Solution: Repaint

The quickest way to make a room (or the entire house) look new again is to add a fresh coat of paint. The best part is that paint is one of the simplest updates with the highest returns. The key is to choose the colour carefully. If you plan to sell relatively soon, consider choosing a neutral colour; this removes your personality and gives potential buyers a better chance at imagining their own lives in your home (which translates into more desire and higher sale prices).

Assuming your home is close to 2,300 square feet (the average-size home in North America), expect to pay about $6,500 to $7,000 to paint your home's entire interior. (This price includes two coats of paint, trim and ceilings by a professional.) For those who want the DIY cost, assume you'll pay $2 to $5 per square foot.

According to data from Zillow, the room dictates the right colour selection. Here's a list of the best colour options by room and their return, based on an analysis of 135,000 homes:

Average Budget: $2,000 to $7,000

Average ROI: 107%

Problem:
Impractical Entry, Foyer or Mudroom

Think of the items you always drop off right away when you get home. If you design an entryway that has places for all of these things to go, you will have less mail piled on the kitchen counter, coats draped over the couch and shoes in the middle of the room. Don't forget to account for handbags, backpacks and random accessories such as sunglasses, baseball caps and umbrellas.

Here's a list of update options for your home's entryway.

Solution: Add Functional Design Elements

Adding mirrors and decorative shelves can do quite a lot for your entryway. For instance, a well-positioned mirror can add light—a critical component for showcasing your home—as well as provide an opportunity to take one last glance before leaving the house. A decorative shelf can offer a place for art as well as clutter control.

Speaking of light: add it. A well-lit room adds to the imperceptible value we place on a room or home—more light subconsciously translates into bigger, more inviting spaces. Plus, it helps us find the stuff we need to get out the door faster.

If you want to let in natural light (the ultimate option) but can't add a window or skylight, consider tubular skylights, which use a rooftop dome to capture the sun's rays and then transfer the light indoors through a highly reflective tube. These skylight options are now relatively cost-effective (starting at $200), although installation will bump up the price to about $1,000 (still half the cost of a skylight).

If your foyer includes a set of basic and boring stairs, a bannister and railings, you'll want to consider replacing or painting these stair elements. Paint a neutral colour that matches the walls to make the bannister and railings "disappear," or opt for a bold, contrast colour to add a bit of style.

Whatever you decide to tackle, here are a few universal tips to keep in mind:

- Lighter colours tend to make spaces look bigger.

- Make sure you have somewhere to put down small things, like keys and the mail, when you walk in the door.

- Add big-style elements to small spaces for functionality and an updated design.

Average Budget: $1,000 or less

Average ROI: variable

Solution: Contain Clutter

The number one issue that comes up in entryways is storage. Lack of storage or ineffective storage means your foyer will end up looking like a rummage sale with shoes, coats and bags strewn all over the place.

If you have a closet, use it. If not, consider adding pieces of furniture such as an armoire and maybe a chest of drawers, along with some hooks, to contain the clutter. If space doesn't permit the addition of furniture, install plenty of hooks to hang coats and include something like a storage bench so you can stash shoes, hats, bags and gloves. It can also serve as a spot to sit down and put on your boots.

To keep piles of paper from taking over the area, add a console table—a thin table typically used in entryways. The table offers a spot to put bags and keys, while storage bins or baskets can be tucked underneath to corral hats, mitts and other items. Since most console tables are 18 inches deep, stick to 12-inch baskets or bins.

Finally, you could opt to invest in a custom build. A built-in bench and slim side table for keys and other essentials can be all that's needed to control clutter, even in the smallest or most awkward space.

Average Budget: $10 to $5,000

Average ROI: variable

Solution: Add a Mudroom

Adding a mudroom to your home can be a big commitment, but in some communities, such as those considered desirable by growing families, the addition of a mudroom may be worth the cost. Mudroom costs can vary dramatically, with insulated but covered space costing less than $2,000, while the addition of a 50-square-foot, fully insulated room costs an estimated $12,000, and large extensions or bump-out additions can be more than $30,000.

Another option is to enclose a porch. Expect to pay around $10 to $15 per square foot—or, for a 200-square-foot porch, budget between $1,000 and $3,000.

Average Budget: $12,000

Average ROI: 25%

Problem: Outdated Bedrooms

Solution: Install a Walk-in Closet

60% of homebuyers would pay extra for a master bedroom with a walk-in closet

Adding a walk-in closet to your master bedroom will mean trying to create space without detracting from your current floorplan. If you have a large master bedroom, you can add a walk-in closet pretty easily with the construction of non-load-bearing walls and the installation of a semi-custom closet. If your bedroom is already on the smaller side, a walk-in closet addition will require you to take space from another area of your home.

Another option for smaller master bedrooms is to add a semi-custom closet system like IKEA's PAX system. For a few thousand, you can get semi-customizable closet space that maximizes storage and addresses your room's specific needs better than a stand builder's grade closet.

- **Average Budget:** $600 to $10,000

- **Average ROI:** 53% to 75%

Solution: Enlarge Your Current Master Suite

49% of homebuyers would pay extra for a master bedroom with an en suite bathroom

Although reclaiming an unused bedroom as part of the master en suite, either as a walk-in closet or as a master bathroom, can create a stunning suite, it can also hurt the value of your home. That's because most buyers will pay more for more bedrooms (up to a certain point), even if your master suite is like something out of a glossy-paged magazine.

Instead of destroying the bedroom, consider design elements that let you combine rooms without destroying the highest and best use of your home.

For instance, instead of converting that unused bedroom into a massive master bathroom, consider turning it into a walk-in closet with a sit-down vanity area. That way, you can install French doors and use the space as you want, but when it comes time to sell, you can convert the layout back to the highest, best use, which is a home with more bedrooms (which appeals more to buyers).

- **Average Budget:** $65,000

- **Average ROI:** 50% to 125%

Problem: Outdated Flooring

Picking the right floor is critical, but that doesn't mean there is one right answer. The right floor will depend on what the room is used for, whether there are temperature and humidity fluctuations and whether the floor will continually be exposed to outside elements.

Here are the most popular flooring options, along with their best uses and costs.

Concrete

($2 to $30 per square foot; average: $8.50/square foot, installed)

Pros:

- Offers excellent water resistance (if sealed with either a sealer or epoxy paint)

- Durable

- Low maintenance

- Beautiful design options (such as the inclusion of dyes, one-of-a-kind finishes, stamps)

- Works well with radiant heated floors (electrical cables or hot water tubes embedded in the concrete to create warm, comfy floors)

Cons:

- Hard under the feet

- Susceptible to below-grade water seepage

- Susceptible to cracking

Tile

($7 to $24 per square foot; average: $11/square foot, installed)

(ceramic is cheaper, porcelain is more popular)

Pros:

- Lots of design options

- Very durable

- Water- and stain resistant

- Low maintenance

- Lasts decades

Cons:

- Expensive to install

- Can crack or chip

- Can be cold under the feet

- Can get slippery when wet

- Harder DIY installation

- Requires additional care (such as sealing grout lines)

Hardwood

($5 to $25 per square foot; average: $8/square foot, installed)

Pros:

- Adds warmth

- Looks fantastic

- Highly valued by potential buyers

- Durable and long lasting

Cons:

- Not water resistant

- Susceptible to warping, splitting, fissures or cracking due to humidity changes

- Not all hardwood is suitable for use as a subgrade floor due to its tendency to swell and contract

Engineered Hardwood

($3 to $17 per square foot; average: $9/square foot, installed)

Pros:

- Adds warmth

- Looks fantastic

- Appealing to potential buyers

- Can be more cost-effective than hardwood (but not always)

- Plywood base makes each plank strong and durable

- Resists water better than hardwood and laminate flooring

Cons:

- Not water resistant and will be destroyed if subjected to prolonged or sustained contact with water

Laminate

($1 to $12 per square foot; average: $4/square foot, installed)

Pros:

- Water-resistant, up to a point

- Very cost-effective

- Easy to install for DIYers

Cons:

- Water needs to be mopped up immediately. If not, water may be able to seep past the first four layers and penetrate the fibreboard layer (the wood fibres and blue layer)

- If fibreboard layer gets wet, the laminate will swell and bend and won't revert back to its original shape and structure (when you start to see warping and bubbling in the floor)

Linoleum

($2 to $5 per square foot; average: $4/square foot, installed)

Comes in sheets and in tiles. You'll pay more for sheet linoleum, as this requires more labour to install, but offers fewer penetration points, which translates to much better water resistance.

Pros:

- Extremely durable (often the go-to choice for daycares, hospitals and some retail stores)

- Naturally antibacterial

- Water resistant

Cons:

- Often considered out of date and old fashioned

- Oil-based product

- Must be recoated with an acrylic sealer once per year (to maintain a durable, water-resistant finish)

Vinyl

($3 to $10 per square foot; average: $7/square foot, installed)

Like linoleum, vinyl can come in sheets or tiles. These days the tiles come in a variety of finishes, including wood-grain look.

Pros:

- Cost-effective (given its durability and water resistance)

- Can be installed by competent handy homeowners (or professionals)

- Exceptionally water resistant

- Used by main retail outlets, including Indigo (the brand uses wood-like vinyl tiles)

Cons:

- If using tiles, the seams have no adhesion, making them susceptible to water seepage

- Can remove the potential for water seepage by using a floor adhesive, but this will require more labour and additional materials (which translates to more expense)

Carpet

($5 to $12 per square foot; average: $8/square foot, installed)

Pros:

- Adds warmth and comfort

- Cost-effective

- Easy to lift up, air out and dry out, should the basement flood

- Durable

Cons:

- Dirt and stains may be hard to remove

- Can be seen as dated or old fashioned

- Not water resistant (but can be dried)

- Can't be used with in-floor heating

Cork

($2 to $12 per square foot; average: $9.50/square foot, installed)

Cork flooring has been around for decades but only recently came into fashion because of its "renewable resource" label.

Pros:

- Soft and cushioned walking surface

- Good insulator

- Can be refinished

- Hypoallergenic, antimicrobial and eco-friendly

- Easy to install

- Easy to maintain

Cons:

- Can be damaged by heavy furniture/appliances and from dropping heavier items onto the floor

- Easily damaged by pets

- Requires water sealing

- Can fade in sunlight

- Relatively expensive

Bamboo

($2 to $8 per square foot; average: $6/square foot, installed)

As a flooring material, bamboo has many of the same benefits and drawbacks of hardwood flooring.

Pros:

- Renewable material

- Easy maintenance

- Can be refinished

Cons:

- Easily scratched

- Humidity swings can cause cracks

- Toxins present in adhesives

Approximate (Before-tax) Professional Installation Costs for a New 800-Square-Foot Floor

- $6,800: Concrete

- $8,800: Tile

- $6,400: Hardwood

- $7,200: Engineered wood

- $3,200: Laminate

- $3,200: Linoleum

- $5,600: Vinyl

- $6,400: Carpet

- $7,600: Cork

- $4,800: Bamboo

As you can imagine, the rate of return will be based on what appeals to the market and the state of the floor being replaced, as well as the wear and tear the floor takes before the home is listed for sale. The cost and value added will vary, but in general:

- **Average Budget:** $700 to $4,000

- **Average ROI:** 50% to 80%

To determine a more precise solution, here are some factors to consider:

Solution: Update or Replace Old Flooring with Hardwood

54% of homebuyers would pay extra for a home with hardwood floors

In previous generations, homes with carpets were considered better, as they added warmth and conserved energy. But younger generations tend to dislike carpets and consider hardwood floors to be the most desirable.

Most homeowners and potential buyers now agree that hardwood is the best option for living rooms and family rooms. There are many reasons for this: it's easier to clean, it looks good, and as a result, it can significantly boost the resale value of your home. The biggest return will happen if you are replacing another flooring type with hardwood.

The average cost to install hardwood flooring (paying a professional) is between $2,500 and $6,500, with labour making up $3 to $8 per square foot of this total price. Keep in mind that this type of flooring installation requires attention to detail. Also, your cost will vary depending on the type of species and the amount of floor space involved.

Average Budget: $1,500 to $11,000

Average ROI: 90% to 110%

Solution: Mudroom or Entryway Flooring

Want the biggest impact in an outdated entryway or mudroom? Update the floor. Since the entryway is the first part of your home potential buyers will see, consider splurging on high-quality, durable floor tile. Tile is waterproof (if installed correctly), durable and long lasting and can add a splash of sophistication or whimsy (or anything else in between). If tile isn't an option, consider hardwood. Although not as durable, hardwood does have a high impact on perceived value in a home.

Unfortunately, not all homeowners have the option to replace the entryway or mudroom floor. Perhaps the entrance pours into the family or communal area of the home, or budget constraints may be a factor. Either way, if replacing the floor isn't an option, consider adding a colourful rug or runner. This will add a splash of colour, and if it's the right material, it can also help protect the floor underneath while making it easy to clean. The best options are natural fibres, such as cotton. Once dirty, cotton rugs and runners can be thrown in the washer and dryer for a full clean. Be mindful, though, as not all natural fibres are great in wet environments. For instance, jute rugs can take on a funky odour if they get wet and can't dry properly.

Average Budget: $100+ or less

Average ROI: variable

Problem: Low or No Curb Appeal

Believe it or not, your home's curb appeal can make or break a possible sale. Still, not all landscape and outdoor projects are worth the investment. For instance, you should steer clear of improvement projects that appeal to only a small number of buyers. For instance, an in-ground swimming pool might be an attractive feature for some, but many homebuyers see it as a hassle, at best, or possibly a money pit. Instead, focus on updating the exterior rather than adding expensive features.

The projects you choose can also vary dramatically when it comes to a return on your project cost. For instance, adding a deck can give you a 75% return on the project cost, while a patio offers only a 30% to 60% return on your project cost.

Here are six options to increase curb appeal, starting with the cheapest.

Solution: Update the Details

Decorative house numbers have come a long way. There are entire font families dedicated to residential houses and commercial buildings. You should try to match your new house numbers with the finish on your exterior light fixtures and the style of your home.

Also, consider upgrading your mailbox, particularly if it can add a splash of colour or a design element that complements your home's style.

Adding new lights near doors and along walkways enhances your home's beauty and security. If you don't want to deal with complicated and expensive wiring, opt for solar landscaping lights.

Another option is to create a welcoming nook on your front porch. Add a pair of lounge or rocking chairs and a small table. You could also upgrade to a sofa set or an outdoor swing.

Finally, add a splash of complementary or contrasting colour with potted plants, hanging planters and flowers in planter boxes.

Average Budget: $25+

Average ROI: variable

Solution: Class Up Your Garage Door

Swapping out your old, beat-up garage door for a new one will go a long way towards increasing your home's curb appeal, and it's relatively inexpensive. Standard single garage doors cost between $600 and $1,500, installed. Standard double garage doors cost $900 to $2,000, installed. More ornate garage doors or options with windows will increase the price.

If a new garage door isn't in the budget and your current garage door isn't shabby or dented, consider adding classy embellishments. Grab a drill and some decorative garage door hardware designed to look like high-end iron hinges and handles. For as little as $25, you can transform a plain garage door into one with a visual impact.

Average Budget: $800 to $2,000

Average ROI: 85% to 95%

Solution: Update Your Front Door

A $30 gallon of paint will freshen up the entryway and make the house seem more welcoming. Opt for something bold and bright, like a cool turquoise, a stately red or a sunny yellow. Just make sure it looks good against your siding, trim and roof. (Also, splash out on good rollers and paint brushes. Good tools will help you get a professional look that doesn't include streaks, blotches or dried drips.)

A 2018 report by Zillow found that homes with front entry doors that were painted charcoal, smoky or jet black sold for almost $6,300 more than comparable neighbouring homes.

Of course, your front door needs to be in good condition and not too dated to make the paint update work. If it's not, consider replacing the door completely. Steel doors are usually the cheapest. Expect to pay at least $1,000 for the installation of a basic steel door and about $2,000 for a fibreglass or standard wood door. Prices on custom wood doors vary considerably, but expect to pay $5,000+ to install.

Average Budget: $1,500 to $10,000

Average ROI: 54% to 72%

Solution: Update Your Landscaping

The best place to start is at the front door. Prune back overgrown hedges, bushes and trees or, better yet, replace overgrown shrubbery with flowering foundation plants. Just remember to mix plant heights and colours for a more dramatic effect.

Consider replacing grass if it's badly damaged. Budget about $1 to $2 per square foot of sod, delivered.

For a more permanent and high-end look, edge the lawn with mulch and a pretty stone divider before planting a few perennial shrubs, flowers and herbs. Don't panic if you know nothing about plants; there are always a few varieties that need almost no maintenance.

Not sure where to start? Local garden centres often offer free design services, or you can ask the neighbour with a green thumb what works for them.

Making Strategic Home Improvements

Average Budget: $1,000 to $3,500

Average ROI: 50% to 100%

Solution: Update Your Exterior

First impressions are everything, and year after year design pros agree that fresh white or grey exteriors win out when it comes to resale value. If you don't like these options, consider neutral colours such as greige (a grey-beige) or grey-blue. Just be sure to pick a colour that complements surrounding homes in your neighbourhood and is in keeping with the architectural style of your home.

The actual material you choose to update your home's exterior will also have an impact on your budget and ROI. Siding can be a quick, durable way to update your home's curb appeal and, on average, offers a 77% return on the project cost. But it's expensive. To replace all the siding on a 2,000-square-foot home, expect to pay $25,000 to $35,000.

Pro tip: Many fibre cement board manufacturers offer a prefinished board, so painting is unnecessary. Plus, these products come with a 20- or 25-year warranty and require little more than an annual power washing for maintenance.

If replacing the siding isn't an option, consider repainting. Houses painted a creamy or yellow-toned colour typically sell for $3,500 less than homes painted other colours, according to data analyzed by Zillow. This isn't a cheap update—with costs ranging from $1,000 to $6,000 for the average job—but it will certainly add a lot to your home's curb appeal.

Average Budget: $1,000 to $35,000

Average ROI: 51% to 77%

Problem: House Is Just Too Big

5% of homeowners complain that their home is too big

There are two primary reasons why an owner would consider their home too big: either they bought a massive home thinking bigger was better but didn't understand what that meant for heating, cooling and cleaning, or the homeowner is now a divorcee or empty-nester and they've outgrown the needs of a large family home.

Starting in 2026, the first wave of baby boomers will begin to turn 80. With such a large population segment facing health and financial concerns, more and more people will scrutinize their housing needs. Many will consider their homes to be too big, and this will mean downsizing.

Solution: Downsizing

To determine if you'd benefit from selling and finding a smaller home, answer these questions:

1. Do you use only 40% to 50% of your home 80% to 90% of the time?

2. Do you dread spending time in the garden since it's always about maintenance work and chores?

3. Do you spend a large portion of the year living in a vacation home or travelling?

4. Does family typically gather in other homes, not yours?

5. Have you taken all the steps required to reduce energy and heating costs but still find your bills too high?

Whether you can't stand the time and money it takes to manage a large home or you want to right-size your living accommodations, you'll need to go through a process. There are tonnes of resources on the internet that can help.

SUM IT UP

If you want to know whether an entire home upgrade or remodel is worth the cost, do the math. To illustrate, let's assume you buy a home for $550,000 with 10% down.

Over five years, you spend $100,000 on home improvements that include:

- $35,000 upgrading two bathrooms;

- $25,000 on a minor kitchen remodel;

- $10,000 on new paint inside and out;

- $10,000 to update siding;

- $9,500 on new hardwood floors in the family room, dining room and den;

- $6,000 on landscaping;

- $3,000 on purpose-bought clutter-control solutions; and

- $1,500 to build a noise-barrier fence in the front yard.

Homes in your area appreciate by 2.5% each year. This is a very conservative estimate and based on typical annual inflation rates; actual average price appreciation, between 2016 and 2020, was closer to 7.1% per year. At the end of five years, you list your home for sale and get the full asking price.

Here's the math:

YEAR 1: PURCHASE PRICE (MARKET VALUE)	$550,000	YEAR 5: MARKET VALUE	$622,275
Down payment	− $55,000	Add 60% return on reno costs	+ $60,000
Mortgage loan	= $495,000	Year 5: Sale price	= $682,275
Add mortgage default insurance fees	+ $15,345	Mortgage debt remaining	$415,065
Total mortgage loan	= $510,345	Total profit	= $267,210

Based on this very simple illustration, which does not take into consideration home expenses and prepayment options, among other factors, **the return on your $155,000 investment was 72%.**

Not bad.

Now consider this: When a fix-and-flip investor renovates a home, they carefully choose their remodelling projects; they focus only on projects that promise cost-effective value.

Homeowners, on the other hand, often take a less strategic approach to remodels and renovations. Decisions are often made based on a wish list and research is done in an ad hoc, piecemeal fashion. What if homeowners borrowed the investor perspective and used the same research techniques and tools? The result would be a plan that develops a list of smart home updates in the four reno project categories (the basics, curb appeal, value-added and personal preference).

Ideally, you'd complete the tasks in category one and two before moving on to the last two categories; however, this doesn't mean you need to complete all improvement projects in category one before moving on to category two. It just means taking the time to strategically map out a general plan of what you will do, when it will get done and how much it will cost. Do this up-front research work, and like all things home reno, it will save you plenty of aggravation and costs in the long run.

TAKEAWAYS

Your Home Is an Asset, Not an Investment. Although your home certainly has value, that doesn't mean spending on your home is an investment. An investment is a decision to use money to earn more money. If your decision to renovate is predicated on the value it will add to your home, then make sure you can back this assertion up with expert insight and data—and be prepared to be wrong.

Investments Can Lose Value, Too. Just because your home doesn't sit neatly in the asset side of your net worth ledger, it doesn't mean you should ignore its value or the reasons it can lose value. Ongoing maintenance and upgrades are smart tactics for slowing depreciation and even adding more value.

You Can Afford Anything, Not Everything. Taking on large amounts of debt to pay for a home renovation or upgrade is a double loss. Not only do you pay interest on a loan that isn't tax deductible, but the asset you're upgrading continues to depreciate. You can still choose to renovate; it just means you need to plan, consider the tradeoffs and make decisions. You *can* afford to upgrade but only if it fits your financial goals and meets your current needs.

The Real Value Is in Problem Solving. Want to renovate and increase the value of your home? Then focus on the problems and their solutions. P&G didn't invent the mop, but Swiffer now dominates the clean-up aisle. Apple didn't release an iPhone but launched a smarter mobile device. Just like best-in-class consumer products, smart renos solve current and future home-owner problems.

5

SAVING ON HOME EXPENSES

TIPS AND STRATEGIES TO SAVE THOUSANDS THROUGH EFFICIENT UPGRADES, NEW HABITS AND REBATES

In the last decade, citizens and governments have become very proactive in looking for ways to cut down on greenhouse gas emissions. These are various gases that have far-ranging environmental and health effects and that help to cause climate change by trapping heat in the earth's atmosphere. This results in extreme weather, food supply disruptions and increased wildfires, among other effects of climate change.

In residential housing, various laws were created to ban chemicals, such as hydrofluorocarbons (found in refrigerators and air conditioning systems), that contribute to greenhouse gas emissions. Across North America, municipalities and districts updated building codes to further increase environmentally friendly ways of building homes.

The move towards sustainability is great news for people already living in their homes. As the former president of the American Institute of Architects Carl Elefante once stated, "The greenest building is the one that is already built."

By choosing certain materials and features, homeowners can help reduce or minimize our impact on the environment. The benefit is that many of these sustainable house ideas help reduce utility costs, increase day-to-day comfort and end up being attractive to potential buyers.

The key is to consider all the ways to save money—and the environment.

If you're planning on completing extensive renovations that include heating upgrades, new windows and doors or better insulation, the best place to start is with a home energy audit.

CONDUCTING A HOME ENERGY AUDIT

A home energy audit is an assessment done by an independently certified evaluator. It shows how efficiently your home uses energy and, more importantly, where that energy is being wasted.

Although different companies may evaluate using different checks, the main test is a blower-door test. This is where they seal off your home and blow a massive amount of air into it using high-powered fans while measuring where and when this air escapes.

Once the energy audit is complete, you get a report that lists your home's energy deficiencies as well as tangible recommendations for fixing these issues to make your home more energy-efficient.

The audit costs anywhere from $100 to $800, depending on your city, your home and the firm that completes the audit. Pricey, right? Not to worry. Many of the energy audit companies advertise their services along with a rebate of this fee; even if the company you select doesn't offer a rebate on the cost, chances are you could find a rebate on this fee from your local, provincial or even federal government. It pays to do a quick search before you pay for the service, and I give a few places to start a little later in this chapter, under "Energy Efficiency Rebates."

Even if you can't find a rebate for the home energy audit fee, it doesn't mean you should skip out on paying for this service. The audit—along with the completion of the suggestions made in the audit—makes your upgrades eligible for provincial and federal rebates, which can add up to some serious savings.

For example, in Ontario, you can get up to $5,000 back on your home energy audit updates. In BC, homeowners could get up to $7,000 back. Then there are the federal rebates, where homeowners across Canada can get as much as $5,000 for completing efficiency upgrades.

To make the most of the audit, and the savings offered on remodels and upgrades to your home, take these steps:

1. Don't undertake major home renos, especially on an older home, without first considering or paying for a home energy audit.

2. To expedite the home energy audit, gather up the last 12 months of utility bills, as your auditor will want to see these.

3. Review the list of suggestions in the audit and see which ones align with your remodel plans.

4. Once you complete the reno, schedule your final audit test, where the company comes and tests your home again to see how much more energy-efficient it is after the completion of these improvements.

5. Get your final report that shows the improvement in your home's energy efficiency.

6. Now submit receipts and paperwork to various federal, provincial and municipal rebate programs. Although it can take up to a year to get the rebate money, it should still feel pretty good to get money back on renovations you were going to do anyway.

If you live in a historic home—built 100+ years ago—it's wise to call in an old-home energy efficiency expert before completing upgrades based on today's standards. Air sealing in a historic home can dramatically affect how moisture moves through a structure, and this could impact the build-up of condensation and the potential for mould, mildew and even rot.

WANT TO SAVE MORE THAN $6,000 EACH YEAR? LET'S GET SERIOUS ABOUT SAVING

According to a recent Bankrate survey, 18% of homeowners considered "hidden home costs" as their biggest pain point. First-time and young homeowners often make up the bulk of those property owners who end up suffering from home mainte-nance sticker shock. According to a survey released by Clever in July 2020, 43% of young homeowners were surprised by the cost of maintaining their homes.

And as we've now established, maintaining a home *can* be a significant expense. The good news is, there are plenty of ways to cut down on those expenses and help reduce our resource use.

To help, here are 36 tips and habits you can adopt. Implement every suggestion, and you could save nearly $6,800 per year on your heating, cooling, water and hydro expenses. Of course, most homeowners can't or won't be in a position to incorporate all of these suggestions. Still, even a solid effort can make a big differ-ence to your bank account and the environment.

How to Reduce Heating Costs?
12 Tips to Save as Much as $2,569/Year

Tip #1: Avoid Short Cycling

Short cycling is when your HVAC system is shifting too rapidly between heating and cooling modes. This energy-intensive switch-ing can happen for several reasons, but the primary reason is when your thermostat's heating and cooling "set points" are too close together.

To prevent this, separate your heating and cooling set points by at least 3°C.

Average Budget: $0+

Average Savings: 10% per year (roughly $68 to $219 per year)

Tip #2: Rearrange the Furniture

Remove furniture that blocks heat registers to prevent heated air from getting trapped in and around the piece of furniture. If you can't move a piece of furniture, consider adding a register air deflector. At $10, this is a cheap fix to help hot (and cold) air circulate easily through your home.

Average Budget: $0 to $50+

Average Savings: $34 per year

Tip #3: Take Out the Window A/C Unit During Winter

Window A/C units are drafty. If they are left in during the winter months, the drafts will suck the hot air right out of your house. If you can't remove the unit, wrap it in an insulated jacket that blocks warm air from escaping. The jackets are hard to find and they don't create a seal so you'll still have drafts, but it's better than nothing.

Average Budget: $0+

Average Savings: $45 per year (per A/C unit)

Tip #4: Seal Windows and Doors

Sealing up doors and windows is one of the most cost-effective methods for improving your home's energy efficiency and helping reduce heating (and cooling) costs.

Leaks can be found around windows and doors as well as foundation cracks, around light and electric sockets and around holes where plumbing pipes enter and exit your home (such as, second floor to attic).

Start by using caulking rated for windows and doors to seal the gaps where your doors and window trim meet interior and exterior walls.

Replace weatherstripping on all doors. Check your attic and basement for significant gaps (for example, around recessed lighting in the attic) and seal with expanding foam. For larger gaps, you may need to use a cut piece of drywall to fill the hole, before using caulking to seal the gap.

Average Budget: $50

Average Savings: $50+

Tip #5: Add Window Coverings

Direct sunlight is the easiest way to heat your home, and it's free! Just open the curtains or blinds during the day. At night, keep more of your home's heat inside by closing your curtains or blinds.

According to an English Heritage study, closing heavy curtains reduces heat loss by 41%, while honeycomb insulating blinds (also known as cellulose blinds) can reduce heat loss by 51%. In the summer, the opposite is true, with closed blinds or curtains blocking up to 65% of the heat entering your home.

Blackout curtains are the cheapest option and can often be found at larger retailers for $50 for a pair. Blinds are more expensive, with custom blinds running thousands of dollars. For off-the-shelf options, check out IKEA or big-box hardware stores.

When buying curtains, make sure they are heavy, preferably dark (or use a blackout fabric on the back) and big enough to touch the ground and walls next to the window—this setup maximizes heat retention in your home. For blinds, try mounting outside the frame, or if that doesn't suit your style, measure blinds to fit as close as possible to each of the window's four sides of the frame.

Average Budget: $50+

Average Savings: up to 25% per year
(roughly $170 per year)

Tip #6: Regularly Replace the Filters in Your Furnace

An outdated filter not only doesn't filter air as well, but it also hurts airflow, meaning your HVAC system has to work harder—and use more energy—to pump out lower quality air. The US Department of Energy measured the impact of dirty filters and found that replacing them with clean air filters can cut energy consumption by 15%.

Average Budget: $100+

Average Savings: $51 per year

Tip #7: Use Space Heaters

Most portable space heaters use a lot of electricity, so if the room you're trying to heat is large or you have multiple heaters in multiple rooms, this can quickly rack up your electricity bill.

However, using a small space heater in a room you can close off can be a cost-effective way to keep your overall house temperature lower, while giving one spot in the house a bit of extra heat. If you use it for an average of four hours a day, a standard 1,400-watt space heater will cost about $17 a month to operate.

To make the most out of this solution, use your space heater in a small or enclosed space. For maximum warmth, place it in the corner of a room and keep all doors to the room shut (to keep the heat in). Remember to turn it off when you leave.

How much you save using a space heater will depend on how you currently heat your home (if you use electricity, it could save you a bundle) and whether or not you turn your main thermostat down a few degrees.

Average Budget: $68 per season

Average Savings: 5% per year
(roughly $0 to $151 per year)

Tip #8: Install Ceiling Fans

When it comes to consistent climate control, moving air is integral. Turns out (pun intended) that fans are much better at moving air than a central air conditioner or a furnace. For instance, a report from the University of Florida Cooperative Extension found that using a ceiling fan will reduce a room's cooling costs by as much as 8%.

If you're worried about using a lot of power by keeping the ceiling fan on, don't. Ceiling fans use about as much energy as a light bulb. For maximum impact, get a fan that can change directions: blowing downwards and quickly in the summer and upwards slowly in the winter.

Average Budget: $75+

Average Savings: $10 per year (per fan)

Tip #9: Plug Up the Fireplace

Old-fashioned brick-and-mortar fireplaces are one of the most inefficient ways to heat a house. That's because every hour, approximately 20,000 cubic feet of heated air is sucked up the chimney and replaced by cold air. It's a process known as the stack effect—warm air rises, increasing air pressure in the home, and the pressure difference prompts a vacuum effect that sucks cold air from the outside into the home. This is the reason why older homes feel so drafty and can account for up to 30% of heat loss.

To stop this, use glass doors, an inflatable draft-stopper balloon or an insert to plug up your chimney. Balloon draft stoppers are the most cost-effective (less than $100), with glass doors the next best option (the cheapest ones start at $270). An insert will not only stop drafts and provide a sealed compartment for the fire; it will also make your fireplace more efficient.

Want to know how much heat you lose up the fireplace from not closing the damper? Open your bedroom window in the dead of winter. Pretty quickly you'll notice a dramatic heat loss, but you'd need to keep it open for 30 minutes to mimic the amount of heat lost up your chimney!

Average Budget: $100+

Average Savings: $180 per year

Tip #10: Use Your Programmable Thermostat

A programmable thermostat enhances heating and cooling efficiency by enabling homeowners to set their climate control systems for the optimal temperature at a minimal cost.

For homeowners with forced air furnaces, installing a smart thermostat is easy. You can buy a variety of brands at just about any hardware store. For those heating their homes with baseboard heaters or radiant in-floor heating, it's not quite as easy but not impossible. For instance, MYSA is a Canadian company that offers an aftermarket smart thermostat for either radiant in-floor heating or electric baseboards. The cost is comparable to forced air programmable thermostats and the installation just as easy.

Electric baseboard heating can account for as much as 50% of your home's overall electricity use, and winter heating bills can be 66% higher than the rest of the year!

Once installed, it's time to maximize the savings. By programming your thermostat to stay at ideal temperatures, you can save anywhere from 20% to 30% on your heating and cooling bills. For those using electric heating, lower your thermostat by 2°C to save 5% or by 5°C to save 10% on your home heating bills.

In the winter or cooler months, program or adjust your thermostat to the following temperatures at the following times:

- 6am to 9am = 68°F/20°C

- 9am to 5:30pm = 60°F/15.6°C

- 5:30pm to 11pm = 68°F/20°C

- 11pm to 6am = 60°F/15.6°C

In the summer or hotter months, program or adjust your thermostat to the following temperatures at the following times:

- 6am to 9am = 75°F/23.9°C

- 9am to 5:30pm = 80°F/26.7°C

- 5:30pm to 11pm = 75°F/23.9°C

- 11pm to 6am = 80°F/26.7°C

If you rely on electric baseboard heaters or your heating and cooling system doesn't allow for pre-programming, then follow these guidelines for lowering your energy bills in the winter months:

Lower your thermostat 2°C to save 5%

Lower your thermostat by 5°C to save 10%

Average Budget: $0 to $200+

Average Savings: 5% to 30% per year (roughly $68 to $219 per year)

Tip #11: Seal and Insulate Ducts

Many duct systems are not insulated properly or have gaps or holes where air can leak out. If your ducts are crooked or not properly connected, you could lose as much as 60% of your heated or cooled air before it reaches a room vent.

A professional back-draft test can help you determine how your home's duct leaks are affecting your home's heat efficiency. However, the test isn't necessary if you know your ductwork is older or incorrectly installed.

Duct sealing technology works by spraying microscopic particles of sealant that form airtight bonds to plug leaks and holes. This solution can save you an average of $250 on your annual heating bill, but the sticker price for the service starts at $2,000.

Another option is to insulate any ductwork that runs through unheated spaces such as an attic or crawlspace. Skip this, and you could be losing as much as 40% of your heated (or cooled) air.

Specialized aluminium HVAC tape, known as UL-181, is tradi-
tionally used to seal leaky ducts, but these standard methods
of duct sealing are virtually impossible in most finished homes
today unless you rip down your walls and ceilings.

Average Budget: $2,000+

Average Savings: $240 per year

Tip #12: Replace HVAC Systems

One big reason for inconsistent temperature is an outdated or
undersized HVAC system. HVAC is short for heating, ventilation
and air conditioning, and as a system, all of these components
work together to keep the climate in your home comfortable and
dry. This system also accounts for a considerable portion of the
average home's energy consumption—on average, 42% of your
home's energy bill.

If your big complaint is drafty rooms in the winter or boiler-like
conditions in the summer, upgrading your furnace and A/C unit
will go a long way towards solving this issue and save you between
20% and 50% on your monthly energy bills.

But this solution isn't cheap. The cost to upgrade your HVAC
equipment—your furnace, heat recovery unit, central A/C and
dehumidifier—varies widely, ranging from several thousand
dollars to tens of thousands of dollars. You may also need to
upgrade your ductwork, which is an added expense.

Costs go up substantially if you're swapping out one type of heat source for another.

But it pays to explore options. For example, upgrading your electric baseboard heaters to a forced air furnace may be too costly, but opting for a ductless heat pump that offers 200% to 300% heat efficiency is a good alternative. Not only is the installation easier, but it could allow you to drop your heating bill from $2,400 per year down to $1,200.

If your A/C unit is at least 10 years old, consider upgrading. Replacing an older unit is likely to yield major savings.

Remember to research local rebates and financing programs offered by all three levels of government and look for ENERGY STAR-rated appliances, marked by the ENERGY STAR® symbol, which is an internationally recognized and trusted mark of high efficiency.

If you are planning an HVAC update, consider paying for an energy audit first. Quite often the difference in energy efficiency as determined by your pre- and post-update audit can make you eligible for additional rebates.

Average Budget: $1,000+

Average Savings: 25% to 101% per year
(roughly $1,200 per year)

How to Reduce Your Water Bill?
6 Tips to Save as Much as $313/Year

Tip #1: Improve the Water Efficiency of Your Toilet

Put an inch or two of sand or pebbles in the bottom of a one-litre bottle and fill the rest of the bottle with water. Put this bottle in the toilet tank, safely away from the operating mechanism. The weighted bottle will sink to the bottom and help reduce the amount of water used with each flush. On average, a weighted bottle can save 19 litres (5 gallons) or more of water *every day* without harming the efficiency of the toilet. If your tank is big enough, you may be able to add two bottles!

An extra step: stop using your toilet as a de facto trash bin! Every cigarette butt or extra tissue you flush away also flushes away 19 to 27 litres (5 to 7 gallons) of water. Use a trash can instead.

Average Budget: $0

Average Savings: $62 to $88 per year (per toilet)

Tip #2: Install Water-Saving Devices

Did you know that more than one-third (35%) of the water usage in your house is due to showering and bathing? Install a low-flow showerhead and you'll only use a maximum of 9.5 litres per minute—about 40 cups of water—compared to the standard showerhead, which releases 12.5 litres per minute, or 53 cups of water. If you take a 15-minute shower with a low-flow showerhead, you could save 190 cups of water, about 12 gallons.

Consider adding faucet aerators to all bathroom and kitchen faucets. These small, round devices screw onto the tip of your faucet to create a more consistent, splash-free stream of water without compromising the water pressure. Prices start at just a few dollars each.

Average Budget: $25+

Average Savings: $39 per year (per showerhead)

Tip #3: Repair or Replace Leaky Toilets and Faucets

Not all leaks are noticeable. For instance, a toilet that continues to run after flushing wastes up to 200,000 litres per year, the equivalent of 1,400 baths. That's like flushing $580 down your toilet each year! Unfortunately, a running toilet isn't a very noticeable leak. To find out if you have a problem, place a few drops of food colouring (or a dye test tablet, but food colouring works just fine) into your toilet tank. Don't flush. After 10 or 15 minutes, check your toilet bowl. If the colour of the water in the bowl has changed, your toilet leaks. You can attempt this fix yourself (there's lots of help online) or spend a few hundred dollars on a plumber.

If you're tackling a leaky faucet, first consider changing the faucet (or fixtures) washer (the rubber or plastic ring that helps create a seal). Again, there's plenty of help online or call a plumber. Just don't ignore it. For every drop of water that leaks from a faucet, you pay approximately $30 extra on your water bill each year. Fixing the leak might not save you a bundle, but it can help reduce the corrosive impact a leak can have on pipes and sink fixtures— and helps save this valuable resource.

Average Budget: $5+

Average Savings: $30 per year/$580 one time

Tip #4: Use Soaker Hoses and Timers in the Garden

If you do have a garden, water your outdoor plants early in the morning or at the end of the day so the water doesn't immediately evaporate in the sunlight. To make this automatic, purchase a water timer—it screws to your outside faucet and lets you set a schedule for when you want to water your plants and for how long. Double up on savings and use a soaker hose at the base of trees, shrubs and plants, and you could dramatically cut your garden's water needs by as much as 35% to 60%.

Another great option is to install and use a rain barrel. These barrels usually come with a spigot at the bottom that allows you to attach a hose and use rainwater to hydrate your garden plants.

Average Budget: $100+

Average Savings: $33 per year

Tip #5: Install a Dual Flush Toilet

Toilets account for 30% of a home's overall water usage. Upgrade to a dual flush toilet, and you could save 20% to 60% on your water consumption each year. Prices start at $200, not including installation, but can climb significantly.

Average Budget: $200+

Average Savings: $200 per year

Tip #6: Cover Up Your Pool

Invest in a pool cover. Not only does it help retain a heated pool's temperature, but it reduces evaporation. The US Department of Energy reports that a pool cover cuts the amount of replacement water needed by 30% to 50%.

Average Budget: $1,475+

Average Savings: $24 to $80 per year

3 HABITS TO ADOPT
TO REDUCE WATER USE

Want to reduce your water use, help save this valuable resource and save money? Consider adopting these three habits and save up to $810 per year.

1: TURN THE TAP OFF WHEN SHAVING, WASHING HANDS AND BRUSHING TEETH

By turning off your tap every time you shave, while you soap and lather your hands, and when you brush your teeth, you can significantly reduce your home's water usage.

- Estimated Cost: $0

- Average Savings: $20 to $30 per year

2: REPURPOSE WATER

One easy solution to reduce water usage is to reuse grey water. Grey water is the relatively clean wastewater that collects in baths, sinks, washing machines and kitchen appliances. To start, place a bowl in your sink. Once you've finished washing and rinsing your fruits and veggies, you can then use this grey water to water indoor plants or your garden. You can do the same with the water that drains down the sink as you wait for the water to heat up. Rather than lose it, use it.

- Estimated Cost: $0

- Average Savings: $20 to $30 per year

3: CHANGE YOUR DIET

It takes a lot of water to grow, process and transport our daily food desires. Much of that water goes to raising animals for meat and dairy products or growing the food to feed these animals.

To reduce your water footprint, you can reduce your meat and dairy consumption, switch to shopping local and grow food in your garden. If more people do these things, they will not only lead to a reduction in total water usage but also less food waste.

Another option, if you don't want to eliminate meat and dairy from your diet, is to get educated about the water footprint of foods. Choosing foods with a smaller water footprint helps to reduce your overall global water consumption (and it could save you a few bucks as well).

Global Average Water Footprint

Global water usage is driven by agricultural and industrial needs. Making decisions to avoid or reduce our consumption of food with high water demands can significantly reduce the overall global average water footprint.[19]

To help illustrate, here is a list of food items and how many litres of water it takes to produce these items:

- 300 g of Beef Steak — 4,500 litres of water

- 500 g of Cheese — 2,500 litres of water

- 1 x 500 g package of Rice — 1,700 litres of water

- 300 g of Pork Steak — 1,440 litres of water

- Large Pizza — 1,259 litres of water

- 300 g of Goat Steak — 1,200 litres of water

- 1 Chicken Breast — 1,170 litres of water

- 1 litre of Milk — 1,000 litres of water

- 1 lb of Soybeans — 900 litres of water

- 1 Pot of Coffee (750 ml) — 840 litres of water

---

19 Waterfootprint.org, https://waterfootprint.org/en/water-footprint/what-is-water-footprint.

- 1 lb of Wheat — 500 litres of water

- Corn on the cob — 450 litres of water

- 1 Bottle of Beer (500 ml) — 150 litres of water

- 1 Bottle of Wine (750 ml) — 720 litres of water

- 1 Apple (100 g) — 70 litres of water

- **Estimated Cost: $0**

- **Average Savings: $750+ per year**

How to Reduce Your Electricity Bill?
9 Tips to Save as Much as $2,574/Year

Tip #1: Swap Out Your Outdoor Lights for Energy-Efficient Bulbs

By switching to energy-efficient bulbs, such as compact fluorescent lamp (CFL) floodlights, metal halide or high-pressure sodium lights, you can reduce the energy you use for outdoor lighting. For example, high-pressure sodium lamps use 70% less energy than a standard incandescent floodlight and last up to 10 times as long.

Switch two 100-watt incandescent lights—operating at three hours a day—to two 25-watt CFLs to save $16 a year.

Average Budget: $10+

Average Savings: $15+ per year

Tip #2: Upgrade Those Holiday Lights to LEDs

Decorating your home with LED lights could reduce holiday lighting electricity use by as much as 90%. Assuming you keep your holiday lights aglow for six hours a day through the entire month of December, you could save almost $30 by replacing the incandescent strands with LEDs (and you don't have to waste your time checking every bulb on the strand to find the bad bulb!).

Average Budget: $30+

Average Savings: $27 per year

Tip #3: Insulate Plumbing Pipes

Exposed, uninsulated pipes located in unheated spaces, such as basements, attics or crawl spaces, lose heat as water travels from your heater to your plumbing fixture. Wrapping these pipes in foam or rubber insulation can make a two- to four-degree difference in the temperature of the water and allows hot water to reach your faucet faster. Insulation with an R-value of three or more will also help protect these pipes during cold snaps, and even better, if you can insulate virtually all your home's hot water pipes, you can drop your hot water tank's temperature by five degrees. Expect to pay about $1 per linear foot for pipe insulation and shave 3% to 4% off your hot water heating bill each year.

Average Budget: $10+

Average Savings: $20 to $30 per year

Tip #4: Maintain Your Fridge or Freezer

Your refrigerator and freezer are the two appliances in your home that use the most electricity. To cut down on their energy consumption, it's important to clean and maintain these appliances.

Start by moving your fridge out from the wall to clean off any dust or debris from the back where the motor is located. When putting it back, make sure there is a gap of at least three inches between the back of the fridge and the wall to allow for air circulation.

Then buy a cheap fridge thermometer to keep track of the appliance's internal temperature. Set at their optimal temperatures—between 2°C and 3°C for a fridge and –18°C for a freezer—can shave $25 off your annual electricity bill.

Every year, check door seals. A cracked, crumbling or damaged seal can let cold air escape and force the motor to work twice as hard.

If your fridge is more than 10 years old, consider budgeting for an ENERGY STAR upgrade. This upgrade alone could shave $40 off your electricity bill each year. Unplug and remove an old, second fridge or freezer and save another $85 per year.

If you need to buy a freezer, consider a chest (top-loading) model, as these are 25% more efficient than upright freezers.

Average Budget: $0 to $5

Average Savings: up to $150 per year

Tip #5: Simple Laundry Tips

Heating water accounts for 90% of the energy consumption of washing machines. An ENERGY STAR front-loading machine can cut water use by nearly 40% and electricity use by as much as 65% when compared to a conventional top loader.

To save on laundry costs, run the washer and dryer only when you have a full load. Do this and save up to $20 per year on hydro costs. Switch to cold-water washes—say three out of every four loads—and save another $20 or more on your annual hydro bill.

If possible, hang dry your clothes rather than use the dryer. If you hung four out of eight laundry loads each week, you would save as much as $65 per year on your hydro bill.

If you must use your electric dryer, be sure to toss a clean, dry towel in with the wet load, as this will significantly reduce drying time. If you're doing seven loads a week, this simple trick could save you $27 a year.

Average Budget: $0

Average Savings: $132 per year

Tip #6: Use Timers and Smart Plugs

Consumer electronics account for 15% to 20% of total residential electricity use in North America. Much of this energy is consumed when these devices operate in low-power modes—the standby mode of all electronics that are not in current use. However, this phantom power use can be reduced with the use of smart plugs.

A study conducted by Ecos, a US-based manufacturer of affordable green products, shows that a smart plug strip used on a home entertainment system could save you about $27 per year. Combine it with a timer, and you could save $61 per year. It doesn't sound like a lot, but when you start adding up all the electronics in your home, it's quite possible to save $100 or more each year on phantom electricity costs.

WHAT DOES AN EXTENSION CORD, SURGE PROTECTOR OR POWER CORD DO?

Adding an extension cord—smart or otherwise—allows you to plug multiple items into an electrical outlet. Surge protectors offer the added feature of protecting your electronic devices from power surges, which happen when electrical storms hit your area or other power grid problems cause spikes and surges in the electricity going into your home. Surge protectors help to protect electronic devices from the impact of surges, while smart or energy efficient power cords can help reduce electricity use, which saves you money.

WHEN TO USE DIFFERENT TYPES OF EXTENSION CORDS, POWER STRIPS, SMART PLUGS AND TIMERS

Not all extension cords and smart plugs are created equal. To maximize the advantage offered by these tools, choose the right type of power strip or extension cord required for your needs. Here's a rundown of each type and their optimal use.

POWER OR CURRENT-SENSING SMART PLUGS

Also known as "load-sensing plugs," they detect a drop in the current that occurs when a control or main device enters a low power mode. These strips work well where there is a central device (a TV or computer) and several peripherals (printer, DVD player, speakers, etc.). The peripherals are disconnected when the central device is off.

When to use:

Best for electronic devices that work in dependency relationships. For example, plug a TV, game console and any other streaming device into a load-sensing plug.

How it works:

These smart plugs detect a drop in the current when the control or main device is switched off. This triggers the smart plug to cut power to the peripheral devices. This eliminates the use and cost of phantom electricity by cutting power to a group of devices all at once.

OCCUPANCY SENSOR SMART PLUGS

Occupancy sensor smart plug strips work well in office cubicles because they can detect the presence or absence of the office worker and turn devices on and off accordingly.

When to use:

In rooms and spaces that are used less often, such as a guest room.

How it works:

These smart plugs will detect the presence or absence of a person and turn devices on and off accordingly.

TIMER SMART PLUGS

Smart plug strips can also turn equipment on and off based on a programmable timer. A timer smart plug strip is great for devices that never need to operate during certain hours.

When to use:

Use with devices that need to operate only during specific hours.

How it works:

You set the timer and based on your schedule, the plug will cut or let power flow to the electronic device. For example, timers are often used for holiday lights.

REMOTE-CONTROLLED SMART PLUG STRIPS

The advantage of the remote-control smart plug strip is that you can control exactly when devices receive power without reaching below desks or around furniture. They are also great for seasonal electricity devices, such as Christmas lights or holiday decorations.

When to use:

Use for devices that are hard or awkward to turn on and off or when you want control over an electronic device without being near it.

How it works:

The remote control triggers the plug to cut or give power to the plugged-in device.

BLUETOOTH OR WI-FI ENABLED

Very similar in application to the remote-control plugs, but rather than rely on a separate control and infrared technology, these plugs let you use a smart device, such as your phone to control the plug and the electrical device plugged into the smart plug. Keep in mind, these only work if your Wi-Fi or Bluetooth connection is reliable.

When to use:

Use for devices or areas where you want to control electronic devices and require this control whether you are present in the room or not.

How it works:

Works by sending a signal to the plug, via Bluetooth or Wi-Fi, to cut or give power to the plugged-in device. Some even operate using a timer feature.

TIPS FOR USING SMART PLUGS AND EXTENSION CORDS

Not all items or devices need to be protected by a surge protector. In general, only use surge protectors on devices with a microprocessor, such as computers, TVs, audio equipment and mobiles.

Wireless handheld devices, such as tablets and phones, charge at lower voltages and this makes surge protection even more important. If possible, set up a charging station for these devices that only uses a surge protector. Also, be mindful of maximum loads. Don't exceed the electrical rating of surge protectors or any smart plug as this will dramatically reduce the plug's life expectancy and could leave your devices vulnerable.

Over time and with every voltage fluctuation, your surge protectors will wear down. You will need to budget for replacements. To make sure you are getting the most protection, replace surge protectors every two to four years.

Average Budget: $0 to $100

Average Savings: $100+ per year

Tip #7: Turn Your Hot Water Tank Thermostat Down and Add a Blanket

Water heating is the third largest energy expense in your home, typically accounting for about 12% of your utility bill. Although most modern water heaters are insulated, some are insulated better than others, and many older heaters aren't insulated at all. A small investment in a blanket for your water heater—starting at $30—will help you save 7% to 16% on your hot water heating bill.

You can buy specialty blankets online, through HVAC suppliers or at big-box hardware stores. You can also use an insulated blanket; just don't cover the water heater's top, bottom, thermostat or burner compartment.[20]

You can also turn your tank's thermostat down a few degrees. According to the Environmental Protection Agency, a water heater set at 60°C (140°F) or higher wastes between $430 and $460 per year. Set the thermostat to 49°C (120°F), and you not only save money but also reduce the corrosive mineral build-up in your water tank and pipes (a build-up that significantly reduces the lifespan of the tank).

If you have an electric water heater and use hot water for only short periods during the day, consider installing a timer to turn the water heater on during high-use periods and off during low-use periods. Most timers allow for multiple on/off periods during the day and include a manual override switch to allow water heating at any time.

---

20 "Savings Project: Insulate Your Water Heater Tank," Energy.gov, accessed June 22, 2021, https://www.energy.gov/energysaver/services/do-it-yourself-energy-savings-projects/savings-project-insulate-your-water.

Average Budget: $30+

Average Savings: $84 to $570 per year

Tip #8: Focus on Your Light Bulbs

Using incandescent light bulbs? Stop it. Assuming a five-year timeline, incandescent bulbs will cost $300, CFL bulbs will cost $70, and LED bulbs will cost about $50. You won't see the savings up front, but you will notice when it comes time to change the bulbs. LED costs the most but lasts 15 times longer than incandescent, while CFL lasts five times longer.

To reduce hydro costs associated with lighting, clean dirt and debris from all bulbs (a clean bulb maximizes light output).

Use natural light as much as possible. Opt for natural light rather than a 60-watt bulb for four hours per day and save about $9 per year.

Another option is to use task lighting. By turning off ceiling lights and using table lamps, track lighting and under-counter lights in work and hobby areas, as well as in kitchens, you can save approximately $6 per year.

Finally, don't forget what your parents told you: turn off the lights! Switching off two 100-watt bulbs for an extra two hours per day can save you $15 per year. If you've already switched to CFLs or LEDs you can still save about $8 to $10 per year.

Average Budget: $0 to $100

Average Savings: $95 to $710 per year

Tip #9: Update Your Electric Appliances

If your appliances are getting old, it might be time for an upgrade. When shopping, be sure to choose energy-efficient appliances. You'll save $85 per year by switching to an ENERGY STAR-rated fridge; choose an ENERGY STAR dishwasher and save $50 per year; upgrade to an ENERGY STAR washer and save $650 per year. Over 10 years, you could save $7,850!

Average Budget: $600+

Average Savings: $50 to $800 per year

6 SMART HABITS TO REDUCE HYDRO
SAVE AS MUCH AS $514/YEAR

1. USE A MICROWAVE, SLOW COOKER OR TOASTER OVEN INSTEAD

Use the microwave, slow cooker or toaster oven rather than your electric stove, and you could shave a few more bucks off your annual hydro bill, as well as a few hours off your meal planning and prep work!

It takes a microwave only 15 minutes to do what it takes an electric oven an hour to do. Use the microwave or other smaller appliance four times a week, instead of the oven, and you'll save time and money.

Costs for a slow cooker start at $25 and go up, while microwaves can start at $70 and go up.

- **Average Budget:** $0 to $70+

- **Average Savings:** $13 per year

2. DITCH THE DESKTOP

Time spent on screens increased significantly as global initiatives required us to stay, work and play at home. As a result, more of us were on desktops and laptops. Although not huge energy hogs, these electronic devices still consume juice, and we can certainly save money with some smart adjustments.

For instance, a desktop computer uses about 60 to 200 watts of power or the equivalent of 0.06 to 2 kWh. If left on all day, every day for an entire year (and left on full power), that computer would cost you roughly $385 per year to run (assumes you pay about $0.20 per kWh for electricity).

An easy way to cut those costs is to turn your computer off— at least for a portion of each 24 hours.

Another option is to switch to an ENERGY STAR desktop computer or, even better, an energy-efficient laptop. Desktops labelled with the ENERGY STAR symbol use 30% to 60% less energy than conventional models. Laptops use even less energy, although monitor size can impact those savings, with a 17-inch monitor using 30% more energy than a 15-inch monitor.

- Average Budget: $500+

- Average Savings: $10 to $190+ per year

3. TURN OFF THE WINDOW A/C

Not home? Turn off your window air conditioner. Leaving a window A/C off for five hours per day for 60 days can help you save a few bucks off your hydro bill.

- **Average Budget:** $0

- **Average Savings:** $20 per year

4. AIR-DRY YOUR DISHES

You can save about 15% of your dishwasher's electricity use by selecting the air-dry cycle or opening the dishwasher door instead of using the heat drying cycle.

Also, consider replacing your older model dishwasher with a newer, more efficient one that could save you up to $40 a year. When searching for an eco-friendly dishwasher, be on the lookout for an ENERGY STAR-certified model. These use 12% less energy and 30% less water than a standard model. Some provinces even offer a rebate for ENERGY STAR products.

- **Average Budget:** $450+

- **Average Savings:** $27 to $40 per year

5. UPGRADE OLDER MODEL TVS AND GAME CONSOLES

To save money, pick a TV that fits your space. Generally speaking, you can calculate the right size TV for your room with a simple calculation:

> Distance between the screen front and the couch ÷ 2.5 = Perfect TV size.

For example, if you sit approximately 8.75 feet (105 inches) from your TV, choose a 42-inch HDTV. Also, consider choosing ENERGY STAR-rated televisions, which use at least 30% less electricity than non-ENERGY STAR TVs.

If you are shopping for a new TV and want to maximize both your spending budget and your energy savings, consider swapping out for a more efficient TV model. Swap out an older model 50" plasma TV for a 52" LCD, and you could save $35 or more per year; upgrade to a 60" OLED, and you can save $50 or more per year (assuming an average of six hours per day of TV at $0.20 per kWh).

Also, consider how and when to use gaming consoles, particularly newer models such as PlayStation5 and Xbox Series X or S. The newer gaming consoles require more electricity because of their increased capabilities. Many of these devices also use significant amounts of "standby" electricity while supposedly in "off" mode. Using a gaming console as a media streaming device to watch TV will require 35% to 40% more electricity than other media streaming devices.

- **Average Budget:** $300+

- **Average Savings:** $35+ per year

6. UNPLUG UNUSED DEVICES

According to Alan Meier, a senior scientist at the Department of Energy's Berkeley Lab, approximately 50 devices and appliances in a typical North American home are continually drawing power—even when they appear to be off.

This consumption adds up. About 15% to 25% of our hydro consumption is used by these devices sitting in idle power mode, according to a study of Northern California by the Natural Resources Defense Council. The easiest way to stop phantom hydro use, and to save money, is to unplug these devices. (Another option is to use smart plugs.)

- **Average Budget:** $0

- **Average Savings:** $50 to $216 per year

ENERGY EFFICIENCY REBATES

When on a quest to save money, always look for rebates, which are cash-back incentives. You can find rebates issued through federal, provincial and municipal governments as well as through specific companies. Most government rebates are long-standing—meaning they have been in place for a long time and will probably continue for a long time. That doesn't mean you should bank on a rebate. Always check the fine print, deadlines and requirements for qualification of all rebates.

Nationally, the three most common rebates are:

#1: New Housing GST/HST Rebate

You may be entitled to a rebate on the federal portion of HST (and GST) if you purchase or construct a new home or substantially renovate a home.[21]

There are a few requirements, such as the home must be intended for use as your primary residence and it must have a market value of no more than $450,000.

#2: CMHC Green Home Refund

Get a premium refund when you buy, build or renovate your home for energy efficiency using the Canada Mortgage and Housing Corporation (CMHC)-insured financing. This financial incentive applies to single-family homes as well as townhouses and condos.[22] Two types of refunds are available:

- Receive a 15% premium refund for a home built to ENERGY STAR building standards

---

21 https://betterhomesbc.ca/rebates/federal-provincial-gst-hst-new-housing-rebate.

22 https://www.cmhc-schl.gc.ca/en/professionals/project-funding-and-mortgage-financing/mortgage-loan-insurance/mortgage-loan-insurance-homeownership-programs/energy-efficient-housing-made-more-affordable-with-mortgage-loan-insurance.

- Receive a 25% premium refund for a home built to R-2000 building standards

#3: Rebates Offered through Home Energy Audit

This is not one rebate but a host of potential rebates. The money is offered as an incentive to help homeowners make more energy- and resource-conscious decisions. For more, check out the home energy audit information in Chapter 5, "Conducting a Home Energy Audit."

For a list of all possible federal and provincial rebates, please see the Natural Resources Canada site[23] or go online to www.zolo. ca/house-poor-no-more for the Rebate Roundup. Keep in mind that the rebates on this comprehensive list are not limited to resale home renovation improvements but also include rebates to builders, business incentives, options for commercial projects and renewable resource upgrades, among other options.

SUM IT UP

Owning a home is one of the most substantial expenses in the lives of most people. Real estate is expensive not only to purchase but also to maintain. Standard costs, such as mortgage payments, utility bills and property taxes, eat into the budget. Add to these costs ordinary home maintenance, such as landscaping, repairing leaky faucets, repainting, and replacing carpeting or flooring, and the cost of homeownership starts to add up over time. Then there's the added cost of more extensive renovations or repairs.

---

23 https://oee.nrcan.gc.ca/corporate/statistics/neud/dpa/policy_e/programs.cfm (choose "Financial Incentives" under "Type of program").

It's not surprising that homeownership often comprises the bulk of a family's monthly budget. As a result, many homeowners look for opportunities to find some home savings.

Taking advantage of the rebates and savings is a great way for homeowners to help offset the costs of maintaining your home. Plus, these incentives typically involve renovations or upgrades that lead to greater future savings by helping reduce monthly expenses by cutting down on energy consumption and the resulting utility costs.

TAKEAWAYS

Start Small for Big Impact. As author James Clear illustrated in his book *Atomic Habits,* small habits build up to big impacts. Trying to make wholesale changes can be overwhelming. Instead, start with one change, like unplugging unused electronics. Once that's a habit, move on to the next change. Taking small steps to reduce our energy consumption may feel like baby steps, but over time, energy goes down and savings add up.

A Dollar Saved Is a Dollar Earned. Start Saving. You don't have to join the climate change debate (is there still a debate?) to hop on the energy savings train. Use your own personal finances to motivate you. Implementing even a quarter of the suggestions outlined in this book would save you over $1,700 per year. Invest those savings for 10 years, at a modest 4% return, and you'll have almost $23,000!

6

FOCUSING ON MORTGAGE AND DEBT MANAGEMENT

SMART STRATEGIES TO HELP YOU TACKLE THE DEBT SIDE OF HOMEOWNERSHIP

What is debt? In the simplest terms, debt is an obligation. This obligation means one party owes another party, and when it comes to a mortgage, it means the home buyer owes the bank the money they borrowed to buy the home.

Simple, right? Except debt can get complicated. Fast.

Most of us have been taught that debt is bad—that it's an obligation to pay back the money and completing this obligation as fast as possible is best. In many situations, this simple assertion is true but not in all situations.

For example, most North Americans who attend college or university will end up borrowing money to pay for tuition. Most will also borrow money to purchase their first (or fifth) car. Are both these debts equal and are both these debts bad? In the simplest terms, yes.

In any situation where you borrow money, you are obliged to pay it back. However, in Canada, the interest owed on borrowed money that is used to invest is considered a tax-deductible cost. So what counts as "investing" borrowed money?

Turns out, money borrowed through federal or provincial student loans (not private bank loans) that is used to pay for post-secondary schooling is considered an investment, since the government believes this is a way for each individual to further their education and earn more money. That means the interest owed on these student loans is a tax write-off. On the flip side, the money borrowed to purchase a car is not a tax write-off.

Although you may feel like a car is a necessary expense, it is not an investment but a "depreciating asset"—meaning it's an asset that loses value the longer it's in use and the older it gets. As a result, the interest on money borrowed to purchase a car is not a tax write-off.

Why do I bother mentioning all of this? Because not all debt is created equal. To borrow the words of a former colleague, Robert Brown (author of *Wealthing Like Rabbits*), "there is bad debt and good debt, and good bad debt and bad good debt."

Does your brain hurt yet? It should. But it's not super-complicated. Here's why.

Although many financial advisors will define debt using four common buckets—secured, unsecured, revolving and non-revolving—a more advantageous way of defining debt is in terms of how helpful it is to you. That's where Brown's "good" and "bad" definitions of debt fall into place.

Bad debt is money borrowed to purchase a consumable or depreciating asset. Most credit card purchases, as well as car or personal loans, will fall into the bad debt category.

Good debt is money borrowed to purchase an asset that will theoretically appreciate. The advantage is that this borrowed money is used to acquire an asset that will increase your net worth. For instance, a mortgage is used to purchase property, which is assumed to grow in value over time. Money borrowed to invest in stocks or bonds, as well as money borrowed to pay for an education, is considered "good debt" for the same reason.

Good bad debt is money borrowed to pay for a depreciating asset that helps you grow your earnings (and, theoretically, your net worth). For instance, if you take out a two-year loan to help pay for a used car, strictly speaking, this borrowed money is bad debt. It's not a tax write-off (unless that car is used for business purposes, but we'll assume it's not for now), and the car won't add to your overall net worth since it loses value with each day it ages and is in use. However, this used car will probably have value once the debt is repaid in two years. If you use it as a way to commute to work, the car also helps you earn money, which is another way of increasing your net worth. Although it's always better to pay for these types of expenses out of pocket, truth be told, most of us end up relying on good bad debt to smooth out expenses over the years.

Bad good debt is money borrowed to purchase an asset that will grow in value and, theoretically, increase your wealth but in terms that prevent this theory from becoming reality. An example is a homebuyer who stretches their house purchasing budget and takes on a mortgage that is too large. Usually, they make this happen by increasing the amortization—that is, the length of time the mortgage debt will be owed—to reduce monthly payments to a manageable amount. It's unlikely the property's value will increase enough to cover the interest costs, and more than likely, the mortgage debt will impede the property owner's ability to save for retirement and continue to grow their net worth. This is bad good debt.

WHAT IS DEBT? DEFINING TYPES OF DEBT

The reason why it's important to understand good and bad debt is that it is almost impossible to live without debt in today's world. Given the eventuality that you will probably become a "debtor" (i.e., someone who borrows and owes a debt), it's important to understand how to classify each type of debt decision and how that decision plays a role in wealth creation.

The key takeaway here is that debt isn't a binary decision or a limited choice between two opposing alternatives. To help you use debt—and, in particular, the debt you owe on your home—to build your net worth, you first need to consider a few important principles when it comes to debt management.

Lesson #1: Debt Is Different for Everyone in Every Situation

The reality is, we all want short, quick answers to complex problems. Should I buy this house, that stock, this car, that bottle of wine, or should I keep my money?

Debt is not the same for everyone, and your circumstance can dictate whether a debt is good or bad. So the first lesson about debt is that you **must** assess according to your own needs, plans and goals. There is no way around this homework.

Lesson #2: Debt Is a Tool, Not a Way of Life

Listen, I didn't get to where I am now—in a light-drenched home office (complete with bookcase and coffee maker) that's a mere five-minute walk to the ocean, my kids' school and old-growth pine trees—without taking on a bit of debt and, at times, a lot of debt.

However, there's a big difference between me accepting debt as a tool to help me achieve some of life's goals and me accepting debt as a way of life. It's also why my husband and I were unwilling to buy a home above a specific price point when we first moved to North Vancouver in 2017. Sure, we qualified for more. Sure, we could've splashed out and bought a larger home that included a rental suite.

Larger, bigger and more debt wasn't part of our overall financial plan. We wanted a manageable mortgage (you know, in case something crazy might happen...like a pandemic), we didn't want the added responsibility of being a landlord, nor did we want the stress of carrying a debt that would deny us current or future choices.

We reminded each other that even "good debt"—like buying a house that fits our lifestyle and budget using a properly structured mortgage—is still debt. Every dollar spent on non-tax-deductible interest is a dollar that could be spent on something else.

To use debt effectively as a tool, we need to account for the cost of that debt and really understand the current and future gains and losses.

Lesson #3: Only Take On Debt if It's Part of the Plan

A crucial step in any financial plan is to pay down "toxic" high-interest debt, such as credit card balances, payday loans, title loans and rent-to-own payments. Interest rates on some of these may be so high that you end up repaying two or three times what you borrowed. Truth be told, such debt can derail both future *and* current plans.

This doesn't mean you should avoid all debt—and focusing only on being debt-free can lead to inefficient planning. Debt has a place, both within your wealth accumulation strategy and within the overall economy.

WHY DEBT IS IMPORTANT

- **Debt redistributes money in the economy.** Debt can enable you to reallocate money to more productive avenues. For instance, someone with excess savings can lend money to someone short on money. Without debt as a financial instrument, there'd be greater imbalances of money that would constrain financial activity. In reality, debt never leads to "lost" money. For every liability, there's an asset to equal it.

- **Debt provides mutual benefits.** Responsible, fair debt employs reasonable interest rates and terms in a way that makes the debt mutually beneficial. The lender gains interest while the borrower gains the money they need in the meantime.

- **Debt is an investment vehicle.** For lenders, debt is an essential investment vehicle that makes it possible for individuals and companies alike to grow their capacity. Think back to the railways that private sectors built by taking on major debt, sometimes for years, before finishing construction and becoming able to repay it.

- **Debt enables homeownership.** Without debt, most people would never afford to buy a home. With a mortgage loan, one of the most major purchases in a person's life can be divided up into payments over a 25-year span (or shorter or longer), making homeownership possible.

- **Debt makes the income cycle work.** Most people will see a curve in their earnings throughout their lifetime, starting as students who often have little in the way of income, yet huge living and education expenses. Those out of college have greater income but potentially higher debt; however, as they grow older, they tend to have less debt and, as they approach retirement, less income. Debt makes the income life cycle work.

The key to the good use of debt is to have a strategy.

DEBT MANAGEMENT AND WEALTH ACCUMULATION STRATEGIES

You need to understand what you gain and give up by taking on debt. The ultimate advantage of debt is that you can use other people's money (OPM). This use of OPM allows you to leverage a little of your money and a lot more of other people's money to acquire assets. When those assets have value—such as property or stocks—then their acquisition is wealth accumulation, and this increases your overall net worth.

Overall, this is a good use of OPM; however, there is a cost. Not only do you have to pay interest on the loaned money, but more of your after-tax dollars are now required to pay back that debt.

DIFFERENCE BETWEEN AFTER-TAX AND PRE-TAX DOLLARS

To understand the power of before-tax dollars compared to after-tax dollars, consider this:

- If you charged $50 per hour and worked 40 hours per week, every week of the year, your annual take-home pay would be $104,000.

- If you lived in Ontario, your average tax rate would be close to 28% (while your marginal tax rate, the tax rate charged on the next dollar you earned, would be closer to 43%).

- Based on these tax rates, your actual earning power is $36 per hour, not $50.

Now, what if you could use the pre-tax earnings of $50 per hour, rather than the after-tax earnings of $36 per hour, to pay down debt and build your net worth?

Plus, other factors of your life are impacted, such as your credit score or your ability to choose what you want to spend your money on. Then there's the risk involved. When you use OPM, you are employing the tool of leverage.

Leverage allows you to multiply your buying power; you purchase a high-value asset by using a small percentage of your own money and a large percentage of the lender's money.

To help illustrate, let's say a buyer purchases a condo for $250,000 with a $50,000 down payment. Five years later, the owner sells the condo for $332,500—for what appears to be a 33% increase. But that's not entirely accurate since leverage was used.

The buyer used $50,000 of their own money to earn $82,500 ($332,500 minus $250,000)—that's an investment return of 65%.

Of course, there are still transactional costs as well as ongoing housing expenses during the time the condo was owned, but this simple example provides a good illustration of how leverage works.

Then there's the downside. What if the condo dropped in value by $50,000 just before the owner sold? A sale price of $200,000 would mean the owner wouldn't get the $50,000 down payment back. Worse, they'd also owe the bank an extra $50,000—the shortfall between the sale price and what's owed to the bank (again, this is a simple example, so we're not including transactional costs or ongoing expenses). In this case, the use of leverage means that while the investment declined in value by just 20%, the buyer suffered a 100% loss on their investment.

Still, for many wealth builders, the use of leverage, OPM and taking on debt are smart ways to grow your nest egg, but only if you know how to strategically deal with the debt.

Here are three core tactics when prioritizing debt and savings in your financial plan:

1. Prioritize savings first.

2. Prioritize debt repayment first.

3. Split the difference and do both.

The tactic to use depends largely on how you answer the following: would you prefer to be debt-free (no mortgage, etc.) or have a solid nest egg built up for retirement (and rainy days)?

The problem is, this question isn't always easy to answer. And don't be discouraged. Even financial experts can't agree if one strategy is better than the other.

To help, consider your answers to these three questions:

#1: Have You Done the Math?

It might sound trivial, but it's nearly impossible to decide without actually doing the work. In this case, it's calculating what you would earn and what it would cost if you were to take on debt to boost your savings and acquisition strategy.

The general rule of thumb is to prioritize investing when rates of return—what you earn—are higher than the cost of borrowing.

One long-time proponent of this strategy is author and educator Talbot Stevens. According to Stevens, it makes sense to prioritize investing when rates of return are higher than mortgage rates. In his book *Financial Freedom Without Sacrifice,* Stevens suggests *not* prioritizing debt repayment until your mortgage rate is 3% or more *above* your potential rate of return on your investments. It also helps provide context as to why our parents and grandparents were so focused on paying down mortgage debt. When my father bought his first home, his mortgage rate was close to 18% (some homeowners had mortgage rates closer to 23%!). He would've had to find oil in the backyard of the property to get a market return that was higher than that rate! So it made sense that he would focus on debt repayment and not retirement savings.

Mathematically, it doesn't make sense to prioritize paying down your mortgage debt since the guaranteed "return" is your mortgage rate (say, 3%). Use your money to invest and you could earn 5% to 6% (or more) instead. Plus, if you invest using your Registered Retirement Savings Plan (RRSP), you'll receive a tax refund that can go either towards debt repayment or right back into your RRSP (an especially powerful strategy if you're in a high tax bracket).

Although the math regarding this decision is important, your mindset counts, too. Some people sleep better when they are plugging away at debt, especially as their retirement party draws near. So you'll need to ask yourself two more questions.

#2: What Type of Saver Are You?

If you paid off your student loans and then used that surplus of cash to invest in your retirement or save for a down payment on a home, then you are a disciplined saver. Disciplined savers benefit more when prioritizing debt repayment over bulking up their investment portfolios.

If, however, you paid off your student loans and then turned around and used that surplus cash to buy a car or go on vacation, then paying off your mortgage (a non-deductible debt) may not be prudent (particularly true in a low-interest-rate environment).

Disciplined savers work best with prioritizing debt repayments since they will naturally switch to saving once cash is freed up. Those who are not as disciplined—most of us—work best when we prioritize saving since it forces us to allocate funds to investing *and* to debt repayment (we always make that mortgage payment, right?).

#3: Are You Nervous Nellie?

Although doing the math and figuring out your saver type is important, the final question you need to ask is how well you sleep at night.

If the idea of debt keeps you up at night, then paying down your mortgage first is smart. On the flip side, if you lose sleep at the thought of poverty in your golden years, then contributing to your RRSP first is a much better option.

Once you have the answers to these three questions, it's time to pick a "debt management and grow your savings" strategy.

To help illustrate how each strategy works, let's use the following assumptions:

- Single-family detached home in Toronto, ON

- Market value of the home is $950,000

- Down payment of 30% (unless otherwise stated)

- Total mortgage debt at the start of the loan is $665,000

- Amortization of 25 years (unless otherwise stated)

- Fixed-rate mortgage

- Mortgage rate of 2.5% (unless otherwise stated)

- No change in mortgage rate over the life of the loan

(not realistic but used to keep calculations simple and comparisons clean)

- Tax rate of 33% (unless otherwise stated)

Strategy #1: Prioritize Your Savings

In this strategy, you focus first on investing for your retirement and make paying off your mortgage a secondary goal.

For this strategy to work, you need to understand and accept market risks and be willing to stay in the market over the long term.

In theory, investing should always earn a better return than mortgage debt repayment, but you need to be a long-term investor who is willing to take risks in the market. That's because choosing to pay off a mortgage slowly and investing your earnings early requires returns that are better than what fixed-income investments, like bonds and GICS, can provide. Why? Because paying off your mortgage early is the equivalent of investing in fixed income—it's a safe, guaranteed return. To justify taking on the risk of market volatility, you need a reasonable expectation of earning more on those funds.

Consider the fees you pay when you prioritize investing over paying down your mortgage. The more your investments cost, the lower your return is because those costs eat into your returns. A low-cost ETF investor with a management expense ratio (MER) under 1% will more likely net better returns than the average mutual fund investor with a MER over 2%.

Also, be mindful of where you invest your money. Non-registered accounts are probably the least beneficial place to invest when prioritizing savings since they offer little to no shelter from taxa-tion. Instead, create a savings strategy that maximizes registered accounts, such as RRSPs and TFSAs. Talk to your financial planner for more options.

One final consideration is the length of your amortization and your risk of default. If you have a longer amortization period left and don't have a lot of equity in your home—especially if you're a new homebuyer who stretched just to buy in—then consider making extra payments on your mortgage first. This helps build up an equity cushion in your home.

Built-up home equity gives you the option to stay in your home and renegotiate lower monthly payments or find ways to make up the monthly shortfall (such as renting out rooms) in the event you lose your job or an income earner dies.

When to Prioritize Investing over Paying Down the Mortgage

- If you can tolerate more risk and market fluctuations that are inherent in investing

- If you have contribution room available in your RRSP or TFSA accounts (using these accounts gives you the added benefit of tax refunds or tax-free growth)

- If you have considerable equity in your home *already* or a shorter amortization period left

Here are three factors to consider when prioritizing your retire-ment savings and investment earnings:

#1: *Create an Investment Plan*

It should go without saying, but I'm going to say it anyway: get an investment plan.

As part of your financial plan, an investment plan considers your circumstances, objectives and risk tolerance. It acts as a guide to help choose the right types of investments to fit your needs, personality and goals.

An investment plan helps you match your financial goals and objectives with your financial resources. Put another way, it helps you figure out what you want to achieve, when and how much you can invest.

The basics of an investment plan include your goals, your time horizon, the resources available to you and how involved (or active) you want to be in the investment strategy.

If this all feels very overwhelming, consider talking to a financial professional, or go online to read a bit about the basics of creating an investment plan. It doesn't have to be complicated, but doing this work will help you find the right path to achieving your personal financial goals.

#2: *Boost Your RRSP Contribution*

Every year, many Canadians scramble to find the money to contribute to their RRSP account. Because this is a tax-deferred account, an RRSP contribution can help reduce and smooth out the amount of tax owed. The question, then, is should you borrow to make that contribution?

Unfortunately, there is no one-size-fits-all solution, but there are some general guidelines that can help you make the right decision for your situation.

First, you need to decide how much you will benefit from an RRSP contribution. A general rule of thumb when it comes to RRSPs is, the higher the tax bracket, the bigger the tax savings. The lower the tax bracket, the lower the tax savings.

For that reason, you should contribute to an RRSP when you are in a high marginal tax rate (38%, for example)—like when you are in a career position, earning a good salary—and take it out when you are in a low marginal tax rate—like when you retire. (Theoretically, you can also tap into your RRSP savings when you are not in a good income-earning year, like when you lose your job, but you'll need to remember that the government charges a 30% withholding fee for withdrawals made before retirement.)

It also means that it might not be a good idea to contribute money to your RRSP, for instance when you are in a low marginal tax rate (25%) or if you believe you'll end up earning more in retirement (putting you in a higher tax bracket).

To help you make a decision, consider the following:

- If your income is below $50,000 (or the upper threshold of the second marginal tax bracket, putting it around $48,500), you won't see any significant tax benefits from an RRSP contribution.

- It's best to calculate whether you anticipate higher earnings in retirement, say from the sale of your business or future sales commissions, which would make an RRSP contribution in the here and now a poor choice.

- When it comes to retirement savings, there can be some drawbacks to a well-funded RRSP account. As your investments grow, you will need to consider your marginal tax rate in retirement as well as your annual withdrawal rate—the percentage of your savings that you'll need to withdraw each year to live. Then calculate how much you'd need to withdraw to smooth out your tax rate in retirement.

- Consider your current annual earnings and then realistically consider future earnings. If you anticipate a bump in your pay cheque soon, consider waiting to make that RRSP contribution. You can carry the RRSP contribution room forward, and by waiting, you're giving yourself more room and a bigger deduction in higher-earning years.

If you do this math and it still makes sense to contribute, you'll want to decide whether to borrow to invest. This will depend on your risk tolerance, your ability to minimize the loan costs and whether you have a plan to pay off this debt.

The *best* strategy is to only borrow an amount that is matched by the refund you'll receive. That way, you are paying little or no interest on the loan and you get the advantage of compounding interest on those savings.

Thankfully there is a fairly easy and quick formula for figuring out how much to borrow (based on your expected tax refund). Here are the steps:

1. Calculate your marginal tax rate. (I use TaxTips.ca, and click on my province of residence.) In this example, let's assume your tax rate is 33%.

2. Divide 1 by your tax rate ($1 / 0.33 = x$).

3. Then subtract 1 from that answer ($x - 1 = y$).

4. Take the final answer (y) and use it to divide the amount of money you will contribute to your RRSP before the investment loan ($\$ / y$ = the amount you should borrow to invest in your RRSP).

For example, let's say Pat has $5,000 to invest in her RRSP and she is in the 33% tax bracket:

1. $1 / 0.33 = 3.03$

2. $3.03 - 1 = 2.03$

3. $\$5,000 / 2.03 = \$2,463$

Based on these calculations, Pat should invest $7,500 into her RRSP this year, which includes the $5,000 she saved as well as the $2,500 she borrowed.

She will get a refund of $2,463, which she can then use to pay back the $2,500 RRSP loan.

Remember, unlike loans for non-registered investments, interest on investment loans used for registered plans, such as RRSP or TFSA, are not tax deductible.

#3: Use a Self-Directed RRSP

You could also loan yourself a mortgage using your RRSP and, in essence, tackle two financial goals at once.

I first learned about this strategy while reading *The Little Book of Real Estate Wisdom* by Garth Turner, one of Canada's biggest real estate bears.

In the Jargon of Market Traders

A bull is someone who buys securities, commodities or other assets in the expectation of a price increase.

A bear is someone who sells securities, commodities or other assets in expectation of a price decline.

The idea is to become the lender and the borrower. You are required to charge the current posted interest rate—let's assume it's 3%—which means regular mortgage payments are made by you to you.

Win-win, right? You still have to borrow to buy a home, but by borrowing from yourself, you pay yourself back and contribute to your RRSP.

Except, the strategy only works if interest rates are high. That's because the primary goal of any investment you make is to maximize the rate of return so that your money can compound and grow for your retirement. The primary goal when borrowing money is to minimize the cost of borrowing. On the one hand, you want a high rate to increase your investment portfolio; on the other hand, you want a low rate to decrease your borrowing costs. These competing goals simply mean that one will lose out to the other.

When you add in the costs to set up and maintain a self-directed RRSP and the fact that you miss out on getting RRSP deductions (that help reduce taxes owed), this option isn't ideal in a low-interest-rate environment.

Of course, there are always investors who will benefit from these more niche options. In this case, if you're an investor who doesn't anticipate relying on RRSP savings to fund your retirement—for instance, a business owner—or you're a *very* conservative investor who is not concerned with maximizing annual tax rebates, a self-directed RRSP that holds your mortgage debt may be the ideal solution.

For those still interested in this option, here are the basic rules for setting it up:

- You must pay the current posted rate as the interest rate on your mortgage.

- Your lender will use your home as collateral in case you default on your mortgage payments.

- Your current RRSP portfolio (or contribution room) must equal or exceed the outstanding mortgage owed on your home.

- You will need to find a lender willing to set up a self-directed RRSP.

Focusing on Mortgage and Debt Management

- You must pay the costs associated with this option:

  * An initial setup fee from your lender of approximately $300

  * Start-up legal fees, which start at $500

  * Annual administration fees, charged by the lender approximately $200 per year

  * CMHC fees (currently around 0.5% of the mor principal), which are mandatory

  * Annual self-directed RRSP administratio' approximately $150

- You must allow a trustee to examine your annual basis.

To help illustrate how this all works, let's example (adapted from Turner's 2002 bo

  1. Start with a mortgage-free hom equity in your home.

  2. Establish a $100,000 non-r

  3. Set up a $100,000 RRSF

  4. If your mortgage rat would be just over equity from your

5. By setting this up, you have created a $100,000 debt paid to yourself over the next 25 years (the amortization of your mortgage).

6. At $700 per month, with a 6% rate of return (before inflation), you will have contributed just over $485,000 to your RRSP in 25 years.

Do all of this, and you can hold your mortgage inside your RRSP—consider it the fixed-income portion of your portfolio holdings—and rather than making mortgage payments to the bank, you make payments to your RRSP. Keep in mind, however, these payments will not qualify for tax deductions and they do not make the mortgage a tax-deductible debt.

rategy #2: Prioritize Your Mortgage

focus of this strategy is to get out of debt before switching ving. The key to making this work is knowing you can rely ur disciplined saver tendencies to carry you all the way h to the end.

st basic way to achieve this strategy is to pay all your expenses, and then use the remaining money to make a ent on your mortgage.

and why this works, it's important to understand how ayments work.

mortgage payment is made up of two parts: the prin- and the interest portion. Ideally, you want to minimize the interest paid and maximize the amount paid toward the principal debt (the actual money you borrowed). A prepayment towards your mortgage debt achieves both these goals and is particularly effective when the pre-payment is made at the start of the loan term.

If you examine an amortization chart, you'll see that in the initial years—when your mortgage debt is at its highest—you pay much more in interest.

YEAR	INTEREST	PRINCIPAL	TOTAL	LTV	BALANCE
2021	$15,110.84	$11,250.63	$26,361.47	78.0%	$428,749.37
2022	$14,713.62	$11,647.85	$26,361.47	75.8%	$417,101.52
2023	$14,303.38	$12,059.09	$26,361.47	73.6%	$405,042.42
2024	$13,876.62	$12,484.85	$26,361.47	71.4%	$392,557.57
2025	$13,435.83	$12,925.65	$26,361.47	69.0%	$379,631.92

Assumptions: $550,000 mortgage; 20% down payment; 25-year amortization, five-year term at 3.5%

As you make your regular mortgage payments, more of the principal debt (the sum you initially borrowed) is paid down. The lower your principal debt, the less interest is charged and the less you owe overall.

There is a general misconception that a pre-payment will reduce the debt owed and that this automatically reduces your monthly mortgage payment. Typically, that's not how mortgages work. An extra payment reduces your total debt. When that total debt is lower, you pay less interest. When you go to make your next regular mortgage payment, there will be less interest accrued (since the total debt is lower), so more of your payment goes towards paying that total debt down further.

DO ALL LENDERS OFFER MORTGAGE PRE-PAYMENT PRIVILEGES?

Not all lenders will offer pre-payment privileges, and those that do, don't always offer the same rules and privileges. For instance, some big banks allow you to make only one lump-sum pre-payment each calendar year, based on a percentage of the original loan—usually 10% to 20%. Other lenders base it on your contract year, so if you signed the mortgage contract in July, then your "year" runs from July to July. Still, other lenders allow you to increase your monthly mortgage payment anywhere from 10% to 100%; the 100% option is known as a double-up payment. Still others allow you to increase your regular mortgage payment, by a percentage, once per year. This means you can increase the monthly amount you pay by 10% each year (for a total of 50% for a five-year mortgage). The key is to shop around and read the fine print.

How to Pay Off Your Mortgage Faster

Want to save 30% to 50% off your house-debt costs? There are eight methods to help pay down your mortgage faster, all of which help reduce the overall cost of borrowing *and* add a high-value asset to your overall net worth. Here's a brief synopsis of each method using the previous assumptions to help illustrate how it works.

#1: Increase monthly payments

On top of your regular mortgage payment, commit to paying an additional sum. Start in the first month of your mortgage contract and you can be mortgage-free years sooner and save tens of thousands in interest costs.

- Regular monthly mortgage payment: $2,979

- Add pre-payment per month: $500

- Reduce time in debt by: 4 years + 8 months

- Total interest paid: just over $182,650

- Total saved (reduced interest payments): just over $46,000

#2: Double-up pre-payment

Commit to doubling your regular mortgage payment each month.

- Regular monthly mortgage payment: $2,979

- Add pre-payment per month: $2,979

- Reduce time in debt by: 14 years + 4 months

- Total interest paid: just over $92,000

- Total saved (reduced interest payments): just over $136,500

#3: *Make an annual pre-payment*

Make one lump-sum payment each year until the loan is paid off.

- Regular monthly mortgage payment: $2,979

- Add pre-payment of $12,000, once per year, every 12 months

- Reduce time in debt by: 7 years + 3 months

- Total interest paid: just over $155,125

- Total saved (reduced interest payments): just over $73,560

#4: *Accelerate the payments*

Rather than make regular monthly mortgage payments, accelerate the frequency to twice per month or once per week, or opt for biweekly accelerated (26 payments rather than 24).

- Regular monthly mortgage payment: $2,979

- Change to biweekly accelerated: $1,490 every two weeks

- Reduce time in debt by: 2 years + 8 months

- Total interest paid: just over $202,555

- Total saved (reduced interest payments): just over $26,135

#5: Choose a shorter amortization

The typical amortization period is 25 years, but it can be as short as 5 years, or as long as 35 years (if you made a down payment of 20% or more on your home).

Forcing yourself to pay off the mortgage in fewer years translates into lower interest costs. The risk, however, is that your regular monthly payments will be much higher.

- Regular monthly mortgage payment on 25-year amortization: $2,979

- Reduce amortization to 20 years, monthly mortgage payment: $3,520

- Reduce time in debt by: 5 years

- Total interest paid: just over $179,720

- Total saved (reduced interest payments): just over $48,970

#6: Choose a longer amortization + add a pre-payment strategy

By selecting a longer amortization, you reduce your required monthly mortgage payment. This is a terrible option if you do nothing else since it extends the amount of time you are in debt and your overall cost of borrowing. But if you use this option alongside a pre-payment method, you'll end up with flexibility and reduced costs.

This flexibility is great if you anticipate lifestyle or income changes over the years—for example, if you plan on starting a family and want to keep monthly bills to a minimum during the child's first year.

Keep in mind, a longer amortization is not always an option. Most lenders require you to have more than 20% equity in a home before increasing the amortization length beyond the standard 25 years. Other lenders won't offer this option unless the home's purchase price is under $1 million. Still other lenders will only offer this option if you're willing to pay the fees on the mortgage default insurance the lender will take out to mitigate their potential loss (should you default).

Still, for disciplined savers or responsible consumers with fluctuating income levels, this can be a good option. For example, increase the amortization to 35 years, and you drop your monthly mortgage payment by more than $600 per month. Add in a double-up payment (assuming you never have to stop this double-up payment), and you could be mortgage-free in less than 14 years.

- Regular monthly mortgage payment on 25-year amortization: $2,979

- Increased amortization to 35 years, monthly mortgage payment: $2,373

- Double-up pre-payment: $2,373

- Total amortization: 21 years + 2 months

- Total interest paid: just over $331,550

- Total saved (reduced interest payments): just over $210,150

#7: Choose to use a lower home down payment

Consider putting less than 20% down on the purchase of your home. Yes, you'll need to add in the cost of mortgage default insurance, but there's a **very good** chance a smaller down payment will get you better mortgage rates, which reduces your overall mortgage debt costs.

The reason why high-loan-to-value (LTV) mortgage loans— loans with less than 20% down—offer the best mortgage rates is that lenders **love** these loans. Since mortgage default insurance is a requirement, this gives lenders a guarantee that this debt will be repaid. If you default, this insurance pays the lender the full sum of what is owed. This is great since it lowers the lender's risk, which reduces their capitalization needs and increases the amount of money they can loan out and make money on. Win-win-win-win.

As a result, lenders compete for high-LTV mortgages. Lenders compete **hard** for these clients, including offering the best possible rates. As we know, the lower the mortgage rate, the more you save on borrowing costs—even after adding mortgage default insurance costs to the overall sum borrowed.

- Total mortgage debt: $760,000

- Regular monthly mortgage payment with 20% down @ 2.5%: $3,405

- Total interest paid: just over $261,363

- Total saved (reduced interest payments): $0

- Total mortgage debt: $760,000 + $21,546 in mortgage default fees

- Regular monthly mortgage payment with 19% down @ 2.0%: $3,310

- Total interest paid: just over $211,290

- Total saved (reduced interest payments): just over $50,000

Despite the fees, you still saved money.

By law, mortgage lenders are required to keep a percentage of their money in liquid assets, such as cash, money market funds or other pre-authorized alternative investments that are considered very, very safe. This "quick cash" is known as the lender's "capitalization" needs, and the specific sum is determined through regulatory formulas.

#8: Use a home equity line of credit (HELOC) or open mortgage

If you anticipate a windfall, have a relatively small mortgage, or need a mortgage only as a temporary stopgap, using a line of credit, a HELOC or an open mortgage can be strategically advantageous. However, there are risks and higher costs associated with this option.

For instance, a less-responsible consumer may feel tempted to dip into a line of credit or HELOC to cover expenses not related to the mortgage. Perhaps you overspent during the holidays? Or you forgot to set aside money to pay your annual tax bill? Or maybe you want that boat? Whatever the reason, this type of "extra" spending can make the flexibility of this sort of loan very, very expensive.

Here's what I mean:

- Opt for a standard fixed- or variable-rate mortgage, and your mortgage rate will hover somewhere around 1.5% to 2.5%—on a $665,000 mortgage at 2%, this results in a monthly mortgage payment of $2,816.

- Opt for a HELOC, and that rate will start getting closer to 3%—resulting in a monthly mortgage payment of $3,147.

- Opt for an open mortgage, and the rate creeps up to 3.5% or more—resulting in a monthly mortgage payment of $3,320.

If you don't take advantage of these flexible loan structures to pay down debt quickly, you could be adding tens of thousands to your overall borrowing costs. However, if you use the flexible terms to pay back the loan, you could save a bundle in borrowing costs.

Ideally, the line of credit, HELOC or open mortgage is best suited for a homeowner who anticipates being able to make significant lump-sum payments towards the debt within the first few years of the loan and, ideally, with a strategy to pay off the entire loan within five years. If this doesn't sound possible, consider an alternative method of tackling your debt.

You can **get into serious trouble** with any of these strategies **if you skip out on the overall intent, which is to pay off your mortgage debt as soon as possible and to minimize your overall cost of borrowing.**

5 TIPS TO HELP YOU SAVE MONEY ON YOUR MORTGAGE COSTS

Here are some tips and tricks to get those debt, borrowing and mortgage details right.

#1: INCENTIVIZE YOURSELF TO READ YOUR MORTGAGE DOCUMENT.

It won't be the most entertaining evening of your life, but before you sign your very thick and full-of-jargon mortgage document, read it. The entire thing. Page for page. Turns out, banks and lenders make mistakes in these documents all the time.

For example, a friend once caught a massive error in the stated mortgage rate, just before he signed. He and his wife had secured a sweet pre-qualified rate and locked in that rate for 90 days. About 60 days later, he and his wife were reviewing the mortgage document, only to find that the rate offered was 75 basis points more than their original pre-approved rate. That's big. Thankfully, my friend is a big believer in documenting conversations and could easily show, through saved emails, that the rate promised was much lower. The bank changed the document, and he and his wife saved tens of thousands in interest payments over the life of the loan.

#2: ASK HOW INTEREST IS CALCULATED.

When considering a new mortgage, ask if the interest is compounded monthly, semi-annually or annually. The less frequently the interest is compounded the better, as you don't end up paying interest on interest. Keep in mind that most mortgages in Canada compound on a semi-annual basis, but ask your lender just to be sure.

#3: IF GETTING A VARIABLE MORTGAGE, ASK WHEN RATES CHANGE.

Most variable mortgages have rates that fluctuate monthly. However, several lenders change their variable rates only once every three months. These less frequent changes certainly offer a bit more protection when rates start to rise.

#4: ACTIVELY SHOP AROUND FOR THE BEST RATE.

You may be tempted to walk into your local bank and sign on the dotted line for the first mortgage that you qualify for, but don't. It really does pay to shop around.

#5: ONLY CONSOLIDATE DEBT IF YOU HAVE A PLAN TO PAY IT DOWN.

Many people refinance to consolidate their debt. In this situation, you're looking to roll high-interest-rate debt, such as credit card balances, into your mortgage to simplify your debt payments and lower your interest rate. By doing so, you could reduce your rate from 19% (the typical rate on a credit card) to 3% or 4% and save thousands of dollars in interest payments.

Don't Cash In Your RRSP to Pay Off Your Mortgage

Let's say you have a $250,000 mortgage at 2.97% and a little over $2 million in investments, but they are all in RRSPs in fairly conservative assets. Last year you made 7% and this year your rate of return will probably be closer to 5%. You are in your early 50s and still working. Is it better to cash out the RRSPs, pay off the mortgage and take the tax hit, or pay the mortgage and hope to make more on your investments?

To answer this question, we need to consider a few factors. First, are you risk averse? If yes, consider the following:

- Paying down debt provides a guaranteed rate of return via the interest you avoid—a return that will increase as interest rates normalize.

- If you are not knowledgeable about investments, paying down debt means you have fewer investments to worry about.

- If you have a high debt level, paying down debt may help get your debt ratios in check.

- If you are in a low tax bracket, RRSP contributions may provide little to no tax benefit and cause a clawback of government pensions in retirement.

- If your spouse is in a higher tax bracket and has room in their RRSP, take advantage of their RRSP room before your own, even if they contribute to a spousal RRSP on your behalf.

There are various implications to RRSP withdrawals. First, you'll need to factor in the withholding tax on that withdrawal. The tax rates are 10% on a $5,000 withdrawal, 20% on withdrawals between $5,001 and $15,000, and 30% on withdrawals over $15,000.

Second, you must add the RRSP withdrawal sum to your income and pay tax accordingly (based on your marginal tax rate). This may exceed the amount of the withholding tax. The all-in tax could be as high as 50%, depending on your province of residence.

These high costs are why most financial planners generally advise against cashing in RRSP savings to pay your mortgage unless you have no other option. It's best to exhaust non-registered investments, TFSAs and other savings before cashing in RRSP money. Instead, consider the tips for paying down your mortgage faster.

Strategy #3: Leverage Debt for Investment Returns

The crux of the debt management dilemma is to figure out how to best use your assets to pay down debt and accumulate wealth. For some, a targeted approach is best: prioritize saving or prioritize debt repayment. Either strategy works because the approach is simple and makes maximum use of your primary tool—the money you earn.

But what about the other tools you have at your disposal? What about the value of time—where younger investors have the fortune of getting in and staying in the market for longer and maximizing the power of compounding? Then there's leverage—a tool virtually all of us use to purchase a home but then never revisit to find out if we can do more (and we can certainly do more).

The good news is, we all have more than just what we earn to accomplish our goals. The third strategy of debt management is about the best use of other tools, in particular our home, the power of leverage and the advantage of deductible debt or pre-tax dollars.

Create a Tax-Deductible Mortgage through a Debt Swap

More than 40% of Canadians are mortgage-free and another large portion has a significant amount of equity built up in their home. For these homeowners, there is an option to use their built-up home equity as a way to boost their investment savings, using a tax-deductible loan.

What Is Home Equity?

Home equity is the market value of what you own in a property. It's the difference between the home's fair market value and the outstanding balance of all debts on the property, such as mortgages or lines of credit.

The strategy is known as a debt swap. The simplest version is to liquidate your non-registered investment accounts and use this money to pay off your non-deductible mortgage debt (this assumes your mortgage isn't already paid off). Then re-borrow, using your home as collateral, and use the money to grow your investment portfolio.

The result of this swap is that your net assets—your home and investment accounts—and your liabilities (the amount you owe) remain the same, but now you've swapped a non-deductible debt for a tax-deductible debt.

To understand, let's assume you are now earning enough to put you in the 45% tax bracket and you still owe $230,000 on your current mortgage but also have $230,000 in an unregistered investment account. If you were to continue as-is, the interest you pay on the remaining mortgage balance is approximately $20,790 (based on our prior assumptions).

Implement the debt-swap strategy, and you can save more than $9,000 in taxes.

Create a Tax-Deductible Mortgage through a Debt Conversion

The debt swap sounds great, particularly if you don't want to prioritize one financial goal, such as paying down the mortgage, over another, such as saving for retirement.

However, most Canadians don't have a large sum invested in a non-registered investment account. That's because most Canadians concentrate on maximizing tax deductions through RRSP contributions and tax-efficient savings using the TFSA. Does this mean the primary benefit of a debt swap—to convert bad or non-deductible debt into good or tax-deductible debt—is out of reach for most Canadians? No!

If you find yourself in this position, you will want to consider the debt-conversion strategy, also known as the Smith Manoeuvre.

WHAT IS THE SMITH MANOEUVRE?

The Smith Manoeuvre was developed by the late Fraser Smith, a BC-based financial planner. Smith was keen to categorize debt and to focus on good forms of debt for wealth accumulation. He believed that good debt beat bad debt. As such, Smith believed the purchase of a primary residence was good debt because it was an appreciating asset. However, he considered mortgage debt as "bad debt" since it had no tax benefits. That's when he realized how important it was to commoditize the Canadian mortgage. By setting up a readvanceable mortgage—a mortgage that provides a line of credit directly proportional to the amount of equity in the home—the money from the line of credit can then be used to invest in non-registered investments.

The debt-conversion strategy allows the homeowner to focus on repaying debt *while* accelerating their investment earnings by using the equity in their home.

To use this strategy, you need to set up a readvanceable mortgage—essentially a mortgage debt attached to a line of credit. Each time you make a mortgage payment, the principal portion of that payment frees up the same amount in the line of credit.

For example, if you make a $2,500 mortgage payment and $1,250 is used to pay interest and the other $1,250 is used to pay down the principal loan, you would then have $1,250 available to borrow from the line of credit. You can then re-borrow what you've paid and use this money to invest in a portfolio of income-producing assets. By doing this, you convert the non-deductible mortgage debt into a tax-deductible investment loan.

The best part is that the tax-deductible debt helps create tax savings that can be further used to pay down non-deductible mortgage debt, which helps to further reduce your overall borrowing costs and frees up more money to invest.

Aside from the standard debt swap and debt conversion, there are four other methods of swapping non-deductible mortgages for tax-deductible debt.

#1: *Kick-start your savings strategy*

If you have equity in your home and you like the debt-conver-sion strategy but want to kick-start your investment portfolio, consider taking out a HELOC. You can use the borrowed money as a lump sum to kick-start the debt-conversion strategy—paying tax-deductible interest on borrowed money that is used to invest.

#2: *Capitalize and maximize cash-flow strategy*

One of the big disadvantages of a debt-conversion strategy is that it requires you to have enough earnings and cash flow to meet your debt obligations. In other words, if you borrow enough to require a $500 per month interest-only repayment, you need to be sure you have that $500 per month to make the payment. However, with the borrow-to-pay strategy, you can avoid that cash-flow crunch by capitalizing the interest. Essentially, this means you borrow from the credit line to pay the interest on the credit line.

Although there are certainly risks to this strategy, there are also two big advantages. First, it doesn't require cash flow to start a debt-conversion strategy. This means you can start this strategy even if money is tight. Second, there is a tax advantage to doing this. The tax rule is that if the interest on your credit line is tax deductible, then the interest on the interest is also tax deductible.

To make this work, be sure you keep track of the money you borrowed so that you can show you used it to pay interest (on the money borrowed to invest).

Also, keep in mind that banks will generally not allow you to set up automatic payments that use the credit line to pay its own interest. This means you'll need to go in and do a manual transaction with each mortgage payment. The easiest way to set this up is to have the interest on the credit line automatically withdrawn from your chequing account. Then withdraw the same amount (to the penny) from your credit line to replace the funds removed from your chequing account. To keep better track of this strategy, set up a separate, dedicated chequing account that is used only for these transactions.

#3: Consolidate strategy

Truth is, you can turn just about any loan into a tax-deductible debt by converting it into mortgage debt. The only requirement is that you have equity available in your home to set up this swap.

What's great about this strategy is that it offers those who struggle to find the money to invest an opportunity to start.

To illustrate, let's assume Pat and Spencer currently pay the following:

- Mortgage payment of $2,000 per month

- Car payment of $500 per month

- Credit card repayment of $300 per month

- Credit line repayment of $200 per month

If Pat and Spencer were to refinance their mortgage, they could roll all the debt into the mortgage. For simplicity, let's assume that by doing this, Pat and Spencer can keep their current $3,000 debt payments. Now, each month they make one payment of

$3,000. Since $1,500 of this payment goes towards repaying the mortgage principal, they now have $1,500 in a line of credit that they can borrow and invest.

Even though Pat and Spencer's monthly payments have not changed, the refinance and consolidation of their debt means they are now repaying all their debts and starting their investment savings.

#4: Prioritize debt repayment strategy

For those who want to prioritize paying off the mortgage debt while still starting a debt-conversion strategy, the best option is to set up a simple strategy (a standard Smith Manoeuvre) and invest in dividend-paying investments.

Historically, a strong dividend company will increase their dividends regularly. This puts more earnings in your pocket. Plus, dividends receive a preferential tax credit, especially if the dividends come from a Canadian-owned company. If you were to take the dividend income earned and the annual tax refund you receive and use it to pay down your non-deductible mortgage debt, then the conversion from bad (non-deductible) debt to good (tax-deductible) debt would go much quicker.

Bottom Line

Regardless of what leverage strategy you opt to use, the minimum rate of return (based on the lowest tax rate and the average annual investment returns of a balanced portfolio[24]) is 23.3%.

---

24 https://www.financialsamurai.com/historical-returns-of-different-stock-bond-portfolio-weightings.

Ask any financial advisor and they'll tell you, this rate of return is really hard to beat.

ADVANTAGES OF LEVERAGING DEBT

Whether you use a debt swap or a debt conversion, the main advantages of these leverage strategies are:

1. Invest in Your Future Without Using Just Your Earnings

The main benefit is the long-term compound growth of investment money. It's why these strategies are best used by those with longer investment horizons or those with a higher tolerance for risk.

2. Tax Deductions

The interest on money borrowed to invest can offer sizable tax deductions that help taxpayers keep more of their earnings.

3. Pay Your Mortgage Off Faster

By converting non-deductible debt into tax deductions, you keep more of your earned dollars, which can then be used to further reduce your non-deductible mortgage debt. Paying off the mortgage faster means lower borrowing costs, which further increases the dollars you have to spend and invest.

4. Use Your Taxable Investment Income However You Want

In general, if you receive taxable income from your investments, such as dividends or a capital gains distribution, you can use that cash for any purpose without affecting the deductibility of the credit line. Just be sure you can trace the cash you withdraw to the taxable income.

WHY INCREASING YOUR PRE-TAX DOLLARS MAKES FINANCIAL SENSE

Why all the fuss about tax deductions and pre-tax dollars? When you compare the spending and saving power of pre-tax dollars to after-tax dollars, it's easy to see why.

For example:

- If you charged $50 per hour and worked 40 hours per week, every week of the year, your annual take-home pay would be $104,000.

- If you lived in Ontario, your average tax rate would be close to 28% (while your marginal tax rate, the tax rate charged on the next dollar you earned, would be closer to 43%).

- Based on these tax rates, your actual earning power is $36 per hour, not $50.

Now, what if you could use the pre-tax earnings of $50 per hour, rather than the after-tax earnings of $36 per hour, to pay down debt and build your net worth?

RISKS OF DEBT LEVERAGE STRATEGIES

Although long-term growth and tax refunds are great, these strategies do come with risks. Here are the three main risks inherent to leverage strategies.

Market Risk

This is the biggest risk. Whenever you invest in the market, you introduce volatility and risk into your savings portfolio. Even though this risk can be reduced with the selection of safer, more reliable or more diverse investment options—such as low-cost index ETFs—market risks still exist.

Magnification of Gains or Losses

When you borrow, you are using leverage—the process of committing a small amount of your own funds, while using a larger amount of OPM, to acquire high-value or income-producing assets. The use of leverage magnifies your gains *and* your losses and can easily double or triple your profit or your loss. You owe the balance of the loan and the interest regardless of how your investments perform.

Compounding Loss Through Emotional Trading

If you are the type of person who might panic and sell during a large market crash, leverage strategies are not right for you. To consider this type of strategy, you need to be able to tolerate the ups and downs of the market and stay invested for the long term, especially if the value of your investments falls below the amount you owe on the credit line.

It's a Long-Term Strategy

If you're considering a leverage strategy, chances are you're looking to invest for at least a decade, possibly longer. During this time, you may face a market crash (or two) and as an investor, you need to be able to stay invested through each crash. Ideally, financial planners only suggest employing a leverage strategy, like the debt swap or debt conversion, if you are willing to invest for 20 years or more.

HOW TO SET UP A DEBT-CONVERSION LEVER-AGE STRATEGY

To start, you'll need to set up a "readvanceable mortgage," which is a mortgage linked with a credit line. Thankfully, most big banks and mortgage mono-lenders offer readvanceable mortgages these days.

To qualify for a readvanceable mortgage, you'll need at least 20% equity in your home. The credit line portion will be capped at a maximum of 65% of your home's value, but the entire mortgage debt can be as high as 80% of your home's current appraised value.

Once set up, you need to be mindful of the rules.

#1: Keep It Legal

Only deduct the interest portion of the money you borrowed to invest, and don't use the line of credit for any reason other than to purchase an income-producing investment. Ignore this rule, and you run the risk of disqualifying your investment loan and being denied the tax deduction.

#2: Keep a Paper Trail

According to the CRA, if you borrow money and claim the interest as a tax deduction, that money **must** be used to purchase an income-producing asset. You can only use the money for investment purposes. And the onus is on you to prove the case. You must provide a paper trail—evidence that every dollar spent was used following CRA rules.

If you do intend to use borrowed equity from your principal residence for any purpose other than for investments, be sure to sever this amount completely and keep all documentation to show that separation. (A great way to do this is to use a collateral mortgage that allows you to hive off segments into different accounts. Just be sure you claim only the interest paid on the line of credit that is used for investing.)

#3: Keep It Real

The CRA is concerned with the "current use" of money borrowed, not the original use. If you borrow to invest and then cash in the investment to spend, your credit line is no longer deductible because the "current use" of the money is your spending.

#4: Keep It Away from Other Tax-Saving Strategies

You cannot use the borrowed funds to invest using a registered or tax-advantaged account. This means you cannot use borrowed funds to purchase ETFs or stocks inside your TFSA or RRSP. If you do, you will not be able to claim the interest deductibility on those borrowed funds.

#5: Keep It Focused on "Expectation of Income"

Whatever investments you select, there should be a reasonable expectation that these investments will earn an income (produce a return). Quite often, investors misinterpret this to mean that the investments must pay dividends or interest. This isn't the case. Virtually all stocks, ETFs or mutual funds are acceptable investments to use in these leverage strategies, even if they don't pay a dividend (as long as its prospectus does not prohibit ever paying a dividend).

#6: Keep the Interest Portion Tax Deductible

If you sell any investments that were bought using borrowed debt strategy funds, the book value of these investments or the proceeds of selling (whatever is lower) must be paid down on the credit line. If you don't do this, the interest on the portion of the line of credit used to buy and then sell these investments could become non-deductible.

#7: Keep an Eye Out for "Return of Capital" Earnings

Check your investments for tax-free "return of capital" payments. If you do receive these payments, be sure to repay the line of credit the equivalent amount. Fail to do this, and the interest on that amount of borrowed funds is no longer deductible.

Can You Borrow Against an Investment Property to Buy a Principal Residence and Still Deduct the Mortgage Interest?

If you use the money borrowed against your rental property as part of your down payment on your principal residence—in essence, borrowing to purchase an asset that does not earn you money—then the debt does not qualify as an investment loan and the interest on that debt cannot be deducted. For more details on strategies to make this work, see "Turn Your Home into a Rental Property" in Chapter 8: Saving on Taxes with Your Home.

HOUSE RICH: HOW TO ACCESS THE EQUITY IN YOUR HOME

Quite often, debt management discussions will focus on how to create tax-efficient debts or how to minimize borrowing costs. These are important considerations when using debt financing to grow your net worth. But this focus does ignore our desire to "make a home our own." It also ignores every other reason why a homeowner may want to tap their home's equity, including the fact that home valuation has increased exponentially over the last decade.

From August 2019 to August 2020 alone, the national average home price was up a record 18.5%. This tremendous appreciation has prompted many homeowners to consider their house as a potential source of quick cash.

There are various reasons and ways to access the equity in your home, from refinancing your mortgage to getting a HELOC, to setting up a reverse mortgage. The trick is determining the best option for your circumstance and then developing a strategy to minimize potential costs and avoid crippling pitfalls.

I've outlined the four most common ways to access the equity in your home, along with tips on how to minimize fees and when you should use each.

#1: Mortgage Refinance

In a year filled with a pandemic crisis, record job loss and incredible home sales activity, it comes as no surprise when government and mortgage lenders try to stimulate the economy and encourage spending through low interest rates. As a result, mortgage rates are now at an all-time low, and many Canadians are now asking, can I save money by refinancing my mortgage?

To help you decide, here are a few tips on when to refinance, along with some highlights on how to qualify for a refinance.

What Is a Mortgage Refinance?

When you refinance your mortgage, you are replacing your current mortgage loan agreement with a new one.

Top Reasons for a Mortgage Refinance

In general, most homeowners will renegotiate the terms of their mortgage loan for the following reasons:

- Get access to the home's equity

- Save money by taking advantage of a lower interest rate

- Consolidate debt (and reduce the amount of cash flow that goes towards monthly debt repayments)

Unlike a renewal—when your mortgage term ends and you can renegotiate a new mortgage loan without penalties or hindrances—a mortgage refinance requires homeowners to reapply and requalify for a mortgage. This reapplication requirement applies even if you are working with the same lender.

As a result, to qualify you for a mortgage, your lender will need to examine the following:

- Your income-to-debt ratio

- The loan-to-value ratio on your current home

- The appraised value of your home

To qualify for a mortgage refinance, you typically need at least 20% equity in your home. However, if you have less than 20% equity and an excellent credit score, some lenders may find a way to approve your refinance application.

When Is It Worth It to Break Your Mortgage?

If you're planning on selling your house in a few years, it's probably not worth it to break your mortgage. After all the penalties and fees, you may barely break even.

On the other hand, if you plan on staying put for the long run, breaking your mortgage to refinance and get a lower rate can help you save a bundle. Just be sure to do the math.

When rates used to be closer to double digits, the general rule of thumb was to not bother unless you could secure a rate that was at least 2 percentage points lower than your current mortgage rate. That rule of thumb no longer applies. Rates have been so low for so long that it's now worth switching for a much smaller drop. Most financial planners and mortgage advisors now suggest considering a mortgage refinance if you can get a rate that is 0.3% lower than your current rate.

For instance, if your original mortgage contract was a five-year fixed at 5.0%, then even a 3.39% rate would be enticing. Even though the difference between the two rates is less than 2%, the rate reduction would translate into a 30% reduction in the monthly mortgage payment. In other words, if you were paying $1,500 a month before, you'd save about $450 every month with the new rate.

Most homeowners would agree that those savings are definitely worth the switch. Like all things to do with personal finance, the key is to run the numbers and do the math.

Penalty Costs for Breaking a Mortgage

When you signed your mortgage document, you agreed to certain conditions, including paying regular amounts to the lender until the end of your term. Breaking this agreement means your lender will earn less in interest payments. So to deter people from taking this route and to recoup lost earnings, lenders charge a penalty.

Not every homeowner wants to break their mortgage, but some find themselves in a position where they have to because of divorce, a death or a sudden need to move. Whatever the reason, breaking a mortgage can trigger serious financial penalties.

Almost 40% of mortgage holders will have to refinance, and when they do, they'll have to pay a penalty.

There are penalties for breaking both fixed- and variable-rate mortgages, but the penalties for breaking a variable mortgage are usually lower. In this case, calculating that penalty is easy. Canada's National Housing Act mandates that for variable-rate mortgages, the penalty is always equivalent to three months' interest.

For example, you have a $200,000 variable-rate mortgage at 3.8%, amortized over 25 years. Let's say your monthly payment is $1,030, and the interest rate portion is $627. Multiply that by three and you get $1,881. That's your penalty.

A fixed-rate mortgage has a much higher penalty, and unfortunately, it's also much more difficult to calculate because it's based on a formula that is unique to each lender. Broadly speaking, this formula, known as the interest rate differential (IRD), is the difference between the rate of your current mortgage and the rate the lender can now charge a borrower if they were to loan out this money. Call your lender and ask them what the penalty would be if you were to break your mortgage.

FORMULA USED TO CALCULATE THE PENALTIES

Once upon a time, the standard in the industry was to charge a three-month interest penalty for early discharges (the term used when you break your mortgage contract before the end of the term).

However, in 1999, the CMHC paved the road for changes when they removed the three-month interest standard from their written policy. These days, lenders still charge three months' interest for the early discharge of variable-rate mortgages, but lenders no longer stick to this penalty limit for fixed-rate mortgages. Now they charge what's called the interest rate differential (IRD), which is a calculation that is proprietary to each lender. The idea behind the IRD is to compensate the lender for any loss due to a mortgage being paid off early (and assumes the funds are being lent again at a lower rate).

If you are faced with having to break a mortgage, consider these three tricks for minimizing the penalties:

1. Use pre-payments.

Annual lump-sum pre-payments usually allow you to make a 10% to 25% pre-payment (based on your initial mortgage amount) against the outstanding debt. By taking advantage of pre-payments, you can lower your loan, which should lower your penalty. Talk to your mortgage advisor or lender to confirm how a pre-payment will impact the penalty charged to break the contract early.

2. Start complaining.

Speak to the bank manager, move up the chain if that doesn't get you anywhere, then try the ombudsman. If that fails, consider getting some cardboard and making a placard. Nothing feels more unfair than a double hit. Like when you have to pay $30,000 in penalties to break your mortgage to sell a home during a divorce. The idea is to prompt the lender to make an exception and reduce your penalty. Hey, we all know that saying, "The squeaky wheel gets the grease."

3. Strategically wait.

IRD penalties can change over time, sometimes quite dramatically. An obvious future change is how this penalty will drop the closer you get to renewal time, but a change in posted rates can also produce lower penalty amounts, particularly if there's a dramatic change.

4. Consider a loophole using a two-step process.

Instead of breaking your mortgage and paying a huge IRD penalty, request a "blend and extend" into a ***new*** five-year fixed term. A new term is critical. Once the new loan is finalized, call your lender and break the mortgage.

At some lenders, the blend and extend can reset the mortgage term and, at the same time, increase the loan comparison rates. The higher the comparison rate, the lower the IRD penalty; sometimes it's so low that the lender defaults to charging the cheaper three months' interest penalty used for variable-rate mortgages.

Keep in mind, this loophole only works with a limited number of lenders and some lenders don't blend and extend into new terms but force you to keep your existing term until the maturity date. **This negates the strategy altogether.**

To be sure, call and confirm if your lender's policies support this strategy. You can run a test scenario using your lender's penalty calculator, or you can just call the lender to ask what your penalty would be if you blended and extended and then had to break the mortgage one month later.

Unfortunately, refinancing midterm or breaking your mortgage isn't very different from applying for your first mortgage, if you are switching to a new lender. You'll still have to fill in an application and go through a credit check. You will be assessed based on your debt ratios and you must pass the mortgage stress test, which requires you to qualify for the mortgage based on the benchmark five-year fixed posted rate. You may also have to do a title search, and there may be appraisal and inspection fees. The process can be quite lengthy and can cost you $1,000 or more in out-of-pocket expenses.

#2: Home Equity Line of Credit

A HELOC allows you to borrow money on an as-needed basis, up to a set amount that you negotiate with your lender. You're required to pay monthly interest only on the amount you've borrowed (although you can pay more if you wish).

The benefit of HELOCs is that the borrowing rates (interest charged on money borrowed) are lower than for other lines of credit because the loan is secured by your property. And unlike a mortgage, there is no schedule of payments on the principal. Keep in mind, however, you'll pay interest on the funds you end up using, plus the interest rate will fluctuate depending on the lender's prime rate.

Since HELOCs use the equity in your home, you are legally capped at up to 65% of your home's appraised value.

Are all HELOCs the same? Surprisingly, no. Some HELOCs give borrowers a single account, and others can be split into sub-accounts. The sub-account HELOCs are preferred because it's easier to file your taxes when all of your investment borrowings are separated from other, non-deductible uses of credit. (Sometimes you can even negotiate different rates for each account.)

HOW TO BANKROLL A HOME RENOVATION

Contrary to popular opinion, most homeowners don't load up on cheap debt to pay for their renovations. According to a 2019 Houzz survey, 76% of homeowners said the money for the upgrades came from savings or personal finances. Only 8% admitted to paying for an upgrade through cash from a mortgage refinance, while another 19% said the funds came from a HELOC. Perhaps the scariest response was that 20% admitted to putting their home reno/upgrade on their credit card—a debt that would be paid off over time.

Consider these three smart ways to bankroll a home renovation or upgrade project.

1. HOME EQUITY LINE OF CREDIT

Using a HELOC means you can access up to 65% of your home's current market value and use this money for any reason, such as a reno.

For instance, if your home is appraised at $500,000, you could borrow up to $325,000 from a lender. If you already have a $300,000 mortgage, this leaves $25,000 in equity that can be used through a HELOC.

The benefit of a HELOC is that it gives you ongoing access to funds at a low interest rate (usually slightly higher than the prime rate, sometimes even lower!).

How it works:

Like a typical line of credit, you can borrow from a HELOC up to the limit, repay and borrow back again. You pay interest on only the funds you use. You have to apply to see if you qualify for a HELOC, and once you do, a home appraisal is done to calculate the home's current value so that you can get the maximum line of credit. Processing fees can run as high as $1,000, and discharge fees (costs to remove the HELOC) can be a few hundred dollars.

2. MORTGAGE REFINANCE

This option allows you to start a new mortgage at a lower interest rate. What's great is that you can even top up your loan amount—essentially adding money to the home's original loan amount (up to 80% of its appraised value). Like a HELOC, you're borrowing against the equity in your home.

How it works:

If your existing mortgage isn't at term, you pay the penalty to break it (typically three months' interest for a variable rate, or the IRD formula for a fixed-rate mortgage) before taking out a new one. Like the HELOC, you have to apply and complete an appraisal. The penalty and fees add up, but it can be worth the trouble for a lower interest rate on your loan.

3. ENERGY AUDIT REBATES

If you're doing extensive renos with energy efficiency in mind, like insulating the basement or upgrading windows and HVAC, you may qualify for municipal, provincial and federal tax breaks.

How it works:

First, you need to complete a home energy audit—a test that will tell you how energy-efficient your home is (or isn't) and then provide a list of upgrades. The audit can cost anywhere from $100 to $800, depending on your city, your home and the company you use. Once you've completed and paid for these improvements, you can submit receipts and paperwork to various rebate programs. It may take up to a year for the money to come in, but if you had to make upgrades anyway, it's nice to get a little cash back for them.

#3: Reverse Mortgage

A reverse mortgage provides you with either a lump sum or a larger up-front amount followed by regular cash payments paid out on a schedule you choose, like weekly or monthly.

In total, the reverse mortgage can be valued at up to 55% of the market value of your home. You'll be charged monthly interest on the amount borrowed. But unlike a traditional mortgage or HELOC, you don't have to make any payments—neither interest nor principal—until you sell the house or die. As long as you comply with the terms of your mortgage, there is no risk of losing your home, and the lender guarantees you will never owe more than the property is worth.

Who Can Get a Reverse Mortgage?

Canadians who are at least 55 years of age are eligible to take out a reverse mortgage on their primary residence.[25]

---

25 https://www.canada.ca/en/financial-consumer-agency/services/mortgages/reverse-mortgages.html#toc2.

Although there are no income requirements to qualify for a reverse mortgage, you must have a minimum of 45% equity in your home.

Snowbirds take note: you must live in your home for at least six months of the year to qualify for a reverse mortgage.

Interest rates are higher for these mortgages. Full loan repayment is due only if you move out, sell or the last borrower dies.

Difference Between a Reverse Mortgage and a Home Equity Loan

In an ideal world, homeowners would proactively apply for a HELOC, even if they don't think they'll need to borrow any money. (This assumes you won't use your home as a bank machine, buying on the line of credit and adding debt to your liabilities list.) The HELOC can act as a type of insurance—giving you access to relatively cheap funds quickly, should you need them.

But not everyone can qualify for a HELOC and it can become particularly hard when you no longer have an income coming in. This is when a reverse mortgage may be a better option.

The qualifications for getting a reverse mortgage aren't as stringent and you don't have to worry about making payments to pay back the loan since the house is collateral and your estate will use it to pay down the debt once you pass away.

SUM IT UP

Many affluent or knowledgeable investors already consider the use of leverage and credit as a wealth management tool—a tool that can help them take full advantage of wealth accumulation opportunities as they arise.

The good news is, there is no one-size-fits-all solution when it comes to effectively integrating the use of debt and credit into the wealth management plan. Better still, the role of credit can evolve—used initially to start an asset accumulation strategy and eventually to grow the value and quantity of those assets.

The ultimate benefit of leverage is that it allows you to build wealth using OPM. It's why those with plenty of money in the bank still choose to carry a mortgage and it's how many of us first start acquiring assets (by borrowing money to buy our first home).

Another significant benefit of using credit is that the use of leverage can boost your effective returns. Although it's true that leverage can magnify your return both on the upside and the downside—meaning you risk magnifying your losses as well as increasing your gains—the potential to boost your returns can really help to build wealth much faster.

Using credit to grow your personal net worth opens up strategies that enable you to take a non-deductible cost and create a tax deduction. This is key when prioritizing wealth accumulation, since taxes eat up 42.5% of our earnings, according to a 2017 Fraser Institute report. (The report was based on an average family with an income of about $83,000 who paid roughly $35,000 in federal, provincial and local taxes.)

Since most of the money we make is earned or used in ways that are not tax efficient, finding and using more tax-efficient strategies can really help.

Whether you are starting out as a first-home buyer or building on a strong foundation as a high-net-worth investor, over time credit can play a foundational role in both wealth creation and protection. Leverage allows you to build more wealth than you could ever achieve alone by utilizing resources that extend beyond your own. It allows you to grow wealth without being restricted by your personal limitations. Leverage is the principle that separates those who successfully attain wealth from those who don't.

TAKEAWAYS

Saving Is Smart. Assuming a Home Is a De Facto Retirement Fund Is Stupid. Buying a home doesn't exempt you from the need to save for retirement, a child's education or anything else. But your home *can* be used as part of a plan to save and invest. Include your home—both the debt you owe and the equity you've built up—as part of your saving and spending plans.

Don't Lead with Your Emotions. Heed Your Emotions. Buying or selling based on fear—either fear of missing out or fear of worst-case scenario—is never good. You might luck out and have it work out, but it's a gamble. This doesn't mean you should dismiss your emotional needs. Even though paying off your mortgage isn't always the optimal use of your hard-earned money, the peace of mind that comes with eliminating debt is huge. The key is to act objectively according to your plan, which was created based on your personal, emotional needs.

Celebrate Small Wins, but Don't Get Stuck at the Party. Paying off a mortgage isn't a goal—it's a milestone towards wealth-building and financial independence. Growing your investments isn't a goal—it's a milestone towards wealth-building and financial independence. Celebrate your small wins, but don't stop at a milestone. Keep forging ahead towards your ultimate goal (however that may look).

Earnings + Leverage Helps You Build More Wealth. Most of us won't get wealthy trading time for money (aka working). Leverage enables you to cut the time, cost and effort necessary to reach your personal and financial milestones. Leverage magnifies your efforts—or your potential losses. Although it's not difficult to master, the key is learning how to use it based on your needs, goals and risk tolerance.

Heed the Three Rules of Debt. #1: Debt is different for everyone in every situation. #2: Debt is a tool, not a way of life. #3: Only take on debt if it's part of the plan.

Borrow to Invest. Pay Cash for Lifestyle Purchases. The interest paid on money borrowed to invest is tax deductible. The money borrowed to purchase a fun experience or toy is not. Focus on borrowing for investment purposes, and use savings for personal purchases.

Home Equity Is a Tool. Use It. For many homeowners, most of their net worth is in their home. From a diversification point of view, this sucks. Leverage this equity by borrowing and investing in equities and fixed income to help diversify your overall portfolio.

Effective Wealth-Building Uses the Entire Earning-Saving-Spending Life Cycle. To build wealth, you need to maximize the use of each dollar earned and invested. In general, the order of priority means paying off all expensive, non-deductible debt (i.e., credit card balances and personal loans) first, then tackle less-expensive non-deductible debt (such as a mortgage loan). Use investment dollars to start building a portfolio in tax-sheltered accounts with a focus on capital gains for long-term growth and Canadian dividends for income. At all times, try to maximize the tax efficiency of every dollar earned and invested. Do this, and you'll be maximizing how effective each available dollar is used in your earn, spend and save life cycle.

7

MITIGATING RISK WITH HOME INSURANCE

WANT TO PROTECT YOUR CASTLE AND YOUR NEST EGG? HERE'S A PRIMER ON HOME INSURANCE WITH OPTIONS AND TIPS TO HELP SAVE YOU MONEY

An integral part of a financial plan is capitalizing on the upside while protecting the downside. In other words, hope for the best, but plan for the worst. In the financial world, this is known as risk mitigation, and it refers to actions an individual or group can take to understand potential risks and prepare ways to reduce exposure to those risks.

As a breadwinner and bill payer, one way to reduce the risk of not being able to pay bills is to get coverage for disability or critical illness. This insurance kicks in if you end up facing an injury or illness that prevents you from being able to work, earn an income and pay bills.

Other ways to protect yourself and your loved ones are through life insurance, which guards those you love against financial hardships in the event of your death, as well as extended health care coverage, vehicle insurance and homeowner's or renter's insurance.

As a homeowner, a good insurance policy should help mitigate the risk of severe financial loss in the event something happens to your home or belongings. It's important to find a good homeowner insurance policy from a reliable provider to ensure you're able to maintain the investment in your home and the things you and your family own.

WHY YOU NEED HOMEOWNER INSURANCE

Loss is unavoidable. It comes in the form of theft, damage, taxes and even death. What is avoidable are the catastrophic consequences of loss. As the Financial Consumer Agency of Canada explains, you need home insurance as it "may help protect your home and its contents in case of theft, loss or damage to the inside and outside of your home or property. It may also help you cover additional living expenses if you're temporarily unable to live in your home."[26]

It doesn't sound all that impending until you come face-to-face with this sort of devastating loss. Just as the residents of Fort McMurray did when their city was ravaged by wildfires in 2016, causing $4 billion in damage. Or the homeowners in Calgary who had to clean up after severe flooding in 2013 caused $3.5 billion in damage. Or the Quebec residents who, in 1998, faced frigid temperatures and severe damage to homes when an ice storm prompted $2.2 billion in residential home damage. Needless to

---

26 "Home insurance," Financial Consumer Agency of Canada, last modified March 28, 2018, https://www.canada.ca/en/financial-consumer-agency/services/insurance/home.html.

say, every single resident who lived through these catastrophic and life-changing events would tell you, home insurance didn't take away the devastation and destruction, but it certainly reduced the financial loss and the emotional stress of that loss.

Even if you don't want home insurance, it turns out most home-owners don't have a choice. Virtually all mortgage lenders will require you to get and pay for an active home insurance policy when you buy a home. It's the lender's way of protecting the asset—your home—that is being used as collateral on the money you borrowed.

HOW MUCH INSURANCE COVERAGE DO YOU NEED?

Quite often, the first question homeowners ask is, how much home insurance should I get?

Turns out, the answer to this question is simple: just enough.

Getting to the details of that answer, however, is not so simple.

For most homeowners, the dilemma is understanding if the terms, coverage and policy premium offered will be sufficient. To make an educated assessment, you first need to understand a few basics about home insurance.

First, don't confuse the value of your policy with the market value of your home, which includes the land your home is sitting on.

Your policy only needs to provide you with the funds to *rebuild or repair* your home—not replace the land. (Of course, there are circumstances, such as earthquakes, where land is also damaged, but for now, let's keep it simple.)

At one point in time, insurance appraisers would drive out and visually inspect your home to determine the rebuild value of your property. These days, the same process is required, but most of it is now digitized or developed using complex statistical equations. Regardless of the method, every insurance provider will calculate the cost to rebuild your current home, based on current building practices, and use it as a base cost for your policy coverage. For example, if you live in an urban city in a detached single-storey home that was renovated and updated in 2015, the replacement value of that home could be between $750,000 and $1 million, while the market value—what you could sell the home for—could be closer to $1.1 to $1.2 million.

Once a rebuild value is established, an insurance provider will decide to offer either guaranteed replacement cost (GRC) coverage or total coverage. GRC means that if the provider's calculations are wrong and it costs more to rebuild your house, the insurance company is on the hook to pay the total rebuild cost. In other words, the provider assumes responsibility if they miscalculate the cost to rebuild your home. The other type, total coverage, will cap repair and rebuild costs to the total policy coverage amount, say $500,000 or $1.5 million.

Although GRC always feels like the safer bet (who doesn't want insurance on your insurance?), it's not always an option. Some providers no longer offer this coverage, some providers only offer it in certain markets or on certain property types, and some providers offer it but at a higher premium, meaning you'll pay more for the assurance offered in a GRC policy than for a total coverage policy.

Although a lower replacement cost means lower premiums, don't be tempted to push for an unrealistically low figure. This is particularly true since underinsuring, if deliberate, can void your policy. The key is to assess the coverage offered based on the costs, and to determine if you will be protected from a total catastrophic loss.

HOW TO ESTIMATE THE VALUE OF YOUR BELONGINGS

Unless you have a basic or no-frills policy, most insurance policies cover both your house and belongings. Known as "contents coverage," this portion of the contract covers the theft or damage of clothes, electronics, appliances, furniture and other possessions. Older policies usually cap the amount you can claim for contents to about 70% to 80% of your home's replacement cost. Some newer policies don't differentiate between costs to replace or repair your home and belongings, as long as the entire claim cost does not go above the policy coverage limit. So if you're insured for $1 million and your home rebuild costs $600,000, you would have up to $400,000 to replace your belongings.

What you need to pay attention to is the way your insurance policy calculates the cost of repairing or replacing your belongings. For instance, if your policy uses **actual cash value calculations**, as older policies do, you can claim the value of those items in cash *minus* any depreciation. If your policy uses **replacement value calculations**, you replace your belongings with equivalent items yourself and submit the receipts for reimbursements. No matter what type of calculation is used, most policies include "special limits" that cap your losses for particular items or types of items, including collectables, jewellery, art and sports equipment.

FACTORS THAT IMPACT HOME INSURANCE

When you're ready to purchase insurance, shop around for rates or make a claim, it's helpful to know what impacts your rates. There are three general categories: building and construction, geographic location and particular insurance needs. The following is a sample list of factors that have a high impact on your home insurance rates. For a full list, please go online to www.zolo.ca/house-poor-no-more.

1. Building and Construction

ELECTRICAL (IMPACT ON RATE: HIGH)

High extra cost: Knob and tube wiring is now considered very dangerous. It's still found in homes built before 1950 (sometimes later). Some insurance companies will add a big surcharge to your policy, while other companies will refuse to insure your home.

Mid-extra cost: Aluminium wiring was used in homes built in the '60s and '70s. Although safer than knob and tube, it's been known to overheat if not installed or connected properly.

Lower cost: Copper wiring is the best because it's stable.

PIPES AND PLUMBING (IMPACT ON RATE: HIGH)

High extra cost: Galvanized or lead pipes were used in homes built before 1960. They pose a health hazard and corrosion can lead to build-up that impacts water pressure.

Mid-extra cost: Kitec (or Poly-B) was used in some new builds after 1970—these plastic flexible pipes are prone to failure.

Lower cost: Copper/PEX/PVC/PB or other plastics are considered superior to other pipe material, as each withstands temperature fluctuations and are resistant to leaching.

Mitigating Risk with Home Insurance

AGE AND RENOVATIONS (IMPACT ON RATE: HIGH)

High extra cost: Older homes with little to no upgrades will have higher insurance premiums, as there's typically a higher chance of accidents and damage due to deteriorating infrastructure.

Mid-extra cost: Older homes with some upgrades and renovations will have additional costs, but not as much since there is less chance of failure on the upgraded systems.

Lower cost: New homes have the lowest premium, as all housing components are at the start of their useful life expectancy and because the home was built using modern construction standards.

STOVE (IMPACT ON RATE: HIGH)

High extra cost: Homes that use wood stoves can prompt higher rates, as there is a higher risk of fire and these units can lead to monoxide poisoning. To keep your insurance, your provider may require annual or biannual qualified inspections.

Mid-extra cost: Gas stoves may prompt higher rates. Some providers will require proof of proper installation or inspection.

Lower cost: No stove or electric stoves offer the lowest rate since there is little to no risk of fire originating from the stove.

HEATING (IMPACT ON RATE: HIGH)

High extra cost: Oil-heated homes are more expensive to insure since there is a higher risk of environmental damage (which is expensive to remedy). The age and condition of the tank will factor into how much higher the premium will be.

Mid-extra cost: Gas-fueled, fixed-space heaters pose significant fire and health risks, particularly monoxide poisoning.

Lower cost: Electric heat or forced-air gas furnaces are widely used options and offer the lowest premiums.

2. Geographic Location

LOCATION (IMPACT ON RATE: HIGH)

High extra cost: If you're a homeowner in BC, AB, SK or MB, expect higher rates. In BC, there is a history of earthquakes and wildfires. In AB, SK and MB, there is a history of flooding, windstorms, and hailstorms, all of which carry hefty claim costs.

Mid-extra cost: If you're a homeowner in ON, expect higher rates due to a history of severe flooding, windstorms, and hailstorms. If you're a homeowner in QC, your rates will be higher due to ice storms and earthquakes.

Lower cost: Homeowners in Atlantic provinces have lower rates, despite some extreme weather.

NEIGHBOURHOOD (IMPACT ON RATE: HIGH)

High extra cost: If you live in a neighbourhood with a high crime rate or a high rate of break-ins, then expect higher insurance rates.

Mid-extra costs: If you live in a neighbourhood with a low crime rate and a history of occasional break-ins, you can expect a moderate rate increase.

Lower cost: Safe neighbourhoods with a very low crime rate and limited to no personal property crimes will have the best rates.

3. Particular Insurance Needs

PROPERTY TYPE AND COVERAGE (IMPACT ON RATE: HIGH)

High extra cost: If you own a house, your rates will be higher, since the policy (and provider) must take into consideration the house and the contents, any detached buildings (such as garages and sheds), all fences and landscaping, and additional items, such as a pool.

Mid-extra cost: If you're a condo owner, you'll pay a bit more for your insurance protection, as you need to cover the loss or damage of all your contents, as well as financial damage due to condo assessments, unit improvements, and potential litigation.

Lower cost: Tenants pay the lowest rates, as their insurance covers only contents.

DIFFERENT TYPES OF HOME INSURANCE

For most homeowners, the best type of insurance to purchase is a comprehensive policy, which covers loss and damage to the house and its contents. However, not all policies are created equal, and all homeowners should research their options when choosing the right policy.

Generally speaking, there are three types of home insurance coverage:

Basic or named perils: This is the cheapest coverage. Basic coverage typically protects only the building and not the contents. Named perils will cover your home and belongings for specific threats that are listed (called "named perils"). For instance, if it doesn't specifically say in your policy that you're covered for smoke damage, then you're not. No-frills policies are a variation on basic coverage and apply to properties that don't meet an insurance company's underwriting standards. For example, you may get home insurance coverage, but any damage caused by old or faulty wiring may not be covered.

Broad: This type of policy provides comprehensive coverage on big-ticket items, such as the building, and named perils coverage on your contents.

Comprehensive: The most popular option is comprehensive coverage. It covers loss or damage on all buildings on the property and your belongings. This coverage includes all risks except those specifically listed as exclusions.

SHOULD YOU GET EXTRA HOMEOWNER INSURANCE?

Many of the risks that your policy doesn't cover are dangers that are best left uninsured, either because you can prevent the damage through maintenance or because the cost isn't worth the coverage. Still, some risks are worth mitigating by purchasing the extra coverage.

Earthquake insurance is not included in a comprehensive policy, but a homeowner in Ontario could add this rider for roughly 50 cents per $1,000 of coverage (based on 2013 rates). A home with a replacement value of $300,000 and maximum contents coverage of $200,000 would cost you an extra $200 to $500 per year in premiums if you added earthquake coverage in most parts of Canada.

A "bylaw" rider covers the repair or replacement of all structures that are no longer compliant with your city's bylaws. Add a bylaw rider if your home was built more than 20 years ago.

Perhaps the most common and important riders are sewer backup and overland flood coverage. Water damage accounts for 40% to 50% of all claim costs. This is because today's basements are no longer unfinished concrete storage areas. They're customized workout rooms, home theatres and second kitchens. Water damage claims can range from $5,000 to $50,000 or more, which is a big out-of-pocket expense for most homeowners. Keep in mind that not all basement water damage is covered by your comprehensive plan or these additional riders. Homeowners in older homes risk water seepage because of clogged weeping tiles, blocked underground drains or cracked foundations. This type of damage is not covered, as it's typically the result of a lack of home maintenance.

WAYS TO REDUCE HOME INSURANCE COSTS

Now that we have a basic understanding of the different types of insurance and coverage, let's look at how to get the right level of protection while finding ways to save.

Don't over-insure. If you think you're over-insured, shop around. Ask each provider to spell out exactly how much coverage you get and how replacement costs are calculated. I've heard from some insurance brokers that homeowners have saved as much as $1,000 per year on their policies just by comparison shopping for equivalent coverage.

An agent is a professional who works for one insurance company. An independent insurance broker works with multiple companies.

Watch the extras. Riders add more protection and coverage but with additional costs. The trick is to figure out what "extra" protection is worth paying for and which riders to skip.

For instance, it's common for homeowners with expensive jewellery to purchase extra insurance coverage. This coverage typically costs 1% to 2% of the jewellery's appraised value. So extra coverage on a $20,000 engagement ring will cost $200 to $400 per year. If this ring is lost or damaged, you'll get an equivalent ring. That's good. But that does not mean the insurance company pays out $20,000. Instead, they'll source the least expensive replacement from a wholesaler or other retailer, pay for the equivalent ring and pocket the difference. There is nothing wrong with this—you get an equivalent replacement even if the insurance provider paid less. However, it does mean that you end up paying for more coverage than you receive.

Not all riders should be avoided. For instance, sewer backup and overland flooding are two types of extra coverage that can be added to most policies. And in virtually all communities across North America, **I would classify them as mandatory** for any homeowner who wants to protect their home and their bank account from financial hardship. On average, these riders add $60 to $300 to your annual insurance premium, but if you end up making a claim, these riders will cover tens of thousands in clean-up costs and damages.

The only way to verify whether you have unnecessary riders is to talk to an insurance professional. A professional broker will know what coverage is in the market and, very often, can find overall savings or better coverage at a similar price based on your specific needs.

Pay a higher deductible. The biggest reason for choosing a higher deductible is that it can reduce your premium. If you choose a deductible of $1,000 or more, an insurance company will typically reward you with a lower-cost premium. By analyzing decades of claims statistics, insurance providers know that higher deductibles deter homeowners from making smaller, more frequent claims. Fewer claims help providers keep their costs low and prevent your coverage from being flagged or cancelled. That's because insurance is a numbers game, or more precisely, it's an industry that relies on statistics. Underwriters—the people who assess and evaluate risk—know that the average homeowner should only make an insurance claim once every 10 years. If you start to make frequent claims, even if they cost little to cover, these underwriters classify you as a statistical risk. More risk equals more cost in the insurance business. Too much risk means denied (or in this case, cancelled) coverage.

Look for discounts. Most insurers offer a 10% discount if you don't make any claims for at least three years. There are also discounts for bundling policies, new-build homes and membership affiliations. Additionally, you may qualify for added discounts based on your age, mortgage status or being a nonsmoker. Policyholders who pay annually instead of monthly also usually qualify for discounts of up to 10%.

Call your provider. By reviewing your policy on an annual basis, you can see changes, omissions or deletions. You can use these to start a conversation with your insurance company or independent broker and let them know that you'll be shopping for a better rate unless they can lower your costs. Quite often, a short call can get you a discount on your current insurance rate or better coverage for the same price.

WHEN SHOULD YOU FILE A CLAIM?

Always make a claim if faced with a catastrophic loss—and that number is different for everyone. For smaller issues, before you pick up the phone, think about how the claim will impact your premium. Making consistent small claims can drive up your premiums and result in a poor relationship with your provider. Take your deductible into account, and determine if you're able to afford repairs or replacement costs without the help of your insurer before making a claim. Also, consider any discounts you currently have. For instance, say your $1,000 bike was stolen (your belongings are covered under your home insurance, even if away from home). To make a claim, you will have to pay your $500 deductible. That means you will recover only $500 from the loss. What's more, you've now lost that 10% discount you got for making no claims within a specified period.

The rule of thumb is to only make a claim for things you can't handle yourself. So $10,000 in damage due to a sewer backup should be claimed, while a stolen camera should not. If you have a good relationship with the broker, call informally and find out how a certain claim will impact your coverage.

HOW TO TELL IF YOUR CLAIM SETTLEMENT IS FAIR

Imagine this scenario: there's a terrible windstorm and as the windows shook and the wind howled, a mature tree fell onto your roof. You call your local roofing company and receive a quote of $17,155 to remove the tree and repair the damages to your home. You call your insurance company and file a claim, but your provider offers you only $11,145—far less than the cost of the repairs.

Does this mean your insurance company is shortchanging you? Not necessarily.

First and foremost, it's important to understand that your insurance policy doesn't include coverage for HST or GST (depending on your province or territory). In the above scenario, $1,974 of your repair costs are for taxes and are your responsibility.

Additionally, you need to determine if your insurance company calculated your claim based on actual cash value or replacement cost. If your policy calculates the actual cash value, that's based on the depreciated value of your roof, meaning that the age of your roof and its life expectancy can reduce your settlement. In the above scenario, if your roof had depreciated by 20%, you would need to reduce the total repair cost (less taxes) by 20%, which leaves you with a sum just below $12,145. Deduct the

$1,000 deductible and you're left with a total cash settlement of $11,145. In this case, your settlement is fair.

If you don't want to be on the hook for added costs, search for a policy that calculates claims based on replacement costs so that you're responsible for paying only your deductible.

CAN YOU LOSE YOUR HOME INSURANCE COVERAGE?

Even though the prospect is frightening, it is possible to void your insurance policy. Watch out for these exclusions that can render your coverage void.

Vacancy. One major reason for the non-payment of claims is vacancy exclusion, which is found in most policies. This exclusion states that if you vacate your home for a specified period (usually listed as consecutive days, but it can be as short as 48 hours), your home insurance is no longer valid, and any loss resulting from an insurable event will not be covered.

Co-insurance. Co-insurance occurs when a home's insurance policy covers up to a specific, declared value, but the damage is greater. Although it may make mathematical sense that you'd be responsible for the extra costs, homeowners are often caught off guard when they find out that the co-insurance clause applies to the entire loss. Although co-insurance is becoming relatively unpopular, check your policy, particularly if you began your coverage over two decades ago. Co-insurance must be listed in bold red lettering on the front page of the policy or the spine of the policy.

Home renovation. Although coverage is usually determined on a case-by-case basis, most insurance providers can deny your claim if your home was or has been renovated and they didn't know about it. Most providers require prior notification of any renovation, even including minor upgrades, like swapping out old laminate kitchen counters for granite countertops.

Running an undeclared home-based business. If you've started a home-based business and you haven't let your insurance provider know, there's a chance your claim may be denied. Inform your provider of any business you conduct at home and alert them to any inventory or assets you store on the property.

SUM IT UP

The best way to save money is to avoid being over-insured—that is, paying more in premiums than you'd receive making a claim. On the other hand, the best way to avoid unexpected losses is to avoid being under-insured or not having adequate coverage for the risks you face. To avoid cancellations to your coverage or denied claims, be honest and up front with your insurance provider, and do your research before making a claim.

If you're a typical homeowner, you'll need to shop around and read your policy at least once a year. It may not be exciting, but to get through it, reward yourself with a glass of single malt, a bottle of Prosecco or a fabulous night on the town. Consider it a well-deserved treat after all that dry reading!

TAKEAWAYS

Insurance Protects Wealth. It Doesn't Build Wealth. Insurance won't help you earn or save, but it will protect your assets. Without adequate home insurance coverage, any loss or damage to your property and belongings could decimate your savings or push you deep into debt.

Don't Over-pay. Don't Under-insure. Assess your risks and coverage needs and only pay for insurance that will cover major losses. Although not as price-competitive as auto insurance, you can still save hundreds or thousands in premium costs by shopping around for home insurance coverage every few years.

Little White Lies Can Cost You Big. Fail to mention to your insurance provider about a material change in your home or how it's used—such as renting out a room on Airbnb, starting a home-based business or renovating your home—and run the risk of voiding your entire homeowner coverage.

8

SAVING ON TAXES WITH YOUR HOME

UNDERSTAND PROPERTY SALES, TAX RATES AND STRATEGIES TO AVOID OR MINIMIZE CAPITAL GAINS TAX

Owning a home in Canada can be very expensive and very rewarding at the same time. Unlike US homeowners, Canadians can't claim costs associated with our principal residence as tax-deductible expenses. However, that doesn't mean Canadian homeowners can't save at tax time.

As a homeowner, there are various ways to save on taxes, but to get the maximum tax deductions you are legally allowed, it's best if we go through a few basics first.

UNDERSTANDING HOW PROPERTY IS TAXED

All property—including your home, cottage, rental units, even stock portfolios—may increase in value over time. This appreciation in the value of an asset is known as a capital gain.

In the eyes of the tax authorities, a capital gain is subject to tax—the tax is known as capital gains tax. (Clever, eh?)

As of 2016, the Canadian federal government now requires every owner to report the sale of the property on their tax return, even if they don't end up owing tax on the sale. Failure to report the sale, whether intentionally or unintentionally, brings the risk of an audit, penalties and interest charges, and it could prompt you to lose important tax exemptions.

HOW TO CALCULATE CAPITAL GAINS TAX

In Canada, profit on real assets, such as property, will trigger capital gains tax. (The property is the capital, while the increase in value from the purchase price to the sale price is the capital gain.)

Unlike ordinary income tax, which accumulates and is owed every year, capital gains tax is only triggered with the sale (or change of use) of the real asset.

As a result, a capital gain—and the tax it triggers—can be an afterthought, making it an unexpected situation you have to deal with when you sell your home, a vacation property or any stocks or shares. It's also why people can be so afraid of capital gains tax; you sell and earn a big profit, but just as quickly you owe a huge chunk of money to the tax authorities.

In the grand scheme of things, capital gains tax is one of the better government levies because it means you are paying tax on only half your profit, at your current marginal tax rate.

Saving on Taxes with Your Home

Capital Gains Tax

A **taxable capital gain** is the portion of your capital gain that you have to report as income on your income tax and benefit return.

What is capital gains tax?

Capital gains tax is the term used for the tax owed on the profitable sale of a capital asset.

A capital asset is a tangible piece of property with a useful life that lasts longer than a year.

This can include stock investments, a business or a property, as well as art or collectibles.

The value of capital assets can either appreciate or depreciate and, as a result, **can trigger owed tax or a potential tax deduction.**

How is capital gains tax calculated?

Capital gain

Selling Price
- Original Price
+ Costs/Fees

 X

50%

Only half
of capital gain
is taxed

 =

**Amount of capital gains
that is taxed**

by your marginal tax rate

When is capital gains tax owed?

Capital gains tax is due when you sell your asset or when you change the use of that asset.

For example, you won't owe tax while stock gains value inside your portfolio. However, once you sell your shares, the profit must be reported on your tax return.

For example, if you own and live in a home but then buy another and turn the original home into a rental property, you will owe capital gains tax as of the date the use of the property changed, but you don't have to pay that tax until you sell the rental property.

For example, if you sell your principle residence for a profit then capital gains tax is owed, but you do not have to pay this tax because of the Principle Residence Exemption (PPE) rule.

How Each Type of Income is Taxed

To determine what type of investment is right for you,
consider how much cash income you can receive,
based on the type of earnings and the tax rate.

To understand, let's assume you want to earn $30,000 from your investments but still stay
in the lowest possible tax bracket for the year. Based on these criteria, here is how much
cash you can receive from each investment type, plus the impact it has on your taxes:

Income Type	After-Tax Earnings	Pre-Tax Cash You Get	Tax Impact
Dividends	$22,000	$30,000	138%
Interest & Foreign Dividends	$30,000	$30,000	100%
Capital Gains	$30,000	$60,000	50%
Deferred Capital Gains (Est.)	$30,000	$120,000	25%

How to Interpret:

Dividends are "grossed-up" by 38%. Multiplying the dividend received by 1.38 means that
$30,000 of taxable income from dividends would result in $22,000 of after-tax earnings.

UNDERSTANDING TAX BRACKETS AND MARGINAL TAX RATES

To appreciate the win-win of capital gains tax, we first need to understand how tax rates are applied and how your marginal tax rate is determined.

In Canada, we have a progressive (aka graduated) tax system that uses tax brackets. This means that lower-income earners are taxed at a lower tax rate than higher-income earners. Theoretically, it means the more money you make, the more taxes you pay. It also means that the first dollar you earn will probably be taxed at a lower rate than the last dollar you earn in a year.

Each tax rate is separated into different tax brackets; as the income earned increases, the tax rate also increases. (The provincial and federal governments also update the income brackets each year to account for inflation.)

To determine how much tax you owe, you first need to consider how much of your annual income and earnings fall into each tax bracket.

To illustrate, let's consider the 2021 federal income tax brackets:

TAX BRACKET	TAXABLE INCOME	TAX RATE
1	First $49,020	15%
2	Between $49,020 and $98,040	20.5%
3	Between $98,040 and $151,978	26%
4	Between $151,978 and $216,511	29.32%
5	Over $216,511	33%

Based on these tax brackets, you would pay 15% tax on the first $49,020 that you earn in a year, 20.5% tax on any income or earnings from there up to $98,040, 26% tax on earnings up to $151,978, and so on.

Since we all pay tax based on a graduated tax system, our total tax ends up being based on our average tax rate. To calculate your average tax rate, divide your total taxes paid in a year by your total taxable income.

Don't confuse your average tax rate with your marginal tax rate, which is the amount of tax you owe on your next dollar of income (or earnings).

For example, if you earned $95,000 last year, the federal portion of the taxes you owe would be 15% on the first $49,020 you earned, then 20.5% on the income earned between $49,021 and $95,000. Now, if you earned an additional $10,000 last year, the first $3,040 would be taxed at your marginal tax rate of 20.5%. Once you reach the income threshold of that tax bracket, your marginal tax rate—the amount of tax owed on the next dollar you earn—increases. In this example, that means you'd end up paying 26% federal income tax on the remaining portion of that extra $10,000 earned.

The term "marginal tax rate" refers to the tax you will owe on the next dollar you earn. You can determine your marginal tax rate by looking up federal and provincial tax bracket rates. The term "average tax rate" is the average rate of tax you pay based on the total amount of taxes you paid divided by your total taxable income. For example, if you earned $10,000 and paid $1,000 in taxes, your average tax rate would be 10%.

CAPITAL GAINS TAX ON PROPERTY SALE

The steps to calculate capital gains tax using your marginal tax rate are as follows:

1. Sale price – (purchase price + adjustment costs) = capital gain

2. Capital gain x 50% = taxable earnings

3. Taxable earnings x marginal tax rate = capital gains tax owed

To illustrate, let's assume your earnings put you in the 33% tax bracket and you decide to sell an investment condo for a total profit of $50,000. On your next tax return, you would report the sale of this condo and end up owing $8,250 of tax on the condo profit. The calculation to determine the capital gains tax owed is as follows:

1. $50,000 x 50% = $25,000

2. $25,000 x 33% = $8,250

If you had earned that $50,000 as income (or as interest), you would owe tax on 100% of those earnings at your marginal tax rate. This reduced tax burden is one reason why investors prefer assets with capital gains rather than other forms of earnings.

But what if I told you there was a way to avoid paying any capital gains tax?

WHY A HOME IS THE OPTIMAL TAX SHELTER

When you sell your principal residence, you owe $0 tax. That's right. You don't need to pay even a dime in taxes if you sell your family home. That's because the CRA provides Canadian home-owners with an exemption from taxes owed on the profit made from the sale of their primary residence.

What Is the Principal Residence Exemption?

The principal residence exemption (PRE) is an income tax benefit that exempts you from paying capital gains tax on the profit of the sale of your principal residence—your home. Generally, the exemption applies for each year the property is designated as your principal residence.

This exemption isn't reserved for just one home or just once in your lifetime. You can designate any residential property owned and occupied by you or your family at any time in a given year as a principal residence. It's the *designation* of a property that is important, as it allows you to shelter the profits earned on the sale of that home from capital gains taxes.

As you would expect, there are legal requirements to qualify for this exemption, and the CRA is **very clear** about these.

Under the Income Tax Act, to designate a property as a principal residence, you must follow these seven PRE rules:

1. A principal residence is generally any residential property owned and occupied by you or your family. This can include a house, townhouse, condominium, cottage, mobile home, trailer or even a live-aboard boat.

2. A family unit can designate only one property per year as a principal residence. A family unit is you, your spouse (or common-law partner) and any children under the age of 18. (Keep in mind that the CRA does apply the plus-one rule; this means that if you sell a home in one year and

buy your next home in that same year, you will not have to pay capital gains tax on either property.)

3. You and your family must "ordinarily inhabit" the dwelling during the year. Despite what's been written to the contrary, the CRA has never specified that a property must be lived in for a certain amount of time to qualify as an "ordinarily inhabited" home. Instead, the CRA will look at all evidence—including the length of time in the dwelling, primary income sources, where you spend your time, as well as patterns of buying, living, moving and selling—to determine if the designation made is factual.

4. You don't need to physically dispose of (or sell) a property to trigger a capital gain. You can change the use of a property—from a family home to rental property—and that will change both the designation of the property and the exemption status.

5. To qualify for the principal residence exemption, the property's primary use cannot be to earn income. So if you own a six-plex and live in one unit, and you sell that property for a profit, you cannot shelter the entire profit using the principal residence exemption. Check with an accountant that specializes in property to determine your best options.

6. The PRE exemption is limited to a dwelling and no more than one-half hectare (or 1.2 acres) of land. That means if you live in a home located on 10 acres of land and sell this property for a profit, you would be exempt from paying tax on 1.2 acres of the land but would need to pay capital gains tax on the remaining 8.8 acres. You can get an exemption for property that is larger than 1.2 acres,

but you will have to prove to the CRA that additional land is required for your use and enjoyment of the property. (Not as easy as you think!)

1. The property you claim as your principal residence does not have to be located in Canada.

HOW TO AVOID OR MINIMIZE CAPITAL GAINS TAX

For most Canadians, the requirement to report the sale of a principal residence is nothing more than a compliance exercise. It's your home. You sell it. You owe no tax.

But what if your situation isn't that simple? What if you and your family own more than two properties? Or what if you are on the deed to your parent's home? What if you rent out a room or a suite in your house? Or you've moved in and out of a home that you also rented out for a period of time?

Life is messy, and the confusion around when capital gains tax is owed and what qualifies for the exemption only makes the application of tax law to real-life scenarios that much more complicated.

To help, here are nine general strategies to legally avoid or minimize capital gains tax.

#1: Buy, Own and Live in Your Own Home

As outlined, all the profit earned on the sale of your principal residence is tax-free, making this one of the most powerful tools in your wealth accumulation strategy.

#2: Maximize Exemption Years

If you own more than one property and both have gone up in value over the years, it's possible to shelter more of your profit by maximizing which years each property was used as a principal residence.

Let's look at a simplified example. Say you bought a home in the city for $250,000 where you lived full time. You also bought a cottage about two hours away for $200,000 to use year-round. The city home appreciates and is now worth $650,000; the cottage also appreciates and is now worth $725,000. Sell both properties without any strategy in place, and you would end up paying capital gains tax on the cottage—the property with the largest appreciation in value. This is standard practice and would mean you sheltered the $400,000 profit from the sale of your home from tax (saving you $66,000 in tax, assuming a 33% tax bracket).

However, if you were to designate your cottage as your principal residence, the full $525,000 in profit would be exempt from tax and this would save you from paying $86,625 in tax. Already, you'd be putting more than $20,000 in your pocket by changing your principal residence designation.

You could go one step further and divide the PRE designation between the two properties, but you would need to confirm that property was used only by you and your family during those years, that no claims were made on tax returns that would exclude one or both properties from being classified as a principal residence, and that the properties were not income-producing during the designated principal residence years. Consult an accountant or tax specialist before selling or changing the use of a property to make sure you can effectively shelter current or future capital gains from tax.

#3: Keep Receipts and Claim Deductions

Keeping receipts and invoices is not integral for homeowners who don't claim house-related tax deductions, such as a home-based business; however, if you do earn income and intend to claim deductions, it's important to keep receipts and invoices.

The CRA may ask you to provide proof of expenses (i.e., receipts and invoices) should they do a spot-check review or a full-blown audit. You may also want to use the expenses to save on taxes owed by increasing your adjusted cost base (ACB).

What Is Adjusted Cost Base?

Adjusted cost base (ACB) is an income tax term that refers to the change in an asset's book value—the original purchase cost—to an updated market value, based on improvements, new purchases or other factors. The ACB is important as it increases the purchase price used to calculate capital gains. For instance, if a landlord purchased a single-family home for $500,000 and spent $100,000 creating two apartments, the ACB of the rental property would be $600,000. When the landlord sells the rental property, they can use the ACB cost, not the original purchase price, to determine the capital gains owed.

#4: Keep Records When Changing the Use of a Property

For homeowners who turn their old home into a rental property, it's important to establish the fair market value of the property at the time the use of the property changed. That's because the home's change in use is a "deemed disposition"—what the CRA considers as the equivalent of a property sale. The fair market value becomes the new "purchase price" and will be used to calculate capital gains when the property is sold or changes use again.

The easiest way to get an on-the-record, fair market value for your property, that is objectively accurate, is to pay for an accredited appraisal report and then keep it on file. This report will cost roughly $150 to $600, depending on the property location and circumstances. Another, cheaper option (but potentially not as accurate) is to ask a local real estate agent for a comparative market analysis, a report that looks at comparable property sales in the neighbourhood and estimates the value of your home based on this comparison.

#5: Gift the Property and Delay Taxes

Canada has no gift tax; however, if you gift property to a family member other than your spouse (say a child or grandchild), the transfer of ownership will trigger capital gains tax.

However, there is one way to delay the payment of that tax. If you transfer property to a family member who is under 18 years of age, the income earned from that property will be attributed back to you, but capital gains (or allowable capital losses) on the subsequent sale of that property are not attributable to you.

As a result, tax specialists will often suggest to clients with assets that are expected to increase substantially in value (such as shares in a corporation, jewellery, art or property) to consider transferring them to an under-age child or family member (such as niece or nephew) or creating a trust that holds the assets with your child as the beneficiary.

In all cases, the owed tax can be delayed and deferred until the property is sold, but for specific advice, always talk to a tax specialist.

#6: Be Strategic About Timing Property Sales

If you do sell a property that is not exempt from capital gains tax, you'll want to be strategic about when you sell since the amount of tax you pay is based on your marginal tax rate.

For instance, if you lived in Ontario and sold property during a high-income earning year, you could end up paying 24.14% of the property sale profit in tax (half your marginal tax rate). Wait until you retire, and you could drop the tax rate charged on the property sale profit to 14.83%.

The general rule of thumb is to time property sales that trigger capital gains taxes in lower-income years.

This doesn't mean you have to wait until retirement. Lower-income years can include sabbatical years (assuming you collect only half your pay), the year you take parental leave, a year when you experience unemployment (chosen or otherwise), or a year when you earn less than anticipated for other reasons.

#7: Amortize the Sale of Property

There are times when it makes sense to structure the sale of a property over a four- or five-year term.

As the seller, this means working out an arrangement with the buyer to receive a portion of the sale funds over a four- to five-year term. By doing this, you eliminate the big one-year earnings that typically occur with a property sale (and typically push sellers into higher marginal tax rates). Instead, you receive a portion of the agreed-upon sale amount each year for four or five years.

Although there are risks involved—such as the buyer defaulting on payments—the big advantage is that you would smooth out the profit over five years and reduce the overall tax owed.

Be sure to talk to your tax professional and legal representative before adopting this strategy.

#8: Plan Ahead to Pay the Taxes

In the event of death, the sale of a property or another major asset can trigger significant capital gains taxes.

To avoid putting your heirs in a position of having to pay a large tax bill, consider planning on how your estate will cover this cost. One good option is to hold life insurance (on you or your spouse). When you pass away, the life insurance proceeds are received tax-free by your heirs, who can then use the proceeds to settle the tax bill.

#9: Turn Your Home into a Rental Property

Quite often, homeowners want to keep their current home as a rental property but move up (or downsize) to find a property that better suits their changing lifestyle.

In these situations, many homeowners assume the equity they've built up in their current home can (and should) be used to help buy their new home. It's a win-win, right? Since the mortgage is on a rental property, the interest paid on the mortgage is a tax deduction. Plus, you now have money to buy a new family home.

Unfortunately, the CRA doesn't see it quite the same. Using a rental property's mortgage money to purchase a new principal residence goes against the "current use" rules required by the tax authorities to keep the tax deductibility of that mortgage. Remember, the "current use" of the borrowed money must be to purchase, own or pay for an income-producing asset. Your new family home does not fall into this category.

This is unfortunate if you're a homeowner who wants to keep a rental property but also needs the equity in this property to buy a family home.

Thankfully, there are ways around this hurdle.

Solution #1: Set Up a Debt Conversion

As previously discussed, you can always set up a debt conversion on both the rental property and the new family home. Every dollar used to pay down the mortgage debt becomes a tax-deductible dollar you can borrow to invest.

By doing this, your cash flow—the money you earn—can be used to pay for the non-deductible mortgage on the rental property and the non-deductible mortgage on your principal residence. Now both mortgages offer you a chance to re-borrow the principal paid on the loans that are then used to invest in income-producing assets. The interest on the borrowed funds is tax deductible, and this setup allows you to pay both mortgage debts *and* still find funds to invest in your future.

Solution #2: Use a Cash-Damming Strategy

Another option is to use cash-damming. This strategy allows you to convert your personal (non-deductible) debt into tax-deductible debt to create tax savings.

The process is to use the income from your rental property to pay the non-deductible principal residence mortgage. Then re-borrow the principal to pay for the rental property costs (including mortgage, maintenance, etc.). Since the re-borrowed funds are being used to pay for an income-producing asset, the interest on those borrowed funds is now a tax deduction. In this way, you've swapped a non-deductible debt for a tax-deductible debt.

Although cash-damming using two separate bank accounts allows you to trace the use of your borrowed money more readily, it is not mandatory.

Solution #3: Use a Promissory Note

There is one final option for turning your former home into a rental property and still accessing the equity to pay for your new home. However, to complete this strategy, you do need to rely on a trustworthy family member (or friend).

This is how it works:

Day #1: Sell your current home to a family member at fair market value.

Rather than take out a loan, ask your family member to pay for the purchase by issuing a promissory note.

To stay on the right side of the tax authorities, make sure each portion of this step is properly documented and legally authorized—i.e., get the promissory note notarized.

Day #2: Reacquire your home from your family member.

Now repurchase your home from your family member. Do this by getting a mortgage on the home.

Give the family member the money you obtained from this mortgage. Don't forget to legally document this transaction. (Use a Purchase and Sale agreement, work with a legal representative, etc.)

Day #3: Your family member pays off that promissory note.

This is when your family member uses the money that was given to them—the money from the mortgage you obtained—and pays the money promised to you in the promissory note.

Day #4: Purchase your new principal residence.

Take the money you've obtained from the repayment of the promissory note and use it as a down payment (or a cash purchase) for your new principal residence.

Because the mortgage you obtained on Day #2 was for the purchase of a rental property, the interest on the mortgage is tax deductible (and used to offset the rental income collected and reported).

The result: you now own a rental property using a tax-deductible mortgage, and you just purchased your new principal residence.

WHAT ARE THE TAX BENEFITS OF OWNING A HOME?

Not paying tax on the profit earned when you sell your home is one advantage of owning property, but this benefit can seem like a lifetime away.

The good news is that tax deductions and credits can also help property owners save money at tax time. Tax credits are the more favourable of the two. Here's why.

Differences Between Tax Credits and Tax Deductions

Tax deductions, or tax write-offs, are deductions you can make on your tax returns to reduce your overall taxable income. Remember, when you reduce your taxable income, you reduce the amount of tax you owe, since less income is taxed at a lower rate.

A **tax credit** is an amount you can subtract from taxes owed. Just as the name implies, you get credit for an amount you've paid, so this amount is deducted from your tax owed.

Tax credits are considered more favourable since the credit reduces what you owe in taxes; however, the value of a tax credit depends on the type and nature of the credit.

For example, a taxpayer in the 33% tax bracket could save $0.33 for every $1 that is reduced using a tax deduction. On the other hand, a taxpayer in the 33% tax bracket would save $1 for every $1 tax credit that's applied.

Put another way, let's assume:

- You earn $60,000 in taxable income, which puts you in the 20.5% federal tax bracket (we'll omit provincial taxes, for simplicity).

- At this point, you owe $12,300 in taxes.

- However, after adding up all your deductions, you can reduce your taxable income by $10,000.

- Now you owe $10,250 in taxes, for a savings of $2,050.

- If you had $10,000 in tax credits instead, you'd have to pay only $2,300 in taxes.

In Canada, there are two basic types of tax credits: non-refundable and refundable. (The United States designates a third type as partially refundable.)

Non-refundable tax credits help reduce the tax owed to $0 but cannot be used further to create (or help boost) a tax refund. Plus, most non-refundable tax credits cannot be carried over for use in future years and often expire if not used.

The most common non-refundable tax credit is the federal personal amount—a set sum that is used to help calculate your tax credit using your marginal tax rate.

Refundable tax credits are awesome. Not only can they reduce the tax owed to $0, but they can also be used to create (or boost) a tax refund and may even be paid to you throughout the year!

For example, those who qualify for the non-taxable refundable Child Tax credit will notice a monthly sum in their bank accounts from the federal government.

By and large, a tax credit is introduced when the government is trying to incentivize taxpayers to take certain actions.

For example, the Federal Home Buyers' Tax Credit (now known as the Home Buyers' Amount) allows qualified first-time home buyers to claim up to $5,000 towards the purchase of a principal residence. The reason for offering this credit is that most North American governments believe that home-ownership is an integral part of overall financial stability and, for that reason, want to incentivize citizens to become home-owners.

Are Tax Deductions and Credits Worth It?

Yes! Finding and applying tax deductions and credits are **worth your time**.

Deductions and reductions in taxes owed help you and your family keep more of your money to spend on your goals and priorities. More money is always a good way to grow your net worth.

To be clear, though, it does take a bit of work to find and apply tax credits and deductions. More often than not, you'll need to keep a copy of the receipts you claim as expenses and invoices you paid. The good news is that the prevalence of digital receipt apps and online accounting software has made this process so much easier and cheaper. Just be sure you keep this documentation for at least six years (from the end of the last tax year you filed).

The key, now, is to know what you are entitled to.

TAX DEDUCTIONS AND CREDITS AVAILABLE TO HOMEOWNERS

Here are some of the federal and provincial tax deductions and tax credits that are directly applicable to being a homeowner.

#1: Home Buyers' Amount (formerly known as the Home Buyers' Tax Credit)

Tax Credit

An individual or couple can claim up to $5,000 (total) on the purchase of a qualifying home (a property registered in your name/spouse's name or both with the applicable land registration system and located in Canada) if both of the following apply:

1. You, your spouse or your common-law partner acquired a qualifying home;[27] and

2. You did not live in another home owned by you, your spouse or your common-law partner in the year of the acquisition or any of the four preceding years.

#2: Home Accessibility Tax Credit (HATC)

Tax Credit (non-refundable)

Claim up to $10,000 in expenses for renovations or upgrades to make a home safer or more accessible for Canadians 65 years of age or older, or for any Canadian who qualifies for the Disability Tax Credit. This credit allows the eligible user to claim 15% of the reno costs as a reduction in their taxes.

Review the expenses eligible through the non-refundable Medical Expenses Tax Credit (METC)[28] before making your HATC claim. In some circumstances, it's best to maximise METC claims first, freeing up more claim room in the HATC.[29]

----

27 https://www.canada.ca/en/revenue-agency/services/tax/individuals/topics/about-your-tax-return/tax-return/completing-a-tax-return/deductions-credits-expenses/line-31270-home-buyers-amount/qualifying-home.html.

28 https://www.canada.ca/en/revenue-agency/services/tax/technical-information/income-tax/income-tax-folios-index/series-1-individuals/folio-1-health-medical/income-tax-folio-s1-f1-c1-medical-expense-tax-credit.html.

29 https://www.canada.ca/en/revenue-agency/programs/about-canada-revenue-agency-cra/federal-government-budgets/budget-2015-strong-leadership/home-accessibility-tax-credit-hatc.html.

#3: GST/HST New Housing Rebate

Tax Credit (non-refundable)

The GST/HST new housing rebate allows you to recover some of the GST or federal portion of the HST that you've paid for a new or substantially renovated house that is for use as your, or your relations', primary place of residence.

You may be eligible for a new housing rebate if the following conditions are met:

- You have purchased a new-build home, constructed a newbuild home or substantially renovated a resale home for personal (or familial) use as a primary residence.

- You've purchased shares in a co-op complex to use a unit as your (or your family's) primary place of residence.

- The fair market value of the new-build or substantially renovated home is less than $450,000.

- The home qualifies as a "primary residence."

#4: Federal Home Buyers' Plan

Tax Benefit

The Home Buyers' Plan (HBP) allows you and your spouse or common-law partner to withdraw up to $35,000 each from your RRSP to help with the purchase or construction of a home. The withdrawal is tax-free for up to 15 years, which is a big deal given that RRSP withdrawals are taxed at your marginal rate, plus a 30% withholding fee if you make the withdrawal before retirement age.

#5: Work from Home

Tax Deductions

If you work from home—and let's face it, quite a number of us do because of pandemic restrictions—there are many expenses you can deduct. The precise list of deductions will depend on several factors like whether you are self-employed, an employee with a home office or a professional who works from home.

Home-Based Business

Typically, work-from-home deductions will include the following:

- Utilities—heating, water and electricity

- Insurance

- Mortgage interest

- Property taxes

- Maintenance and repairs

- Internet

- Office supplies

- Phone

- Cleaning supplies

- Other (you will need to describe)

The amount you can deduct for each of these expenses is based on the size of your home office. For instance, if you live in a 2,000-square-foot home and your home office is 200 square feet, then 10% of each of the above expenses can be used as a tax deduction.

However, there are circumstances where you can deduct a higher percentage on some expenses. Usually, this happens when you use the product or service more for business and less for personal purposes. Take telecommunication services, such as the internet and telephone. If you run an internet-based business, it's reasonable to consider deducting a higher percentage of your internet costs; after all, you probably use these services largely for your business. If you have a business phone line you use only for work, you can deduct 100% of the cost. The same goes for office supplies so long as you use them only for your business activities.

To qualify for any of these home-based business deductions, you need to meet the criteria as set out by the CRA:

- You must use the home-based office space as your principal place of business. That means you must spend more than 50% of your work time in that space.

- You must use the space occupied by your office or workshop almost exclusively to earn business income. In other words, if you use a corner of the dining room table in the daytime, you can't claim that space on your tax return.

- The expenses you claim cannot have been claimed elsewhere.

As a tax deduction, work-from-home expenses cannot be used to create or boost a tax refund. That means you can only claim up to the amount of income your business generates. For instance, if your home business brought in $10,000 one year but you had $15,000 in deductible expenses, you can only claim a deduction of $10,000.

The good news is that unused home-based business tax deductions do not expire and the loss can be carried forward to be used in future years.

If your home office space is used for more than just business, you will need to adjust your expenses to reflect "mixed use." In simple terms, it means finding the percentage of business use and using that to determine how much you can deduct.

For example, let's assume you operate your business from 9 a.m. to 4 p.m., five days per week. This would mean the business operates 35 out of 168 total hours in a week. Multiply your total home-business expenses by 21% (35/168) to determine your total business deductions.

Employee with an Office at Home

Now, if you work from home but you're a salaried employee or a commission paid employee, there are more restrictions for claiming your home office expenses. You can only claim a home office expense when your employer requires you to pay for it. Also, you cannot deduct a cost that your employer reimburses you for, and your employer must file the proper paperwork certifying your obligation to use part of your home as an office on **Form T2200, Declaration of Conditions of Employment**.

You'll want to make sure you keep all receipts for repairs and maintenance on your home office since 100% of these costs can be claimed as a tax-deductible cost.

Record Keeping for Business-Use-of-Home Deductions

As a taxpayer seeking a deduction, you must keep records of each business expense. You should keep receipts, invoices and documentation for any expense you plan to claim. This includes electricity bills, receipts for office supplies and invoices from your cleaning service. Do you pay rent? If so, be sure to ask your landlord for a receipt so you can prove your expenses to the CRA.

To make tax filing easier, consider tracking your expenses in a program such as QuickBooks Online. These records can help you calculate your total deductions each year. If you're audited, an organized system can help you prove your deductions to the CRA, which makes the process move faster.

How Does the CRA Verify Home Office Deductions?

When you claim deductions for your home office expenses, it's important to be accurate and truthful, particularly when it comes to the size and usage of your work area. If your kids use your office as a playroom, for example, it might be tempting to claim you use it exclusively as an office.

However, if the CRA looks through your public social media accounts and sees multiple photos of your children playing on the computer or watching TV, they may dispute your claim. They may also go through your receipts, check your income figures or even send an official to your space during an audit. If you claim exclusive business use of space on your tax return, it's a good idea to keep the entire space free of personal items.

As a small business owner, tax deductions make a great way to reduce your net income and your taxes. By tracking and deducting the expenses you pay for your home office, you can enjoy a lower tax burden when you file your annual return.

#6: Rental Income

Tax Deductions

Want to stay on the good side of the tax authorities and enjoy the benefits of being a landlord or homeowner with rental income? Then you'll need to learn how to declare your rental income and tax deductions accurately. Usually, the part that causes the most grief is knowing what is and isn't deductible.

CURRENT EXPENSES VERSUS CAPITAL EXPENSES

A current expense generally reoccurs after a short period, such as the cost of painting. A capital expense generally provides a lasting benefit, such as renovations that extend the useful life of the property or improve it beyond its original condition. These expenses are deductible but not necessarily in the year the expense was incurred. Rather, they are spread out over the anticipated life of the expense based on guidelines provided by the CRA. The annual deduction is called the Capital Cost Allowance.

Eligible Deductions for Rental Income

You can deduct any reasonable expenses incurred to earn rental income. The two basic types of expenses are current expenses and capital expenses. For homeowners with a secondary or rental suite, be very careful about using capital expenses to reduce taxes owed. Although there may be exceptions, these deductions are primarily used by owners earning a business income from property, and if you claim your home as a business, you can no longer shelter it from capital gains taxes owed.

The good news is, you don't need to claim business-related capital costs to find expenses that can be used to reduce the taxes owed on your rental income. There's plenty of options when it comes to deductions. For instance, you can claim the cost to advertise your suite, a portion of the home insurance premium, any legal or accounting fees and any cost to repair or maintain the suite, among many others (go online for a full list[30]).

---

30 "Rental Expenses You Can Deduct," Government of Canada, last modified April 1, 2021, https://www.canada.ca/en/revenue-agency/services/tax/businesses/topics/rental-income/completing-form-t776-statement-real-estate-rentals/rental-expenses-you-deduct.html.

BUSINESS INCOME OR RENTAL INCOME?

There appears to be a bit of confusion around how to declare income earned from renting your home—whether it is short term via a service like Airbnb or long term (more than six months at a time to the same family).

What we do know is that the CRA requires Canadians who collect income from renting out their property to declare it on their income tax return. But is it declared as rental income or business income? When does rental income become business income? What deductions can you claim?

In most cases, the CRA establishes the difference between rental and business income based on the number and kinds of services that you provide for the tenants. When you provide a space plus what the CRA considers to be "basic services," such as heat, light, parking and laundry facilities, the income earned is rental income.

If, however, additional services are provided to tenants, such as cleaning, security and meals, the CRA believes that you are carrying on a business and no longer earning just rental income.

The more services you provide, the greater the chance that a rental operation will be classified as business income, which means you need to include self-employed business income when filing income taxes.

#7: Short-Term Rentals

Tax Deductions

In the eyes of the CRA, any income earned by renting out your home or other property is considered to be rental income—even if it's just for a night or two, every once in a while. Like other types of income, the money you make from your rental must be reported on your tax return. The good news is that since you're reporting the income, you may deduct expenses related to that income. Just make sure to keep all of your receipts!

Some of the more common expenses you can deduct when earning Airbnb or short-term rental income include items purchased to furnish or supply the unit, as well as household items used for upkeep, such as laundry soap and disinfectant. You can also review the rental deduction eligible expenses list and claim all that apply, such as advertising costs, insurance and portions of your property tax and home insurance premiums.

If the Airbnb unit is located within your home, remember that only a portion of the claimed expenses can be used as a deduction. This portion is determined by the amount of property that is used to earn rental income and the length of time, such as the number of days per year, the rental unit is used to earn that income.

For example, if you rent out your cottage only on the weekends, your cottage is rented out for 104 out of 365 days. That means you would need to take your entire list of expenses related to earning the rental income and multiply that by the percentage of time your cottage is rented out. The calculation is as follows:

> # of days rented / # of days available = % of time property is rented out

For our example, this means 28.5% of expenses incurred with the cottage can be used as tax deductions.

> 104 / 365 = 0.285 = 28.5%

For homeowners who rent out a portion of their home, you'll first need to calculate the percentage of the home used for rental purposes, then the percentage of expenses related to the rental.

Let's assume you have a five-bedroom home and you rent out two rooms for 60 days and, after one year, your total eligible deductions are $5,500.

> # of rooms rented / # of rooms total = % of property used for rental income

> 2 / 5 = 0.4 = 40%

Now:

> # of days rented / # of days available = % of time property is rented out

> 60 / 365 = 0.164 = 16.4%

Finally, it's time to calculate eligible deductions that can be used to reduce short-term rental income:

$5,500 x 40% = $2,200

$2,200 x 16.4% = $360.80, meaning you could claim $360.80 in deductions on your tax return.

Quite often, online tax programs will do these calculations automatically for you, but it doesn't hurt to understand how these deductions are calculated and what's eligible.

Short-Term Rentals and GST/HST

Unlike standard rental leases, short-term rentals are subject to GST or HST.

You will need to collect and submit GST or HST if your short-term rental income is earned on bookings that are less than 30 consecutive days (one month) and the rent you charge is more than $20 per day.

Unfortunately, most short-term rental sites, such as VRBO and Airbnb, do not collect GST/HST for you, so it's up to you to add GST/HST to whatever rate you charge, track this and then pay the government at tax time. Rules change if you earn less than $30,000 per year. Turns out, the tax authority has a "small supplier" rule that exempts income earners from having to register for GST/HST if your revenue remains under $30,000 in a calendar year or in any single calendar quarter (a quarter is three months, such as January, February and March). However, you may want to consider registering for the GST/HST voluntarily, as paying and claiming the tax credits could prompt a refund.

TurboTax has a great guide on GST that can help part-time land-lords and small business owners figure out the details.[31]

#8: Moving Expenses

Tax Deductions

Did you buy a home and move at least 40 kilometres (by the shortest usual public route) closer to your work (including a new at-home business) or school? Then you can claim the tax deductions associated with moving expenses.[32]

Like all deductions, moving expenses allow you to reduce your income before calculating taxes, plus it can be carried forward to the next year if you don't have enough income to deduct all your moving costs. (This also means you cannot use this deduction to create or boost a refund.)

#9: Provincial Tax Credits

There are a few provincial tax credits that directly apply to home-owners.

---

31 "The Complete Guide on Collecting GST/HST for Self-Employed Canadians," TurboTax Canada, September 29, 2020, https://turbotax.intuit.ca/tips/self-employed-taxes-collecting-gst-hst-8730.

32 "Line 21900—Moving Expenses: Expenses You Can Deduct," Government of Canada, last modified January 18, 2021, https://www.canada.ca/en/revenue-agency/services/tax/individuals/topics/about-your-tax-return/tax-return/completing-a-tax-return/deductions-credits-expenses/line-21900-moving-expenses/line-21900-expenses-you-deduct.html.

British Columbia

Home renovation tax credit for seniors and persons with disabilities

If you were a resident of BC and you paid for improvements to your principal residence (or the land your principal residence is on) to allow for a senior or a person with an eligible disability to safely live in the home, you may qualify for up to a $10,000 tax credit based on qualifying expenses.[33]

Manitoba

Education Property Tax Credit

Homeowners who pay property tax may be eligible to save up to $700 with the Manitoba Education Property Tax Credit (EPTC), which helps pay for the school taxes portion of your property taxes. This credit is only available if your household family income is less than $63,500.[34]

School tax credit for homeowners

You can claim this credit if all of the following conditions apply:

---

33 *British Columbia Information Guide*, Canada Revenue Agency, last modified January 18, 2021, https://www.canada.ca/en/revenue-agency/services/forms-publications/tax-packages-years/general-income-tax-benefit-package/british-columbia/5010-pc/information-residents-british-columbia.html#L14.

34 *Manitoba Information Guide*, Canada Revenue Agency, last modified January 18, 2021, https://www.canada.ca/en/revenue-agency/services/forms-publications/tax-packages-years/general-income-tax-benefit-package/manitoba/5007-pc/information-residents-manitoba.html#P271_29388.

- You were 55 years of age or older at the end of the calendar year.

- Your family income is less than $23,800.

- You or your spouse or common-law partner owns, is buying or is a life tenant of a principal residence (the home you normally reside in during the year).

- The assessed school tax for that residence is more than $160 for the year.[35]

Seniors' school tax rebate

You can claim this rebate if all of the following conditions are met:

- You (or your spouse or common-law partner) were a resident of Manitoba at the end of the year.

- You (or your spouse or common-law partner) were 65 years of age or older at the end of the year.

- You (or your spouse or common-law partner) own your home or are liable for paying the school taxes on your property.

- You (or your spouse or common-law partner) lived in that property as your principal residence on the municipal property tax due date.

---

35 *Manitoba Information Guide*, https://www.canada.ca/en/revenue-agency/services/forms-publications/tax-packages-years/general-income-tax-benefit-package/manitoba/5007-pc/information-residents-manitoba.html#P334_37509.

- You (or your spouse or common-law partner) paid the school taxes on your property for 2020.

- Your family income is less than $63,500.[36]

Green Energy Equipment Tax Credit

You can claim this credit if you installed a geothermal ground source heating system or solar thermal heating equipment on your property.[37]

The credit gives you a 15% refund on the eligible installation cost of the geothermal ground source heating system (not including the cost of the heat pump), plus 7.5% of the cost of the qualifying geothermal heat pump (if it was manufactured in Manitoba).

If you install solar thermal heating equipment, you're eligible for a 10% refund on the installation costs.

New Brunswick

Seniors' Home Renovation Tax Credit

Seniors 65 years or older in New Brunswick can qualify for a tax credit to help with the cost of making their homes safer and more accessible. The New Brunswick Seniors' Home Renovation Tax Credit is a refundable personal income tax credit for seniors and

---

36 *Manitoba Information Guide,* https://www.canada.ca/en/revenue-agency/services/forms-publications/tax-packages-years/general-income-tax-benefit-package/manitoba/5007-pc-information-residents-manitoba.html#snrs_schl_tx.

37 "Green Energy Equipment Tax Credit," Manitoba Tax Assistance Office, accessed June 22, 2021, https://www.gov.mb.ca/finance/tao/green.html.

family members who live with them. Seniors who qualify can claim up to $10,000 worth of eligible home improvements on their tax return. The amount of money they get back for these expenses is calculated as 10% of the eligible expenses claimed.[38]

Newfoundland

Resort property investment tax credit

Although not associated with your primary residence, this tax credit does give Newfoundland residents a maximum claim of $50,000 per tax year (lifetime maximum of $150,000) if they invested in a registered resort development property in 2020 (or later). This credit cannot be used to create or boost a refund but can be carried forward to be used in future years.[39]

Quebec

Home Buyers' Tax Credit

You may be entitled to a maximum $750 tax credit if you were resident in Quebec at the end of the calendar year and, during the tax year:

- You or your spouse bought a qualifying home for the first

---

38 *New Brunswick Information Guide*, Canada Revenue Agency, last modified January 18, 2021, https://www.canada.ca/en/revenue-agency/services/forms-publications/ tax-packages-years/general-income-tax-benefit-package/new-brunswick/5004-pc/ information-residents-new-brunswick.html#nw_brnwck_snrs_hm.

39 "T1297 Newfoundland and Labrador Resort Property Investment Tax Credit (Individuals)," Canada Revenue Agency, last modified January 18, 2021, https://www. canada.ca/en/revenue-agency/services/forms-publications/forms/t1297.html.

time and you intend to make it your principal residence (note that you are considered to have bought a home for the first time if neither you nor your spouse owned another housing unit in which you lived during the tax year or the previous four years); or

- You bought a qualifying home and intend to make it the principal residence of someone related to you who has a disability. (Keep in mind, the new residence must either be more accessible for the disabled person, set up to help the person be more mobile or functional, or provide an environment better suited to the person's personal needs and care.)[40]

Saskatchewan

First-time home buyers' amount

A legally qualified first-time home buyer (or family unit) can get up to a $10,000 total credit if purchasing a qualifying home (which is a home registered in your and/or your spouse's or common-law partner's name with the Land Titles Registry and located in Saskatchewan).

You cannot claim this credit if you obtained a loan through the Graduate Retention Program First Home Plan.[41]

---

40 "Home Buyers' Tax Credit," Revenu Quebec, accessed June 22, 2021, https://www. revenuquebec.ca/en/citizens/tax-credits/home-buyers-tax-credit.

41 *Saskatchewan Information Guide,* Canada Revenue Agency, last modified January 18, 2021, https://www.canada.ca/en/revenue-agency/services/forms-publications/ tax-packages-years/general-income-tax-benefit-package/saskatchewan/5008-pc/ information-residents-saskatchewan.html#FTHB.

ANSWERS TO COMMON TAX QUESTIONS

Life is what happens as you're making other (tax) plans.

Every year, I get a lot of requests asking how taxes will impact a person or family based on a set of unique circumstances. When you strip away the particulars, the result is a set of universal situations many Canadians could face in their lifetime.

To help with tax planning, I've distilled the most common "uncommon" situations into 11 scenarios with tips on how to avoid paying more tax than needed.

#1: How Long Must I Live in a Place for It to Be Considered a Home?

Q: I bought a pre-construction condo, but now I've fallen in love and want to sell and move closer to my partner. Will I have to pay capital gains tax on the sale of the condo since I only lived in it for less than six months?

This is probably one of the most pervasive myths in Canadian tax folklore: that you need to live in a home for a specific period of time for it to qualify as your principal residence and avoid paying capital gains tax on the profit from the sale of that home.

Wrong.

The CRA is very clear: There are **no timeline requirements** regarding the designation of your home as a principal residence. You can live in a property for one day and still designate it as a principal residence.

The key is to keep paperwork and have a paper trail to show your intentions. As long as you can clearly show the CRA that you intended to buy and live in a property as your primary residence, you can claim PRE on the sale of that property. Keep in mind, tax investigators take into consideration your profession, your expertise and your past actions; in other words, if you're a real estate pro and you've "fallen in love" three times in the last three years, chances are the CRA won't see this as a case of bad timing but an act to hide income.

#2: How to Avoid Forcing a Family Member to Pay Capital Gains Tax

Q: How can I pass on my home tax-free to my kids?

Probably one of the most common dilemmas any homeowner must face is how to leave property to adult children. There are usually two solutions:

1. Add the adult child to your home's deed while you are still alive.

2. Sell the home to your adult children while you are still alive.

Although both options will achieve your ultimate goal—to leave the home to your child(ren)—both options have tax implications that you may or may not like.

For instance, if you were to add your adult child to the title of your property, your child would immediately become a co-owner of the property. If that child already owns a home, then your property becomes a secondary property. If you are still alive and you sell your property, you will not have to pay capital gains tax since it's your principal residence; however, your adult child will owe capital gains tax, since the capital gains on this second property are not sheltered under PRE.

The second option is far more straightforward. By selling your home to your adult child, you trigger capital gains tax but don't have to pay since you sold your primary residence. On the surface, it seems like a win-win—parents sell their home to their child at less than market value, no tax is paid and the adult child gets a deal. Except, the CRA won't see it this way. The CRA states that if you "sell property to someone with whom you do not deal at arm's length and the selling price is less than its fair market value, your selling price is considered to be the fair market value."

This isn't a problem if your adult child doesn't already own property. However, if they do own property, the purchase of your home becomes a secondary property. If they buy it at a deflated price, the capital gains on this second property will be all that much greater—and not a win for your child.

#3: Can Adding a Rental Suite Threaten My Home's Tax Exemption?

Q: Will adding an income suite to my home result in losing the PRE?

Probably the biggest incentive to invest in a home is that any appreciated value—the capital gain on the asset—is protected from tax through the Primary Residence Exemption (PRE).

A short while ago, a very prominent tax firm stated that any home-owner who added an income suite to their home was running the risk of losing the PRE and, as a result, would end up paying capital gains tax when the home was sold.

The warnings were directed at homeowners who opted to convert a portion of their home into a rental suite (aka mortgage helper). These tax experts pointed to CRA statements that said, "The entire property retains its nature as a principal residence, [only if] there [are] no structural change[s] to the property to make it more suitable for rental or business purposes."

That's a scary proposition for just about any homeowner.

But I've read the tax law and I wasn't convinced. To be 100% accurate, I asked the CRA to clarify their position.

The answer was as I suspected: you will not lose the exemption from capital gains tax on your principal residence if you add or have a rental suite in your home as long as the income suite is **not** the primary use of the property.

According to the CRA answer, any rental suite within your home must be "ancillary" in nature to the property's primary purpose as a family home.

November 2019 CRA response: "In the view of the CRA, an entire home retains its nature as a principal residence when the rental income is secondary to the main use of the home as a residence."

But how does a homeowner—or the CRA—know if a rental suite in a family home is secondary? And what constitutes a structural change that would trigger the loss of this tax shelter?

Sadly, there are no hard-and-fast rules when it comes to the definition of a "secondary" suite.

To combat this ambiguity, tax specialists will develop "best practice" guidelines. For example, Toronto-based real estate accountant Cherry Chan tells her property clients to keep the square footage of secondary suites in a principal residence to less than 50% of the home's total square footage. As she explains, you want to show that the rental suite is auxiliary to the primary use, which is to provide a home for you and your family. She adds that the criteria are purposely vague because it allows the CRA wiggle room to allow for a case-by-case analysis.

Now, when it comes to renovations and modifications to a home to create a rental suite, the strict interpretation of CRA criteria could mean that any homeowner who adds a set of stairs or an external door to create a rental suite could find themselves faced with capital gains tax owed on the rental portion of their home.

As the CRA explained, "Whether adding a window or stairs is considered a structural change is determined on a case-by-case basis."

Those who are worried about the ambiguity, may I remind you that the CRA isn't targeting homeowners who add a mortgage-helper income suite. By and large, the tax authorities are good with you earning a bit of income and claiming related deductions; what's not cool is using these generous tax incentives to hide income and skip out on paying taxes. The wiggle room allows the CRA to capture tax cheats and allows the rest of us to add a door or a set of stairs to that newly renovated basement suite.

#4: Either Your Home Is a Home or It's a Business

Q: *My home is depreciating in value; can I claim that loss as a tax deduction?*

In Canada, property owners are allowed to reduce their payable tax by claiming the Capital Cost Allowance on any real property. This deduction applies to buildings as well as vehicles, equipment and other tangible assets.

The idea is to allow business owners, entrepreneurs or professionals to claim the depreciation of an owned asset that is used to earn income. It's the CRA's way of acknowledging that these assets will depreciate over time and that reduction in value is a real loss to the business asset list. As a result, the CRA allows the cost of these capital assets to be used as a deduction over several years. This yearly deduction is known as the Capital Cost Allowance (CCA) and, as a tax deduction, can help reduce the overall tax owed.

At some point, a few well-intentioned homeowners saw this as an opportunity to save a bit on taxes and decided to claim the CCA on their primary residence. Bad move.

The primary purpose of a principal residence isn't to generate earnings. For that reason, the CRA does not consider a rental suite inside a primary residence as a business. Since CCA is a business tax deduction, it cannot be used to reduce a homeowner's income tax (even if some of that taxable income comes in the form of rent).

If a homeowner *does* claim CCA, even once, the CRA may designate the rental suite as a business, rather than an ancillary use of a primary home, and **require that homeowner to pay capital gains tax on a percentage of the profit from the sale of the**

home. In other words, trying to get a yearly tax deduction based on the depreciation of your home's value could result in a big tax hit when you go to sell the home and end up having to pay capital gains tax.

#5: They're Not Making Any More Land, but They're Certainly Taxing It

Q: Will I pay capital gains tax on land I subdivide and sell?

To qualify for the exemption from capital gains tax, a principal residence must meet all CRA criteria, including not exceeding the maximum lot size of 0.5 hectares. Assuming that this is the case, any portion of land that is sold with a home is exempt from tax.

But what if you sold vacant land? Land with no structure on it? It's impossible to designate this land as a primary residence since tents cannot be designated as a principal residence. That means you would owe capital gains tax on the profit earned on the sale of the land, whether it's subdivided or not.

But it's not just capital gains tax you need to consider. Land sales can often trigger GST/HST.[42] If the land you sold was undivided and only used for personal use, you would not have to pay GST/HST. If you sold one of the divided parcels of land to a family member for their personal use, you wouldn't have to pay GST/HST. However, if you sell subdivided vacant land—even land used only for personal use—to a third party, you would have to pay GST/HST collected from the buyer in that transaction.

---

42 "Sale of Vacant Land by Individuals," Canada Revenue Agency, last modified June 22, 2017, https://www.canada.ca/en/revenue-agency/services/forms-publications/publications/gi-003/sales-vacant-land-individuals.html.

#6: Determining Tax Owed on Shared Property

Q: Who owes the tax on property owned by siblings?

The most common form of shared ownership of a property is when adult siblings co-own a family cottage. This type of ownership is known as "tenancy in common," which means that each owner is independent of the other. Each owner can buy more "ownership" (buy another owner's share) of the property or sell their portion independently. It also means that upon death, the ownership of that property transfers to the deceased person's estate, not the other owner(s). This is different from joint tenancy, where the rights of survivorship automatically transfer to your spouse.

Assuming all co-owners already own a primary residence, the sale of this shared-ownership property would trigger capital gains tax if the property was sold for a price that was higher than the value when the property was acquired.

Even if you decide to transfer ownership to another owner, the tax authorities consider this a deemed disposition, or as good as a sale, and this means you would owe taxes on any profit.

#7: One Family, One Home, No Exceptions

Q: My spouse and I live in different cities for work; can we claim two homes at tax time?

Quite often, we end up finding our life partner a little later in life. As a result, one or both of you may already be property owners. In more extreme circumstances, two spouses (or common-law partners) end up sharing life but, due to work, must live in separate accommodation. Under these circumstances, is it possible to claim two principal residences?

Unfortunately, the answer is unequivocal no. The CRA is very strict about the "one principal residence per family per year" rule.

For spouses who live in separate residences, that means that unless you are living separate and apart due to "a judicial separation or a written separation," you are considered a family unit and can designate only one property as the principal residence.

As a family unit, you would need to decide which house to designate as the principal residence and which house to sell as a secondary property and pay capital gains taxes on. The good news is, you can maximize tax savings by designating exemption years.

For instance, say you bought City #1 home for $250,000 five years ago and bought City #2 condo for $200,000 at the same time. City #1 home appreciates and is now worth $650,000; City #2 condo also appreciated and is now worth $725,000. Sell both properties without any strategy in place, and your family would save $66,000 in capital gains tax owed on City #1 home but end up paying $86,625 in capital gains tax on City #2 home (assuming a 33% tax bracket).

Simply by reversing the designation—claiming the City #2 condo as your primary residence and City #1 as the secondary property—you'd put more than $20,000 back in your bank account.

Go one step further and divide the PRE designation between the two properties. This is a much more complex strategy and you'd need to be sure that no claims were made on tax returns that would exclude one or both properties from being classified as a principal residence, but it's worth it to consult an accountant or tax specialist (preferably before selling or changing the use of property) to learn how you can effectively shelter current or future capital gains from tax.

#8: When Flipping Homes Becomes a Business

Q: Why can't I buy, renovate, sell, move and repeat to earn tax-free money?

A few years ago, the federal government decided to target real estate flippers—investors who specialized in buying, renovating and then quickly selling homes to earn a profit. Turns out that some of these flippers were using the PRE to earn tax-free money. The CRA didn't agree with their use and designation of a principal residence (which allowed these flippers to earn a tax-free profit) and, as a result, cracked down.

One regulatory change that came from that crackdown was the introduction of property sale reporting rules. Before 2016, every time a Canadian sold their primary residence, they didn't have to report the sale to the CRA. This change in reporting regulations now meant that every sale, including the sale of your principal residence, must be reported to the tax authorities.

With these changes came a crackdown. Investigators began to look for patterns—people who frequently bought, moved in, renovated and then sold—and began to hit them with back taxes and penalties. The argument was that the money earned wasn't a byproduct of a lifestyle choice but the result of business decisions; the money earned couldn't be sheltered from capital gains tax because it was income.

Now the new reporting requirements force every homeowner to justify the "ordinarily inhabited" rule—do you live, spend time, get your mail at this property? Plus, to avoid paying income tax on sold property, you'll need to prove that the property purchase wasn't a method or tool to earn income.

With these regulatory changes, the CRA made it very clear: House flipping is a business and not eligible for the PRE. Property bought and sold by flippers is inventory, making the profit earned business income.

#9: Renting Out Your Former Home While Waiting to Sell

Q: We bought our new condo and tried to sell our family home but decided to rent it out and wait for a better offer. Will we end up paying tax?

When it comes time to move up or downsize, homeowners can find themselves in a strange squeeze. Buy during a down market, and you could get a great deal on your new home but a not-so-great sale price on your current home; buy in a busy or accelerated sales market, and you could feel the need to maximize your current home's sale price, which prevents you from accepting any lower-priced offer.

It's a situation any downsizer faced during 2020 and going into 2021 when many potential buyers took to lowballing their purchase offers to capitalize on market fears.

Quite often, the solution to this dilemma of two properties is to rent out the older home. The rationale is that the rent helps pay for the costs associated with that home, and in simple terms, this logic is sound. Sure, there's more paperwork since the rent you collect must be reported to the CRA as income, but there are also deductions that potentially reduce your tax owed on that rental income to zero. Win-win, right?

Not so fast. What if your former, now-rented home doesn't sell for another six months or a year? What if the market continues to stay strong and property values increase during that time? It's a situation one South Surrey couple found themselves in when they went to file their taxes.

They originally listed their family home in early March 2020 for $1.2 million, and if they got their list price, they would've earned $600,000 in tax-free profit. But two weeks later, the global coronavirus was official and the Canadian real estate market slammed to a stop. Stuck with two properties, the couple moved into their new condo and started to rent out their home for $1,500—just enough to cover expenses.

A year later, the average home price in the area was up 27%; the couple sold their home for $1,524,000, for a total profit of $924,000.

After they filed their taxes (and assuming they are in a 33% tax bracket), the CRA hit them with a tax bill of $53,460.

By renting out their home, the couple had changed the use of their home and could no longer shelter any profit earned in that year from capital gains tax.

This does not mean you can't rent out your property; it just means you need to understand all of the implications. For complex or unusual situations or just to be accurate, it's always worth paying for a consultation with a professional. Even if the consultation costs close to $1,000, if it can save you $50,000, isn't it worth it?

#10: Avoiding Tax Through Reinvestment

Q: I can avoid paying capital gains tax if I reinvest the profits, right?

The myth that you can postpone or avoid paying capital gains tax originated with the inaccurate application of American tax law to Canadian tax-saving strategies.

That's a mouthful.

In a nutshell, it means that Americans may have a chance to reduce taxes owed through the reinvestment of earned profits, but Canadians do not have this option.

The Internal Revenue Service (IRS) has multiple tax rates for capital gains depending on how long the American taxpayer held the asset before selling. To qualify for the more favourable long-term capital gains rate, Americans must hold the asset for more than one year. Sell before the year is up, and the taxpayer pays a higher capital gains tax rate (known as the short-term capital gains tax rate). The idea is to incentivize American investors to hold assets for longer periods.

But the CRA doesn't see a difference between capital gains earned on an asset held for a long time or a short time and doesn't give taxpayers a break if they opt to reinvest the profits.

#11: How to Avoid Paying Capital Gains Tax on a Home You Don't Live In

Q: I own a home in one city but moved to a different city for work, where I now rent. I finally decided to sell the home I own to buy in this new city. Will I have to pay capital gains tax on the profit of that sale?

For homeowners who changed the use of a property, from home to rental, but **do not own another property** (which would automatically default to become their primary residence) **but rent instead**, the CRA will allow the homeowner to claim the PRE on the sale (or deemed disposition) of that property.

However, **to claim this credit, the renter must mail a letter to the CRA—it cannot be emailed or faxed**. In the letter, you should state that under Article 45(2), you are electing to continue to designate your property as your primary residence even though it is currently rented out. Although it won't save you the income tax owed on the rent collected, it will shelter the capital gains on that property from taxes owed using the PRE. You will have up to four tax years following the change of use to shelter gains from tax; after that, the property is not considered a principal residence and you cannot shelter capital gains from tax.

SUM IT UP

When you're offered money to help you build a strong foundation for your life, why wouldn't you accept it? Yet, taking the time to investigate what homeowners' tax credits and deductions you qualify for isn't at the top of most homeowners' lists. It should be.

Although answering the question of how your home can help you save at tax time isn't the first (or second, or third...) perk you may think of when choosing to buy and own a home, it can be a powerful strategic tool to help find and manage your money and grow your net worth.

Homeownership can mean qualifying for tax credits, rebates, deductions and benefits that can help put cash back in your pocket—cash that can go towards your bigger plans, such as savings, paying down debt or increasing your overall net worth.

TAKEAWAYS

Think After-Tax Returns, Not Before-Tax Earnings. When you tally it all up, all that matters is how much you keep, not how much you spend or how much you pay to the government.

All Property Is Taxed. Tax is triggered with every property sale. Whether or not you end up paying this tax depends on the type of asset, the primary use, your circumstances in life and your profession.

Reducing Your Tax Burden *Is* a Priority. The average Canadian household pays roughly $40,000 in taxes each year—more than the combined cost of clothing, food and shelter. When reviewing ways to cut your expenses, make tax planning and the use of legitimate tax strategies a priority.

Tax Planning Isn't Just for the Wealthy; It Helps Build Wealth. Learn how taxes are calculated and your marginal tax rate for every dollar invested in every type of investment. Use this information to invest in tax-efficient investments and to strategically use tax-sheltered accounts, like the RRSP and TFSA. For long-term investments, invest for capital gains since these earnings are taxed at only 50% of your marginal tax rate.

Side Hustles Can Cost You. Learn the rules about tax deductions, particularly when it comes to home-based businesses. Claiming the wrong type of deduction can eliminate powerful and important tax shelters—and end up costing you, big time.

Professional Help Costs Way Less Than Bad Planning. Get professional help to minimize your tax costs each year and over time. Tax laws can change and some are complicated. Unless you're willing to keep up with the legal details, it pays to get professional help.

9

YOUR HOME: YOUR CASTLE, YOUR CASH

A SUMMARY OF HOW TO BE
A SMART HOMEOWNER

In this book, I've presented advice on how homeownership can help grow your net worth.

Despite ongoing affordability issues in most major North American markets, property continues to be a solid foundation for the growth of middle-class homeowner net worth. It's a truth that has withstood critique and analysis.

In a study published by Harvard University's Joint Center for Housing Studies, the authors set out to determine if property ownership did help raise individual wealth accumulation. In particular, they analyzed the impact of homeownership on low-income and minority households—demographics that historically and currently face the biggest systemic challenges when it comes to asset accumulation. Their theory was that the observations made in the early 1990s—that homeownership was a way to increase personal net worth—were no longer valid because of the changing real estate market landscape. Instead, the authors found that there

> ...continues to be strong support for the association between owning a home and accumulating wealth. This relationship held even during the tumultuous period from 1999 to 2009, under less than ideal conditions.[43]

The authors went on to state:

> Even after the tremendous decline in housing prices and the rising wave of foreclosures that began in 2007, homeowner-ship continues to be a significant source of household wealth, and remains particularly important for lower-income and minority households. As has become painfully clear, owning a home is not without risk. But even during a time of exces-sive risk taking in the mortgage market and extreme vola-tility in house prices, large shares of owners successfully sustained homeownership and created substantial wealth in the process.[44]

The aim of this book is not to justify one position over another. Becoming a homeowner or staying a renter should not be a zero-

---

43 Christopher E. Herbert, Daniel T. McCue, and Rocio Sanchez-Moyano, "Is Home-ownership Still an Effective Means of Building Wealth for Low-income and Minority Households? (Was It Ever?)" (paper presented at Homeownership Built to Last: Lessons from the Housing Crisis on Sustaining Homeownership for Low-Income and Minority Families, Boston, Massachusetts, April 2013), 2, https://www.jchs.harvard.edu/sites/default/files/hbtl-06.pdf.

44 Herbert, McCue, and Sanchez-Moyano, "Is Homeownership Still an Effective Means of Building Wealth for Low-Income and Minority Households? (Was It Ever?)," 48.

sum decision with one side considered right and the other wrong. This book aims to help everyone who decides to become a homeowner make more strategic decisions that will help reduce risk and increase their wealth accumulation.

This is important given how heavily promoted homeownership is in North America. If you buy into the hype—*you must be a homeowner to grow your net worth* or *it's foolish to buy in such a hot market*—you'll likely end up making a bad decision.

Just ask anyone who sold their stock portfolio or their home between 2009 and 2011.

Of course, if you can recall the headlines back then, it's easier to understand why people liquidated their assets. By November 2008, the Dow Jones year-over-year loss was more than 40%, and market investors recorded losses of more than $50 trillion globally. Reports, like the one released by the AARP, a not-for-profit US-based seniors' advocacy and charitable organization, reinforced how critical everything felt at this time: "The economic downturn underway is likely to be the worst since World War II. Its impact on older Americans could be devastating."[45]

It took a few years before the dire pronouncements about the impact of the Great Recession began to slow (and eventually disappear). No doubt, it was a very hard time particularly for the most vulnerable groups—children, the elderly and the poor.

Amazingly, though, the vast majority of North Americans recovered all or nearly all of their losses by 2012—**but only if**

---

45   Sandy Mackenzie, "The Impact of the Financial Crisis on Older Americans," *Insight on the Issues*, AARP Public Policy Institute, December 19, 2008, https://assets. aarp.org/rgcenter/econ/i19_crisis.pdf.

they stayed in the market. That meant not liquidating their stock portfolio, cashing in their GICs or selling their real estate holdings.

It meant not reacting to a volatile situation based on fear or any other strong emotion. Unfortunately, this is exactly how we react.

For example, look at how the market responded to the dot-com bubble in 1999 and early 2000. At that time, the NASDAQ was up over 85% in just one year. Examining just the market activity of stock mutual funds, a record $29 billion USD in net inflows (money going in minus money coming out) poured into these funds by the end of 1999. In January 2000, another $44.5 billion USD poured into stock mutual funds, and by the end of March 2000, more than $140 billion USD of market money jumped into stock mutual funds. We now know that March 24, 2000 was the peak of the dot-com bubble. By October 2002, the S&P 500 was down 50% from its highs—and the market couldn't get out fast enough. That October marked the fifth month in a row that investors pulled more money out of stock mutual funds than they invested. Most moved their money into bonds, which at this point, were selling at 46-year record highs. See a pattern?

What's this got to do with homeownership and wealth accumulation? Nothing. And everything. To accumulate wealth and be a smart homeowner, we all need to learn to tune out the noise and double down on solid financial decisions. Being a smart homeowner means knowing how your property is valued and how to maximize and *use* that value to grow your net worth. It's about using your home—and your smarts—to make wise decisions when it comes to housing, lifestyle consumption and wealth accumulation. It also means ignoring the zero-sum mentality that you need to choose *between* homeownership and other, just as important, wealth accumulation goals.

To turn **property ownership into smart homeownership**, we need to break down all the misconceptions about buying a home. To start, here are six overall concepts—takeaway lessons—offered in this book:

#1: THERE'S NO SHAME, SO STOP THE BLAME

Over the last two decades, rising home prices across Canada have provided somewhat of a retirement windfall for older Canadians. That's the good news for the baby boomers and—according to most news reports—bad news for younger adults, particularly millennials and Gen Y. So why do younger Canadians keep buying homes? Because the primary motivator for becoming a homeowner is not financial. And it doesn't need to be.

Given all that we've discussed, it is perfectly acceptable to buy a home for purely emotional or psychological reasons.

The real difficulties arise when we try to deny our reasons for buying a home and settle on rationalizations and justifications. The same problems occur when we tackle these desires and decisions around home upgrades, renovations or even buying that boat, car, dress, suit or next piece of back-country gear.

In all these situations, we would do better if we just stopped and honestly accepted our reasons for wanting to buy a home (or anything else, for that matter). Shaming and blaming a person for an emotional or psychological want or need is ridiculous— even if that want or need comes with a large price tag.

Instead, we need to concentrate on being OK with what we want. Then we need to make smart decisions about making it a reality. So if your desire to become a homeowner feels more of a push than a solid financial plan, don't worry. You're in the same boat as just about every other homeowner. You've also got the same set of tools and techniques—some of which are outlined in this book—to help you make the smartest decisions about getting your biggest needs met.

#2: STOP TIMING THE MARKET AND START LIVING YOUR LIFE

Never buy real estate in a hot market. This is probably the most overused statement of the last decade. And like all good lies, there's a shred of truth to it.

The truth is, it's possible to make a smart housing purchase in a hot real estate market; it just requires a different focus and strategic planning.

If you were to focus on market cycles, you could be setting yourself up for a long wait or an ill-timed execution. Remember, all real estate markets move in cycles, but those cycles can be very long. Alternatively, you could experience microcycles in specific, targeted markets within the overall real estate market.

To illustrate, let's assume you decided to sell in 2009 because the market appeared too volatile. The idea was to jump back in when things stabilized.

But prices never did stabilize. They just kept going up. So you kept waiting. And waiting. Now it's 2021, and once again, you're convinced the market will correct and stabilize. Even if it does, you will never get the chance to buy a home at 2009 housing prices.

My advice: stop trying to time the market. Buy and sell your home based on your financial plans. If these plans are well structured, you have wiggle room to amend your plans should the market go against you. But at no time will you be forced to put your plans on hold so the market can "catch up" to your predictions.

By shifting your focus, you end up paying more attention to making homeownership work for you and your wealth accumulation goals. This strategic planning can include the best strategies for saving up a down payment and finding the right home and a clear idea of what is and isn't realistic for your house-buying budget and what the purchase means for your overall financial goals. The best part is, the planning and execution can occur at any time.

#3: BUBBLES BURST, CYCLES CONTINUE AND NEW BENCHMARKS ARE SET

It's true, home prices do go down. After periods of rapid price appreciation, the market will correct and prices will revert to their long-term average rates of appreciation. This is known as mean reversion—a return to the average for an entire dataset, in this case, residential housing prices. This return can be quick or slow, and it happens with any asset, including stocks and bonds. Each time, however, a new benchmark is set.

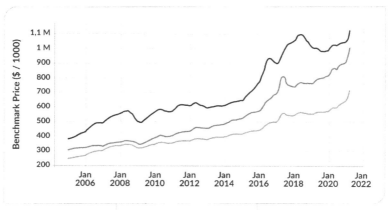

Aggregate - Composite - Actual   Greater Vancouver - Composite - Actual   Greater Toronto - Composite - Actual

What Is a Bubble?

All assets have an intrinsic value—a fundamental, objective value expressed as a price. When the market price exceeds an asset's intrinsic value, an economic or asset bubble can occur. Although these are temporary events, housing bubbles can still last for several years.

For current and prospective homeowners, the choice to include property as part of your wealth accumulation strategy needs to factor in the impact of market cycles (and, roughly, where you are in the market cycle). That means if you bought during a period of price appreciation, you probably shouldn't bank on your home's value continuing to rise at such a rapid rate in the near or far future. It also means you need to figure out how to keep the value of your home strong while using the asset to grow your net worth through diversification. This is where smart debt management strategies can help.

#4: FORCED SAVINGS PLANS ARE GOOD. SERIOUSLY.

I love how many people roll their eyes or dismiss the importance of a forced savings plan, particularly when someone uses the argument to justify the purchase of a home.

I used to be one of those people, arrogantly dismissing the choice because I valued the discipline of saving above all else. Then I became a parent. Suddenly, my budget exploded. Sure, we could reduce our expenses if we didn't have our hobbies, but life has taught both my husband and me the importance of enjoying today, not just planning for the future.

Plus, the realities of this world we live in change. Employees can no longer count on pension plans to fund their retirement or bank on staying in the same career (let alone the same job) for decades or even years. Many in the younger generations can't even secure steady, full-time employment; instead, they settle for stringing together gigs and contract work.

Add stretched budgets and stressed people, and I'm no longer surprised when someone opts for a bit of disciplined saving. Unfortunately, that discipline isn't always intuitive or innate. As a nation, we still don't have a nationalized financial literacy education plan. The result is that many of us lack basic financial skills. And the responsibility for saving and paying for our future years rests squarely on our shoulders.

Truth be told, automatic saving is a cornerstone of sound financial planning. Taglines like "Pay yourself first" or "Commit the first 10%" dominate financial guides. The idea is to develop a system that automatically takes money from your earnings and allocates it to savings. It's a principle that everyone should learn and use, not just homeowners.

Although I don't agree with buying a home as the primary way to fund your retirement, I do believe that all Canadians should include some form of automatic or forced savings plan in their overall financial strategy. The difference is that homeowners can use their property as a fallback should things go wrong.

#5: PAYING RENT IS NOT LIKE THROWING MONEY AWAY!

We often justify the purchase of a home by stating that renting is like throwing money away. It's not.

Owning a home is a financial liability. It takes money out of your pocket every month, and in almost every situation, you'll spend more of your after-tax dollars on housing as a homeowner than you do as a renter.

Used wisely, renting can be a very smart strategy for wealth accumulation. (Just read Alex Avery's book *The Wealthy Renter*.)

Used poorly, housing can be a quick way to become house-rich and cash-poor.

So it's not the act of switching from paying rent to paying a mortgage that puts you in a better financial position. No matter how you do it, paying for a home isn't throwing money away.

Although many of us may start our wealth accumulation through the purchase of a home, it's when we move from default ownership to smart ownership that we begin to use the asset to grow our net worth.

#6: IT'S *ALWAYS* POSSIBLE TO GET INTO THE PROPERTY MARKET (WHEREVER YOU MAY LIVE)

Let's not kid ourselves. Housing is unaffordable in many of the larger or in-demand North American cities. Even at the height of double-digit interest rates, our parents and grandparents didn't have to allocate almost a third of their income to pay for housing.

	YEAR	
	1982	2020
Median after-tax family income	$62,800	$84,900
Average house price in Canada	$72,500	$621,525
Average five-year fixed discount mortgage rate	19.4%	2.49%
20% down payment	$14,500	$124,305
Monthly mortgage payment	$911	$2,225
Housing cost as % of annual income	17.4%	31.45%
% of 1st mortgage payment that goes towards paying off the principle debt	3.8%	16.2%

The result of increasing housing costs has meant that some now rush into the market out of a fear of missing out, while others steer clear and admonish those who leap.

Then there's the silent majority: the bulk of Gen X, millennials and even Gen Y buyers who quietly took the plunge to become homeowners, even in the hottest North American markets. These buyers—of which I am one—ignored the idea that you can't buy in a hot market or that it's impossible to afford anything. The results have been creative and inspiring. For some, it meant buying a vacation property while continuing to rent in the city. For others, it meant co-ownership with friends or family. Still others sought out different property types to buy within their budget. My husband and I opted to let go of our dream home and, instead, buy a good home—a property that met our needs and our budget.

FINAL THOUGHTS

I have a confession. I love my job. Not because I get to write for a living. Not because I get to talk to interesting and incredible people (although it is a big perk). Not because I know a lot (there's always someone who knows more than me). I love my job because it allows me to learn: Every. Single. Day.

A day rarely goes by when I don't learn something new about a financial strategy, a new construction method, an inventive zoning bylaw adaptation or a different way to achieve independence.

Turns out, this approach to work and life now has a catch-phrase: growth mindset. If you strive to expand your knowledge or skill and risk making mistakes, you have a growth mindset. This is the approach we all need to take when it comes to homeownership and wealth accumulation.

Even after all these years, there's plenty I don't know about being a homeowner and even more, I don't know about wealth-building. And that's exciting. Because none of us will know it all, do it all, or get it all. **What we can do is help ourselves and each other.** Join a forum, ask a question in a chat room, DM (direct message) your favourite personal finance influencer, read a book, watch YouTube lessons or take a class. It doesn't matter what you decide to do, where you want to jump in or how you decide to acquire that knowledge or skill, but make it a habit to learn something new about homeownership and financial independence: Every. Single. Day.

If this sounds tedious to you, make it fun: find out fun facts about building and zoning laws. For instance, did you know that Amsterdam homes were built using small footprints but many floors (tall and skinny) because taxes were based on ground-level square footage?

Remember, to really grow your net worth, you need to use all your assets, not just your earned income and your responsible approach to saving.

Good news for those of us who aren't earning buckets of money or may not be naturally disciplined at saving.

It means there are more tools in your wealth accumulation toolbox including, but not limited to, your heart, your head, your home and the use of leverage.

Reading this book should give you techniques to use your tools to make intelligent decisions. Whether you're buying for the first or fifth time, deciding whether to renovate or looking to refinance, the tips and suggestions laid out in this book should help.

That said, don't get frustrated if the process appears slow at times. Good habits take time, and developing strategies to leverage your earnings into homeownership and then homeownership into wealth accumulation is a lifelong process, so enjoy it.

APPENDIX

DETAILS OF SAMPLE HOUSE USED FOR PER SQUARE FOOT CONTRACTOR (PSFC) METHOD

To calculate maintenance and strategic update costs—and to create a baseline for the PSFC method of home maintenance budgeting—I've used a sample house in a sample environment valued at $750,000:

- A single-family detached home with 2,000 square feet of living space

- Three bedrooms, two bathrooms and one kitchen

- No income suite

- Single-car garage

- Attached to municipal water and sewer with curbside garbage and recycling pickup

- Four-season environment (winter has snow, summer is

dry season, with spring and fall providing wetter, cooler conditions)

- Three external doors and 10 windows

- Finished basement (that is part of the 2,000 square feet of living space)

- Roof calculations are based on 1,500 square-foot roof and 250 linear feet of soffits, and 250 linear feet of gutters and 250 linear feet of fascia

- One-time costs are amortized based on 25 years.